LITERATURE, TECHNOLOGY, AND MODERNITY, 1860–2000

Industrial modernity takes it as self-evident that there is a difference between people and machines, but the corollary of this has been a recurring fantasy about the erasure of that difference. The central scenario in this fantasy is the crash, sometimes literal, sometimes metaphorical. Nicholas Daly considers the way human/machine encounters have been imagined from the 1860s on, arguing that such scenes dramatize the modernization of subjectivity. Daly begins with Victorian railway melodramas in which an individual is rescued from the path of the train just in time, and ends with J. G. Ballard's novel *Crash* in which people seek out such collisions. Daly argues that these collisions dramatize the relationship between the individual and modern industrial society, and suggests that the pleasures of fictional suspense help people to assimilate the speeding up of everyday life. This book will be of interest to scholars of modernism, literature, and film.

NICHOLAS DALY is Lecturer in the School of English at Trinity College, Dublin. He is the author of *Modernism, Romance, and the Fin de Siècle: Popular Fiction and British Culture, 1880–1914* (Cambridge, 1999), and of articles in *Novel, ELH, Victorian Studies*, and *New Formations*, among others.

LITERATURE, TECHNOLOGY, AND MODERNITY,

1860–2000

NICHOLAS DALY

Trinity College, Dublin

160101

CAMBRIDGE
UNIVERSITY PRESS

PUBLISHED BY THE PRESS SYNDICATE OF THE UNIVERSITY OF CAMBRIDGE
The Pitt Building, Trumpington Street, Cambridge, United Kingdom

CAMBRIDGE UNIVERSITY PRESS
The Edinburgh Building, Cambridge, CB2 2RU, UK
40 West 20th Street, New York, NY 10011-4211, USA
477 Williamstown Road, Port Melbourne, VIC 3207, Australia
Ruiz de Alarcón 13, 28014 Madrid, Spain
Dock House, The Waterfront, Cape Town 8001, South Africa

http://www.cambridge.org

First published 2004

Printed in the United Kingdom at the University Press, Cambridge

Typeface Adobe Garamond 11/12.5 pt   *System* LATEX 2$_\varepsilon$ [TB]

A catalogue record for this book is available from the British Library

Library of Congress Cataloguing in Publication data

Daly, Nicholas.
Literature, technology, and modernity, 1860–2000 / Nicholas Daly.
p.   cm.
Includes bibliographical references and index.
ISBN 0 521 83392 2
1. English literature – 19th century – History and criticism.   2. Technology in literature.
3. Literature and technology – Great Britain – History – 19th century.   4. Modernism (Literature –
Great Britain.   5. Railroad travel in literature.   6. Machinery in literature.   7. Railroads in
literature.   I. Title.
PR468.T4D35   2004
820.9′356 – dc22   2003055728

ISBN 0 521 83392 2 hardback

Contents

v

Illustrations

Acknowledgments

This book started out as an article I wrote to give myself an excuse to put off the redrafting of my PhD thesis. Eventually I did return to that inevitable project, which has meant that there has been quite a long period between the writing of that first article (begun in Providence, RI in 1995), and the completion of this slim volume (in Dublin in 2003). I have used that time to amass as many debts as possible, intellectual and otherwise, to friends and colleagues, and even a few unfortunate acquaintances. Some of those names I really must give here, though this is far from being a comprehensive roll-call.

For assistance with research materials I am grateful to staff at the British Library, the Newspaper Library at Colindale, the British Film Institute, the Harry Ransom Center for the Humanities at the University of Texas, Austin, the Imperial War Museum, the Museum of London, the New York Public Library, the National Library of Ireland, and, of course, the Library of Trinity College, Dublin. My editor at Cambridge University Press, Ray Ryan, has once again been a pleasure to work with, and Tara Dairman was tireless in the pursuit of illustrations.

Present and former colleagues at Trinity College, Dublin, especially Daniel Anlezark, Aileen Douglas, Nicholas Grene, Judith Mossman, Stuart Murray, John Nash, and Raluca Radulescu have helped this project along in various ways. Darryl Jones deserves a whole sentence to himself as a small monument to his support – including his providing a few of the epigraphs. I am grateful to the students who took my Literature, Technology, and Modernization seminar for forcing me to clarify my thoughts on machine culture. Also in Dublin, the members of the Red Stripe reading group have offered intellectual support outside the academy over the last few years.

Among the international set, Nancy Armstrong pointed out a few pitfalls to avoid at the start of this project, though I am not sure I have managed to avoid them all. David Glover deserves a special mention for his intellectual generosity, as do Neil Lazarus, Caroline Reitz, Jen Ruth, Talia Schaffer,

Brenda Silver, Leonard Tennenhouse, and Cynthia Tolentino. This project has also benefited from the comments of participants at various conferences and seminars: NEMLA 1995; the staff seminar of the English Department at the University of Wales, Cardiff in 1996; the Leeds Centre for Victorian Studies in 1997; the Popular Literature Conference at Almagro in 1998; EFACIS 1999; and the Technotopias Conference at the University of Strathclyde in 2002.

Foremost among my benefactors have been my family, but quite a few others should be listed here for providing assistance, material and otherwise: Mike D'Arcy; Miriam O'Brien, Brian Murphy, and Zoe Summer Gold, who housed this project for, well, quite a while; Carolin Hahnemann; Catherine Kirwan; Claire Connolly and Paul O'Donovan; Nicole Goldstein; Margaret Kennedy and John Tarpey; Moggs Kelleher and Michael Vallely; Denis Burke and Dorothy O'Connell; Claire O'Sullivan; and the McAuliffe and Tarrant families. Stephanie Rains had the good sense to miss the earlier versions of this project, but the final draft has benefited considerably from her cosmopolitan interests.

The research for this book was in part made possible by generous support from the Provost's Fund and the Arts and Social Sciences Benefactions Fund at TCD, and the Harry Ransom Center at the University of Texas, Austin.

Versions of chapters 1 and 2 appeared as 'Blood on the Tracks: Sensation Drama, the Railway, and the Dark Face of Modernity', in *Victorian Studies*, 42.1 (Autumn 1998/9), 47–66, and as 'Railway Novels: Sensation Fiction and the Modernization of the Senses', in *ELH*, 66 (1999), 461–87. I am grateful for permission to reprint this material.

Introduction

Here are three tableaux of people and machines. 1868. A man is lying unconscious on the tracks of the London underground; an express train is hurtling towards him, its lights cutting through the gloom; a second man makes a heroic dash, seizes the prostrate figure and rolls with him to safety as the train rushes past. 1904. A group of men are sitting in a railway car in Glengariff, near Cape Town, South Africa, telling stories. One of them, a petty officer in the British navy, tells the story of a warrant officer who goes to see an early moving picture show. In one actualité he sees a woman he knows disembark from a train at Paddington station in London. Mesmerized by her projected image, he goes to see the show every night. He becomes increasingly distraught and eventually deserts and disappears into the South African interior. 1973. Two men are driving in a Lincoln Continental. One reveals his ultimate car fantasy, which is to die in a crash with film star Elizabeth Taylor. He believes that this deadly collision will release some powerful libidinal energy bound up with the body of the star, and that whoever dies with her will achieve a kind of immortality.

The first of these scenes is from Dion Boucicault's *After Dark* (1868), but similar situations provided the climactic 'sensation' scenes to numerous plays in the 1860s, including Augustin Daly's *Under the Gaslight* (1867). The second episode is from Rudyard Kipling's enigmatic short story, 'Mrs Bathurst' (1904), though it also recalls accounts of the way early audiences reacted to the cinematograph, including such self-reflexive films as Robert Paul's *The Countryman's First Sight of the Animated Pictures* (1901). The last scene is from J. G. Ballard's 1973 *succès de scandale*, *Crash*.

Literature, Technology, and Modernity is an attempt to link these three images of people and machines by considering the relation between modernization and culture from the 1860s to the later twentieth century. The earliest scene relies on a cultural imaginary in which the impact of the machine, or industrial modernity more generally, on the human is a source of trepidation, or even terror, though also of fascination. With modernity represented synecdochically by the train, the hero (or heroine in some versions) is one who can beat the machine on its own turf. The scene offers a pleasurable fantasy of escape from industrial time, while paradoxically also drawing the protagonist, and indeed the audience, further into that temporality. The second episode places the narrator within one machine, the train, and frames another, the Biograph, or cinematograph, as itself a marvellous but maleficent technology, one that has the bewitching power to make copies so powerful that they rival and even outdo the originals. Those who are represented, and in some cases those who simply see the representations, are altered by the new machine. The last and most recent episode again places the speakers within the machine, but it also appears to deliberately evoke the first tableau, albeit with variations. Apart from its substitution of the automobile for the train it also suggests other departures from the nineteenth-century railway scene. Bodies and machines are more intimately linked, and the body of the star is no longer simply that of the woman, Elizabeth Taylor, but also the mythic superbody that has been generated by the film industry. The most obvious change is that the collision with the machine that was to be avoided at all costs in 1868 now seems to be sought out.

It has been argued from various perspectives that modernity relies on the intellectual separation of people and things.[1] In this light we might suppose that industrial modernity, beginning in the second half of the eighteenth century, is predicated on the intellectual separation of people and machines. This book suggests that the corollary of this is a modernity that obsessively replays the meeting of the two. The most extreme image of this meeting is the collision of flesh and steel in the crash, but other and less fatal encounters are also imagined. Cutting across some of the familiar divisions of literary and cultural history – between British and North American material, and between Victorian and Modern, and Modern and Postmodern – this book joins literary history and film history to argue that particular ways of imagining machine-transformed subjects are carried over from the mid-nineteenth century and linger, albeit with variations, well into the second half of the twentieth century. People were coming to terms with industrial modernity for a very long time, if they are not doing so still. One might even posit the existence of a long nineteenth century, if there were not already so many other extended centuries for the cultural historian to contemplate.

In following the adventures of a certain trope, though, I also want to suggest that literature and film are actively involved in modernization, rather than simply mirroring it. My earlier book, *Modernism, Romance, and the Fin de Siècle* (1999), took its impetus from that part of Fredric Jameson's account of modernism in which he argues that aesthetic pleasures have played their part in 'making us increasingly at home in what would otherwise . . . be a distressingly alien reality. Viewed in this way . . . modernism can be seen as a final and extremely specialized phase of that immense process . . . whereby the inhabitants of older social formations are culturally and psychologically retrained for life in the market system.'[2] Then I was arguing for a species of 'popular modernism' in the adventure fiction of late nineteenth and early twentieth-century Britain, claiming that the novels of that period assisted their readers to acclimatize to certain historical shifts in social organization, imperial power, and commodity culture. While I retain the idea of a 'popular modernism,' here the focus is on a different aspect of modernization, what might be termed the mechanization of everyday life. (This study is less directly concerned with literary periodization, but it is worth noting that the appearance of a species of machinic 'popular modernism' from the 1860s on might suggest one reason why later international high modernism did not entirely 'take' in Britain, having to some extent been pre-empted.[3]) Again, though, I am suggesting that literature, and later film, play a part in facilitating that modernizing process. Speed, suspense, and mystery are the first hallmarks of this early literature of modernization – the more general set into which I would place what we usually call modernism. Thus form, whether that of the sensation novel or of the sensation drama, is itself brought up to speed, which in turn means that the reading or viewing process comes to make some of the same demands as the industrial task. This is easy enough to see in the case of an industrial entertainment of the kind that film becomes, where technology is central to the medium (as Walter Benjamin argued many years ago), but it can also be true of literature and drama.

I am not proposing a single 'functionalist' role for cultural texts – their role at different times may be to narrate change, supply popular theories of it, purvey compensatory fantasies, enable some sort of cathexis, or indeed to provide critique. To argue that literature and film take part in modernization is to take a more general position on the politics of culture and what Mark Seltzer has succinctly called 'melodramas of uncertain agency': are texts, or films, *about* their culture, or simply a mirror of it?[4] The first position holds out possibilities of resistance and agency, if not transcendence; the latter, deriving at least proximally from New Historicism, seems to confine the text to a sort of prison-house of culture. Apart from the implications for our understanding of the past, the debate obviously has implications for the critical work of the present: if the texts of the past were totally part of, or totally conditioned by their culture, what is the position of the critic in the present? I hope it will be clear which position I lean towards, though it is also worth noting, as Seltzer does, that the aporias of agency of cultural criticism are already present in, even constitutive of, the texts of nineteenth-century machine culture with which I begin.[5] What, after all, is the fantastic image of a human being racing against a train to save someone, if not an image of human agency in the face of an increasingly mechanized (for which we might also read bureaucratized, rationalized, administered, commodified) world? If we find ourselves still interested in, if not altogether spellbound by, such melodramas of agency, it suggests that we still like to revisit the theatre of nineteenth-century machine culture.

As any study of the interplay of culture and modernization must be, this book owes a good deal to the foundational work of Georg Simmel, Walter Benjamin, Norbert Elias, Siegfried Giedion, Dolf Sternberger, Michel Foucault, and others, as well as to more recent work on technology and modernity, including that of Tim Armstrong, Christoph Asendorf, Tom Gunning, Lynne Kirby, and Mark Seltzer.[6] A more immediate influence was Wolfgang Schivelbusch's *The Railway Journey* (1977), and a little later, Alain Corbin's *Time, Desire and Horror: Towards a History of the Senses*. Schivelbusch's work convinced me that the way in which the middle class as much as the working class went through a species of 'retraining' in order to survive in an industrialized society was a fruitful field of enquiry. My choice of the 1860s as a starting point owes much to Corbin's claim that that decade represents a watershed in European history insofar as it saw the modification of the habitus to fit the contours of modernity, including the creation of 'new thresholds of the tolerable' and new corporeal regimes.[7] (At one level this might be taken to include, say, the end of public executions in Britain, but in a less Foucauldian vein one might point to such diverse phenomena of the 1860s as the building of the London underground; the huge increase in the numbers of patents sought for new inventions; the use of aniline dyes to produce such 'new' colours as mauve; and, the example I use here, the vogue of sensation literature.) My aim has been to trace some of the ways in which literature, and later film, played some part in this modification of the habitus, or what Jonathan Crary has termed the 'modernization of subjectivity'.[8]

I am assuming a certain transparency to the terms literature and technology, but modernity is a term that needs some glossing. By modernity here I mean in fact industrial modernity, the period ushered in by industrialization in the second half of the eighteenth century, though obviously this break is underpinned by earlier developments, such as the appearance of Enlightenment thought, the work of the Royal Society and the growth of scientific method, and the rise of capitalism itself. I have concentrated on one aspect of industrial modernity, the response to new technology, but that response cannot be understood without some sense of the other aspects: commodification; the break with traditional ways of life; urbanization and the concomitant sense of rootlessness; individualism; the expansion of democracy; the growth of commercialized leisure; the separation of work and home and the ideal of domesticity; new ideologies of gender; the growth of bureaucracy; the integration of more and more territory into the capitalist world system – the myriad ways in which all that is solid melts into air.[9] As will become clear, the response to new technologies often condenses fears, anxieties, and longings in the face of these other changes. In using the term industrial modernity I am, of course, also downplaying the divisions among Victorian, Modern, and Postmodern, and assuming that there is not so much a radical break between nineteenth-century and late twentieth-century modernity as a shift of intensity.[10]

I begin not with the industrial revolution itself, and with the Romantic response to it, but with the mid-Victorian period, by which time industrial technology was becoming part of the fabric of everyday life. Accordingly, I deal primarily not with responses to the industrialization of production per se, but with the industrialization of transport, communications, and entertainment – what one might also regard as the industrialization of consumption and leisure. Leisure was transformed by industrial technology in obvious ways, such as the availability of cheap railway excursions, but reading and viewing patterns were also retooled. The ways in which narrative pleasures, inter alia, altered might be seen to be part of the long shadow cast by the more general retraining of subjects for productive roles within industrial modernity, though one should not forget that such new pleasures may also have contained utopian moments.

Beginning with the response to the railway in the 'sensation drama' and 'sensation novels' of the 1860s, this study moves to consider the way in which the cinema – the last machine, as it has been called – was assimilated in Britain at the turn of the century. To move from the railway to the cinema as agent and icon of modernity is to move from the body nervous to two different kinds of body: the body of the spectator that in some ways recalls the nervous railway body, and the body that is filmed, at once de-realized and made eerily present. Chapter 4 pursues the role of the cinema in twentieth-century culture by following the late Victorian novelist, Elinor Glyn, to the Hollywood of the 1920s, exploring her part, together with actress

Clara Bow, in the invention of a film-mediated concept of sexuality – 'It'. The final chapter deals with J. G. Ballard's 1973 shock-novel, *Crash*, and David Cronenberg's film version of it, which reinvent nineteenth-century fantasies of people and machines, but also dwell on the darker side of film-produced charisma and sexuality. There is a rough division, then, between the first two chapters, which focus on the subject accelerated, and where time, speed, suspense, nervousness, and escape are central motifs, and chapters 3 and 4, which deal with what we might term the subject de-realized, where fantasy, reverie, uncanniness, desire, and the erotic are central, and where the image is primary. The last chapter attempts to reunite these two sides of the culture of modernization.

The opening two chapters on the 'sensation' plays and novels of the 1860s deal with the work of Dion Boucicault, Augustin Daly, Wilkie Collins, and M. E. Braddon in relation to mid-nineteenth-century machine culture. While accounts of the Victorian period often assume that industrialization disappears into the background after the industrial novels of the 1840s and 1850s, I hope to show that literature and drama continue to be preoccupied with Victorian machine culture, and in fact that they play an important part in the accommodation of new technologies. Chapter 1 looks at the popularity of elaborately staged 'railway rescue' scenes in the drama of the 1860s (more familiar to us now from the silent film era), arguing that the historical roots of these scenes, and indeed of spectacular melodrama in general, are in the experience of industrial modernity, including the industrial accident. I first discuss melodrama itself as a form aligned with modernity, before putting the spotlight on one particular treatment of the railway rescue, that in Boucicault's *After Dark* (1868), which kept London audiences on the edges of their seats from August 1868 to the following May. As Jonathan Crary has shown, attention becomes a keyword of modernity only in the second half of the nineteenth century, as modernization came up against the limits of subjective human perception, and the possibilities of distraction and fatigue. In this light we can see that theatre audiences in search of an escape from their cares were being brought to new levels of attentiveness by on-stage industrial spectacle.[11] And yet Boucicault's play deploys a fantasy of *escape* from Victorian modernity: what holds people's attention is a scene in which people triumph over industrial time – the hero always gets there on time to avert the industrial accident. Moreover, as we shall see, *After Dark* uses this fantasy to perform quite distinct cultural work: to escape the train will also be to evade an alien and menacing modernity associated with London's underworld as well as its underground.

If one popular form of the 1860s was providing compensatory fantasies of managing, or even evading, machine culture by beating it on its own ground, another form seemed to be more concerned with the creation of mechanic readers. In the sensation novel as in sensation drama, we also see an attempt to represent the accelerated railway age. But the sensation novel, I suggest, does not represent individuals escaping from a hostile machine culture. Even more than the sensation drama, it works to acclimatize its readers to railway time and space, and it is through its deployment of nervousness – shown in its characters, elicited in its readers – that it seeks to perform this acclimatization. If industrialized time and space threatened to overwhelm the human sensorium, then, they also came to offer new aesthetic pleasures in the form of suspense, even if these new pleasures in turn helped to synchronize the reader to industrial time.

Chapter 3 moves from machine time to mechanical images and from industrial transport to industrial entertainment, that is, from the railway to the cinematograph as itself a late Victorian machine. This is not quite the jump-cut it may at first seem: as Kirby, Friedberg, and others have shown, the initial response to the cinema is continuous in many respects with the response to the railway, not least because the latter offered an experiential paradigm that helped the first spectators to accommodate the cinematograph.[12] At a more literal level, the commodity experience of the railway excursion yielded to the 'phantom rides' of Hale's Tours and similar attractions, in which long tracking shots were used to give the viewer an experience of virtual mobility.[13] The railway was assumed to have the capacity to produce modern, nervous, and accelerated bodies, but the cinema apparatus was also perceived as transforming the human frame. Indeed, more than in the case of the railway, the cinema has been presented as a magical technology, even an uncanny one. What we see in the photographic image is not simply a copy of its referent but an emanation of the past that pursues its own career independently of its original, making of the photographic or filmic image something uncanny. The capacity of the camera/projector/screen to spellbind its audience by conjuring up a world of phantasmatic doubles took on a special resonance in a Britain that had to simultaneously assimilate the new medium of moving pictures and the military catastrophes of the distant Boer War (the early cinematograph was even called the 'Boerograph'). Here I explore this phase of early British cinema and responses to it, including a contemporary short story, Rudyard Kipling's 'Mrs Bathurst' (1904). Kipling's story explores the magical power of the new image technology, which transmits the unique force of personality – Mrs Bathurst's 'It' – across thousands of miles, causing one character to lose his wits at the sight of his old flame. I want to argue, though, that Kipling's cinema story is also a war story, and that it complexly links the new technology to the trauma of the Boer War, Britain's first experience of industrialized warfare.

Kipling anticipates two overlapping aspects of twentieth-century modernity: the development of a vocabulary of sexual attractiveness independent of beauty per se – 'It,' or 'sex appeal' – and the seeming capacity of the cinema to turn mere mortals, even very flawed ones, into powerful screen icons. By the 1920s Hollywood had already secured its dominance of international cinema, and was producing its own brand of popular modernist material, which, no less than the texts of high modernism, worked to train subjects for modernity. In the United States, and to a lesser extent in Europe, the cinema colonized the sphere of intimacy: it is scarcely an exaggeration, indeed, to say that twentieth-century sexuality was routed through the cinema apparatus. In Chapter 4 I look at a particular stage in this technological reshaping of sexuality, during which Kipling's 'It' is modified and united with the iconogenic power of the cinema and modern publicity. In 1926 two very different women meet and play their part in this project, the popular novelist and self-styled expert in psychology, Elinor Glyn, and the Brooklyn-born actress and star-in-waiting, Clara Bow. A key figure of modern sexuality, the '"It" Girl', is the result. By this time the nervous kineticism of the sensation-novel body has been replaced by something quite different as a figure of the modern – the 'fast' flapper. Like the flapper, the '"It" Girl' is dynamic, but she also possesses a sexuality that is at once earthy and light. Here I look at the connections among modernity, mobility, and sexuality as they appear in the 1927 film, *It*, in which Bow plays the lingerie sales-girl who translates 'It' into love and marriage to the boss.

In the final chapter I turn to a late twentieth-century narrative that meditates one last time, as it were, on pre-microchip machine culture: J. G. Ballard's car-culture fantasy, *Crash*, which revisits and puts in play the themes that I have explored. Since I begin this study with a set of texts that staged the avoidance of human/machine collision, I end with one in which the collision is finally allowed to happen – in which, in fact, such industrial accidents are longed for. The collisions imagined are not just those between bodies and machines, but between bodies and cinema stars, those who have been given a second body, a body filmic, as it were, through the industrial magic of the cinema. Rather than imagining the complete mechanization of society, and the colonization of the unconscious through industrial entertainment, *Crash* envisages a newly ritualized world of crash fans and dead but immortal stars. I finish by considering Cronenberg's film version of *Crash*, which highlights the mythic significance of the film star's super-body, as well as self-reflexively considering its own nature as industrial entertainment.

CHAPTER I

Sensation drama, the railway, and modernity

> The nineteenth century, when it takes its place with the other centuries in the chronological charts of the future, will, if it needs a symbol, almost inevitably have as that symbol a steam-engine running upon a railway.
>
> (H. G. Wells, 'Locomotion in the Twentieth Century')[1]

3 October 1868. The *Era* in its regular column, 'The London Theatres', reports that the Victoria Theatre is staging a 'locomotive engine and railway terror. The late Mr T. Moncrieff's drama of *The Scamps of London* has been put under contribution for the purpose, and with a little alteration, and some efficient scenery, is found to answer to the purpose precisely . . . [T]here are now 5 theatres in which the same incident is nightly exhibited.'[2] That 'same incident', the 'terror' itself, was a spectacle more familiar to us now as a stock situation in early cinema: someone is tied to, or lies unconscious on, the railway tracks while a train approaches at full speed; at the very last minute the hero or heroine snatches the intended victim away to safety, and the train rushes past, leaving us to shudder at what that narrowly averted collision of metal and flesh would have been like. In the autumn of 1868, London theatre audiences flocked eagerly to see variations on that basic scene presented at, among other venues, the Victoria, the Surrey, the East London, the New Standard, and, for the more upmarket, the Princess's on Oxford Street.[3] The 'terror' drew crowds to Moncrieff's *The Scamps of London* (an older play updated to include a railway rescue), Watts Phillips's *Land Rats and Water Rats*, George Spencer's *Rail, River and Road*, Alfred Rayner's *Danger*, and, the most successful of all, Dion Boucicault's *After Dark; A Tale of London Life*. The *Era*'s description of the railway scene from *Land Rats and Water Rats* gives some idea of how this situation was staged for maximum effect:

The desperate ruffians . . . seize Hetty [sc. the heroine], and place her insensible across the railway line as the whistle and faint puffing of the express is heard, and they depart trembling and ghastly, already anticipating the horror of their crime. Louder and louder the panting of the approaching train is heard; nearer and nearer it comes like a doom. The red lights just gleam on scene when in answer to Hetty, who with half-restored consciousness cries faintly for help [the hero, Richard] Mavis's voice is heard in the toolshed [where he has been locked]. Its window is dashed open, the peril is seen and comprehended, a weapon is found, the wooden door flies into splinters, and as the fierce scream of the engine sounds its note of terror, Hetty is grasped in the arms of Mavis, who clutches her from the line, as, with a shriek, the baffled death rushes by.[4]

The 'trains' themselves appear to have been painted wooden flats, mounted on rails, with much of the illusion created by lighting effects and smoke.[5] If early productions did not always quite pull off the special effects, occasionally attracting critical derision, audiences were indulgent. *The Times* tells us of Boucicault's *After Dark*, for example, that the house was raised to 'a perfect fever of excitement'.[6]

The railway craze of 1868 started in neither the West End nor in the less fashionable 'transpontine' and East End houses. As the *Era* reported, an American play, Augustin Daly's *Under the Gaslight*, had already featured 'the sensational incident of the man bound and left to be cut to pieces by an express train'.[7] This play had been performed in New York in August 1867 at the Worrell Sisters' New York Theatre, before showing up at the Tyne Theatre, Newcastle (20 April 1868), and eventually at the Whitechapel Pavilion in London in July 1868. But as is often the case with popular nineteenth-century theatre, the question of origins is more complex than this. A slightly different railway rescue had provided the climactic scene of Charles Bolton's *The Engineer* (Victoria, 23 March 1863), which was imitated in the anonymous *The London Arab* (Victoria, 29 March 1866) before appearing in a French adaptation at the Porte St Martin Theatre in Paris, reappearing in Daly's play in New York, and finally being reimported back into Britain.[8] In Bolton's play the heroine escapes 'in a ballast truck, which is drawn up the cutting at the moment that Markham [sc. the villain] madly attempts to overset the locomotive [containing the hero], but is immediately prostrated and passed over by the flying engine'.[9] *The London Arab*'s railway sensation scene is at once more gory and more far-fetched: during the rescue sequence heroes and villains fight it out on the lines 'while a train, with the glaring fire and loud snorting and puffing of its engine rushes up, and runs over some of the combatants'.[10] To render the issue of origins murkier still, when Daly obtained an injunction to prevent Boucicault's *After Dark* being performed in New York on grounds of plagiarism, it was alleged that *Under the Gaslight* had stolen the key scene from a magazine story, 'Captain Tom's Fright', which had appeared in *The Galaxy Magazine* for 13 March 1867. The court, though, was not in the end convinced by this argument, deciding that 'nothing . . . adduced on the part of the defendants affects the validity of the plaintiff's copyright, on the question of the originality and novelty of the "railroad scene"', and Daly won his case.[11]

In retrospect, Daly's claims to originality may seem suspect, but Boucicault himself was not above preserving his literary property with equally specious claims. Having borrowed the sensation scene in *After Dark*, he derived its plot from earlier plays of city life, either Grangé and Dennery's *Les Bohémiens de Paris* (1843), or one of its English adaptations, such as Moncrieff's highly successful *The Scamps of London* (1843), and not from the less well-known *Les Oiseaux de Proie* as he claimed. (As the critic in *The Mask* acidly noted, '*Les Oiseaux de Proie* has no more to do with *After Dark* than it has with *Black-Eyed Susan*.'[12]) Yet this did not embarrass Boucicault in the slightest when he objected to William Travers's use of his original title for *After Dark*, *London by Night*, for another play of sordid city life. Evidently annoyed at such hypocrisy, and critical of Boucicault's alterations to Moncrieff's play, *The Mask* urged other playwrights to follow Boucicault in wedding Moncrieff's plot to Daly's sensation scene to produce their own railway rescue dramas.[13] Whether as a result of this encouragement, or, as is more likely, the wish to emulate Boucicault's success, this is effectively what several other playwrights did in 1868.

Legalistic definitions of literary origins do not help us very much in a historicizing project, nor is it particularly useful to know whether Boucicault and his peers were borrowing their high-tech show-stopper from *Under the Gaslight*, 'Captain Tom's Fright', *The London Arab*, *The Engineer*, from each other, or some combination of all of these. What *is* significant, I would argue, is that the railway rescue was so popular, thrilling audiences on both sides of the Atlantic, and at both fashionable and cheap houses. Such popularity suggests that the scene was putting in play some very pressing cultural fears, anxieties, or indeed longings. To historicize this enormously popular staging of Victorian modernity would be to trace the roots of such affects, to locate the 'structure of feeling', as it were, within which such scenes made dramatic sense.

Without wishing to anticipate too much, I will be arguing in this chapter that the historical roots of the popular railway rescue, and indeed of spectacular melodrama in general, are in the broader experience of industrial technology and modernity. In one of the key accounts of nineteenth-century modernity, describing the relation between Baudelaire's poetry and the historical experience from which it springs, Walter Benjamin argues that 'the crowd, of whose existence Baudelaire is always aware, has not served as the model for any of his works, but it is imprinted on his creativity as a hidden figure'.[14] Benjamin thus offers a way of relating the literature of modernity and its historical ground that does not depend on a logic of representation: the crowd, and behind it, the kaleidoscopic experience of urban modernity, is not the subject of Baudelaire's work, but something like a determining absence for that work. This, I would argue, is also true of Victorian melodrama, where what we see on stage only makes sense within the context of the experience of off-stage modernization – not just direct human/machine encounters, but also urbanization, bureaucratization, and the more general acceleration of the pace of everyday life. And yet, attractive though Benjamin's formulation is, it only tells part of the story: in melodrama modernity is often rendered peculiarly *visible*. Such is the case with the railway rescue scene, where the human/machine encounters of industrial society are quite literally produced on stage as spectacle. Not only did audiences want dramas of contemporary urban life, they demanded to see the very artifacts of modernity, or as close a representation as was possible. As one critic remarked of the audience at the Princess's in 1868, they 'would applaud a real gaslight louder and longer than they would a sea-scene painted by Stanfield'. This appetite for the real, for 'representations of locomotives and steamboats, racecourses and chimney-pots', suggests that spectacular melodrama contributes in quite a precise way to the more general commercialized frenzy of the visible in the second half of the nineteenth century.[15]

It is worth noting in passing that this vogue for the real coincided with another aspect of modernization: the disappearance from British life of that 'traditional' spectacle, the public hanging. The year 1868 saw the first of the new 'private' hangings, which had its own railway connection as it happens: in August of that year a railway porter was hanged at Maidstone Gaol for the murder of another railway employee. From then on the urban crowd was deprived of such real-life drama, though it could still read all about it in sensational newspaper accounts. And of course it could see all the delightful villains it wanted on stage.

To recover the historical dialect within which the railway rescue made sense, I want first to discuss briefly melodrama itself as a theatrical form aligned with modernity, before putting the spotlight on one particular treatment of the railway terror, that in Boucicault's *After Dark, A Drama of London Life* (Princess's, 12 August 1868). I will be arguing that while we can discern in Boucicault's play a general fantasy about Victorian industrial technology that is shared by other versions of the railway rescue, *After Dark* uses this fantasy to perform quite distinct cultural work. In particular the play works to link its gloomy portrait of new technology to a nightmare vision of urban modernity, and the undermining of Englishness by 'alien' modern forces.[16]

THE MODERNITY OF MELODRAMA

Melodrama, whether conceived as a theatrical form or as a more transgeneric 'mode', has for some time now been recognized as essentially modern, with its roots in the French Revolution and the industrial revolution – in political modernity and technological modernity. (Ben Singer traces this strain in theatre scholarship to the 1960s, though he sees it as drawing on a much older conception of melodrama.[17]) That melodrama is a theatre of sharp contrasts, sudden reversals, and improbable sensational incidents, is the less surprising when we consider the historical shifts that gave rise to it. René Pixerécourt, often pointed to as the 'father' of melodrama, was a minor gentry figure who fought first against and then for the army of the new French Republic; he wrote his first plays during the years of the Revolution, and witnessed the Terror at close quarters. Besides leaving its mark on Pixerécourt, the Revolution may also have shaped the taste of the audience for the new drama: in Frank Rahill's words, 'nothing was improbable to people who had lived through Thermidor'.[18] Peter Brooks sees the affinity between the Revolution and melodrama as closer still, arguing that the language of the Revolution itself was in a melodramatic register, and that the task of both the oratory of the Revolution and melodrama was the telling of moral truths in a post-sacred world, shorn of church and monarchy.[19] The 'melodramatic imagination' he describes, which is not confined to stage melodrama, attempts to resacralize a disenchanted world, while at the same time testifying that that resacralization can now only be expressed in personal terms, as heroism and villainy. Divine justice, as Singer suggests, becomes poetic justice.[20]

Brooks's account is tailored more to post-Revolutionary France than Victorian Britain, where religion and monarchy co-existed more contentedly with modernity. Nonetheless, the industrial revolution no less than the French required a renegotiation of the terms on which self and society met. Thus for Martha Vicinus, Victorian melodrama, again defined in transgeneric terms, derives most directly from 'the working out in popular culture of the conflict between the family and its values and the social and economic assault of industrialization'.[21] Elaine Hadley has argued likewise that a melodramatic mode emerged 'as a polemical response to the social, economic, and epistemological changes that characterized the consolidation of market society in the nineteenth century', forming in effect an alternative public sphere in which older familial and communal bases of identity were defended against the logic of commodification. Some of the more recent work in this line stresses that this is a public sphere defined by commercial sensation, not enlightened rational discourse, and that it is the shocks of everyday industrial modernity as much as the reverberations of political or social modernity that are registered. Here I will be interpreting modernity quite broadly to mean the disruption of a traditional social and political order, as well as the creation of a new experience of time and space.[22]

If melodrama is rooted in modernity, most accounts suggest that it was a mode that was at the very least ambivalent about the modernity that produced it. But despite its pastoral moments, stage melodrama drew much of its social energy from the kaleidoscope of city life, and rendered the texture of urban modernity with bold strokes.[23] On stage, the nineteenth-century metropolises of Paris, London, and New York appear as sites of stark contrasts: fabulous wealth and acute poverty lie side by side; comfortable homes, shrines of domestic virtue, are always only a quick scene-change away from the foulest sinks of vice, and 'respectable' characters can be shuttled rapidly from shrine to sink. Such scenic heterogeneity correlates with the epistemology of the melodramatic city: the modern metropolis appears to be unfathomable, a resort of mystery and darkness. Inter-subjective connections, often represented *in parvo* within the drama as family ties, become difficult to establish: parent and child, brother and sister, pass each other in the street and never know it. One of the most successful plays of the nineteenth century, Adolphe Philippe Dennery and Eugene Cormon's tear-jerker of 1874, *Les Deux Orphelines* (*The Two Orphans*), which recounts the trials and eventual triumph of two vulnerable young protagonists, Henriette and Louise, when they arrive in anonymous and corrupt Paris, may be seen as exemplary of the way melodrama treats human relations in the city. Upon arrival in the city Henriette is kidnapped with a view to making her work as a prostitute in a brothel run by a depraved aristocrat. She is saved by the aristocratic hero, De Vaudrey, but while her star (temporarily) ascends, Louise, her sister, or rather adopted sister, suffers the most awful privations: the blind Louise is seized upon by the sinister La Frochard (derived from La Chouette in Eugene Sue's *Les Mystères de Paris*), and made to sing and beg in the streets. Louise, though, is really the daughter of De Vaudrey's aunt, the Countess de Linieres. In Act 2, Louise sings and shivers in front of the Church of St Sulpice, while the Countess passes and repasses her, never knowing that her long-lost daughter is before her in rags. When they do finally meet, and just when recognition seems about to dawn, La Frochard interposes and claims Louise as her own, and mother and child are once more sundered.

This city of lost children is no more confined to the stage, of course, than is melodrama itself as a mode. One thinks of *Bleak House*, where Esther passes the room of her long-lost father in Krook's house without knowing how close she is to discovering the secret of her birth (Mrs Wood's *East Lynne*, where the disgraced mother returns in disguise to act as governess to her own children, might be seen as a more baroque variation on this theme).[24] But while abject isolation corresponds at some level to the off-stage experience of the inhabitants of the Victorian metropolis, on stage it always leads to the scene of sudden recognition and the restoration of kinship: in melodrama lost children are always found in the end. In *Les Deux Orphelines* the blind Louise is restored to her aristocratic mother and adopted sister, and is even half-promised the restoration of her sight. (Dickens's Esther finds her mother too, after a long pursuit, though it is of course too late.) Moreover, the vulnerable orphan often turns out to be surprisingly resilient; a creature of 'glass and steel', in Nina Auerbach's phrase, the orphan is protected as well as endangered by his or her innocence.[25]

The possibilities of isolation and community inherent in the melodramatic city were not without their comic side. In Boucicault's collaborative play, *The Poor of New York* of 1857 (one of several adapations of Edouard Brisebarre and Eugène Nus's *Les Pauvres de Paris* of 1856), isolation and recognition are condensed into one day. Three members of the same impoverished middle-class family, the Fairweathers, separately roam the streets in search of work or alms. When both the mother and the daughter, Lucy, finally swallow their middle-class pride and pluck up the courage to ask a man on the street for money, he turns out to be none other than the son of the family, Paul:

> Mother
> ALL: My brother
> My son (Act 4.1)[26]

Boucicault's over-performance of the recognition scene should also serve to remind us that Victorian audiences were no more blind than ourselves to the comic possibilites of melodrama, yet even here one senses that there are tears behind the laughter. However hyperbolic they might now seem, episodes of deracination (orphanhood, or apparent orphanhood) and dislocation (in an unfamiliar city) touched a chord in those whose lives had been transformed by the economic upheavals of the industrial revolution and its attendant social effects. The strokes now seem rather broad, but perhaps fine brushwork was not what was wanted.

But if the individual adrift, the orphan in the metropolis, is often a focus of dramatic attention – the middle-class[27] audience recognizing itself in the lost orphan as it refused to see itself in the grasping villain – it is the city *crowd* that lies at the heart of melodrama. Whether represented on stage or not, the crowd, and thus modern city life, is the precondition for the action of modern melodrama, but not infrequently the crowd appears on stage as the very sign of modernity. Grangé and Dennery's much-imitated *Les Bohémiens de Paris* (Théâtre de L'Ambigu-Comique, 27 September 1843), for example, itself derived from Eugene Sue's *Les Mystères de Paris* (serialized 1840–2), and a principal source for Boucicault's *After Dark*, opens with a crowd scene in front of the Messageries Royal, the main terminal for coaches. Besides some of the principal characters the crowd contains '*Un afficheur, un marchand de chaines de sureté, un décrotteur . . . avec sa sellette, un marchand de cannes, passants, crieurs*' (a bill sticker, a seller of safety-chains, a shoe-black with his foot-rest, a walking-stick vendor, passers-by, hawkers). The spectacle, but also the din of commercial city life is presented. As the curtain rises the peddlers shout their wares: street guides to Paris, chains, matches, two sous a box. The life of the modern city provides more than mere local colour here: what are being represented, albeit synecdochically, are the very conditions which melodrama tries to render intelligible through its improbable plots, violent reversals, and sheer pace.

It is the disreputable margins of city life, the intermediate zone of *la Bohème*, if not the actual criminal underworld, that attracts the Victorian dramatist. To an extent this strain can be traced to Sue's *Les Mystères de Paris* (itself partly inspired by Eugène François Vidocq's *Mémoirs* of 1829), and the play derived from Sue's work, *Les Bohémiens de Paris*.[28] But this theatrical slumming is not altogether a Parisian import, since it also stems from Pierce Egan's *Life in London* (1821) and its many stage adaptations.[29] The fascination that colourful scenes of low life held for what were often middle-class audiences supports Jerrold Seigel's view that a still amorphous middle-class culture sought its own distorted reflection in the fantasy of Bohemia.[30] At any rate, the city as it appears in Victorian drama is very much a fallen world where country, or even suburban innocence is at risk, and where it is the villains who are most at home. In the Victorian urban imaginary, the impenetrable geography of the city, and indeed the urban crowd, provide a natural habitat for crime.

SENSATION DRAMA

That melodrama drew its life-blood from the modern was already evident enough by the end of the 1850s. But Dion Boucicault (sometimes Bourcicault, 1820–90) seems to have exploited this fact more assiduously and self-consciously than any other dramatist. What audiences desired, he realized, were 'the actual, the contemporaneous, the photographic'.[31] Having enjoyed early success in London with the comedy of manners, *London Assurance* (1841), Boucicault found himself in New York in the late 1850s, in desperate need of a hit. He found it with the melodramatic *The Poor of New York*, which he adapted from *Les Pauvres de Paris*, but using recognizable New York locations, and utilizing the financial panic of 1857 as part of the plot.[32] Back in England a few years later and again in need of a hit, Boucicault took up the same play and turned it into *The Poor of Liverpool*, again adding flavour with local and contemporary references. In turn this play became *The Poor of Leeds*, *The Poor of Manchester*, *The Streets of Islington*, and eventually *The Streets of London* (Princess's, 1 August 1864). Boucicault would put the contemporary to work in numerous subsequent plays, including *After Dark*, which one reviewer said contained 'a rapid picture of events which might possibly have occurred in the capital during the very week the drama was in rehearsal'.[33]

But the other ingredient that Boucicault recognized as crucial for melodramatic success was sensation. Again, Boucicault was not the first to utilize the spectacular possibilities of the nineteenth-century stage – the on-stage spectacles of earlier nautical drama, and, indeed, the equine extravaganzas of Astley's circus, anticipate his sensational effects. Nonetheless, Boucicault realized the full potential of sensation, and is generally credited with introducing the idea of the 'sensation scene', in which all the resources of the Victorian theatre could be employed to electrify the audience by creating suspenseful spectacle. *The Poor of New York* may be seen to mark an epoch here too. Audiences turned up in droves to see the second scene in the final act in which a house goes up in flames and a real fire engine arrives on stage to extinguish the fire. The repentant villain, Badger, escapes the doomed building in the nick of time, carrying with him, in the best melodramatic tradition, the vital document that will incriminate the far more villainous Gideon Bloodgood. The stage directions tell the story:

The house is gradually enveloped in fire . . . bells of engines are heard. Enter a crowd of persons . . . Badger . . . seizes a bar of iron, dashes in the ground-floor window, the interior is seen in flames . . . Badger leaps in and disappears. Shouts from the mob . . . the shutters of the garret fall and reveal Badger in the upper floor . . .

Badger disappears as if falling with the inside of the building. The shutters of the window fall away, and the inside of the house is seen, gutted by the fire; a cry of horror is uttered by the mob. Badger drags himself from the ruins . . . (Act 5.2)

Here we have a play that is not simply contemporary in its appeal, but that also utilizes every stage technology available to achieve its sensational visual effects. This intoxicating cocktail of the contemporary and the spectacular became known as 'sensation drama', a term popularized by Boucicault himself, though it appears to be of American origin.[34] In the *Cornhill Magazine* of September 1861, William Makepeace Thackeray refers to Boucicault's *The Colleen Bawn*: 'At the theatres they have a new name for their melodramatic pieces and call them "sensation Dramas".'[35] Pointing to this passage, Richard Altick argues that the term 'sensation' entered the general vocabulary from the drama.[36] Whether or not this is the case, in the same period 'sensation' also came to designate a certain sort of novel, as we shall see in chapter 2, and a certain sort of journalism, becoming 'one of the keywords of the popular culture of modernity'.[37] 'Sensation drama' itself became a highly successful subgenre, its popularity lasting at least until the end of the nineteenth century, when its role was partly usurped by the cinema. Boucicault continued to mine the sensation vein in subsequent plays. In a play dealing with Southern slavery, *The Octoroon; or, Life in Louisiana* (1859), a ship goes up in flames on stage at the end of Act 4. In *The Colleen Bawn; or, the Brides of Garrywoen* (1860), Act 2 ends with the comic-hero, Myles-na-Coppaleen, making a spectacular dive into a lake and rescuing the drowning heroine, Eily O'Connor. In *Arrah-na-Pogue; or, The Wicklow Wedding* (1864), Shaun the Post escapes from prison by climbing an ivy-covered tower, which sinks into the stage as he climbs, thus giving the impression of a cinematic tracking shot.[38] The sensation scene of *The Flying Scud; or, A Four-Legged Fortune* (1866), features the Epsom Derby (though only using one actual horse on stage); that of *Formosa; or, The Railroad to Ruin* (1869), the Oxford-Cambridge boatrace. If spectacle was not in itself something new to the stage, the high production values of Boucicault's theatre of attractions gave spectacle such a central role that it began to seem to some playgoers that the spectacle *was* the play. As in present-day action films, the storyline sometimes appeared to exist only to motivate the device of the special effects.[39] Other dramatists followed Boucicault's lead and produced increasingly spectacular scenes. As Michael Booth records, in *The Red Scarf* (1869), the villain ties the hero to a log in a saw-mill, sets the saw going and sets fire to the mill, while in *The Ruling Passion* (1882) a balloon containing the heroine, an escaped lunatic, and his keeper rises

from the Crystal Palace and eventually lands in the sea, before the occupants
are rescued by an eight-man lifeboat.[40]

Boucicault placed technology itself centre stage in a number of plays. *The
Long Strike*, derived from Mrs Gaskell's *Mary Barton*, contains a scene set
in a telegraph office, in which a vital witness is brought back by the use of
the wire. In *The Octoroon*, the only witness to the murder of one of the
slaves is a camera (with a 'self-developing liquid'), which photographs the
villain as he stands by the body of his victim to read a letter. But in the play
that I wish to focus on for the rest of this chapter, *After Dark*, it is the new
underground railway that provides Boucicault's 'sensation scene'.

STAGING TECHNOLOGY

The railway is more than just another piece of Victorian technology: for
Victorian Britain it was both an agent and icon of modernization. Wolfgang Schivelbusch's study, *The Railway Journey: The Industrialization of
Time and Space in the Nineteenth Century*, illuminates the ways in which
the railway transformed the nation, dramatically reshaping the landscape,
blurring the lines between rural and urban, facilitating the growth of the
major cities, sweeping away local times, and introducing its own standard
time – in effect, 'annihilating' an older perception of time and space.[41] For
the members of the Victorian middle classes it often provided their most
direct experience of the discipline of the new industrial technology: what
the industrial worker learnt on the factory floor they learnt on the station
platform and in the railway carriage; in this sense it quite literally brought
people up to speed.[42]

The railway intervenes directly in Victorian theatre history. The mid-
nineteenth century was very much the growth period for Victorian theatre,
the late 1860s in particular enjoying a boom in theatre construction. In
part this was a delayed reaction to the end of the monopoly of the patent
theatres in 1843, but it was also due to the transport revolution ushered
in by the railways and the omnibuses – quite simply, regular visits to the
theatre became possible for those large numbers of people who lived some
way outside the theatre district.[43] The people who came to see the 'railway
terror' in 1868 would in many instances have come by train, perhaps even
by the new underground railway, which appeared in the 1860s as London
began to develop the infrastructure of a modern metropolis, overhauling
its transport system along with its sanitation network.

So deeply is the railway imbricated with the Victorian period that the
histories of most Victorians, eminent or not, intersect with the history of

the railway. Boucicault's life, though, was more closely bound to the railway than most. Boucicault's presumed father, Dionysius Lardner, the compiler of the 134-volume *Cabinet Cyclopedia*, was also an engineer involved in the early days of the Great Western Railway. He wrote a book on the early railways, *Railway Economy: A Treatise on the New Art of Transport* (1850), which included such sagacious advice as 'never attempt to get out of a railway carriage while it is moving',[44] and engaged in public dispute with Isambard Kingdom Brunel about the danger that would be posed to passengers by the latter's planned two-mile box tunnel outside Bath. According to L. T. C. Rolt, Lardner was 'one of the most tiresome and menacing of the early [railway] experimentalists', individuals who in the days before proper safety standards were allowed private trains with which to conduct experiments.[45] Thus in September and October of 1838 Lardner's train was at large on the main line; rather unsurprisingly this led to a series of collisions, in the second of which his assistant was killed.[46] Fanciful though it may seem, this could have been Boucicault himself: up to the beginning of 1838, when he began his career as an actor, Boucicault was apprenticed to Lardner as a civil engineer.[47] (Boucicault's eldest son, Willie, was not to be so lucky: in January 1876, some years after his father's great railway rescue success with *After Dark*, he was killed along with thirteen others in an infamous accident involving three trains at Abbot's Ripton, near Huntington.[48])

But if we can understand the iconic significance of the railway to Victorian audiences, and to some extent speculate about Boucicault's own attraction to the railway theme, we have yet to explain what it was about this particular play, and this particular scene, that drew London audiences to it from August of 1868 to the following May. Augustin Daly's *Under the Gaslight* was a success in London, but Boucicault's play was a smash hit. First we have to consider the dramatic appeal of the (narrowly avoided) railway accident. By the 1860s the railway had been more or less assimilated into Victorian culture, but, as Schivelbusch has argued, the rapid naturalization of the train meant that original anxieties about its dangers were very quickly brought to the surface again by any minor incident. Initially, the railway's abrupt displacement of a transport technology, and a sense of time and space, that had held their places for generations, made the new system a source of considerable anxiety:

The ever-present fear of potential disaster remained, however, only until the railroad had become a part of normal everyday life. By the time Western Europe had culturally and psychically assimilated the railroad, that is, by the mid-nineteenth century, these anxieties had vanished . . . [But] if the normal functioning of the railroad was thus experienced as a natural and safe process, any sudden interruption of that functioning (which had become second nature) immediately reawakened the memory of the forgotten danger and potential violence: the repressed material returned with a vengeance.[49]

While the return of the repressed could be the result of a variety of causes (two murders on board a train created a veritable international panic), accidents were the most obvious triggers.[50]

In 1868 there was a very vivid evocation of the potential danger of the railway. On 20 August, ten days after *After Dark* opened, one of the worst railway accidents of the nineteenth century took place between Abergele and Llanddulas in Wales. In its regular column on the theatres, the *Illustrated London News* for Saturday 29 August reported that 'The Princess's still prospers with *After Dark*.' The same page carried an article, 'The Burning of the Irish Mail-Train', describing the Abergele railway disaster. Abergele dominated that issue of the *News*, providing the lead story ('A new horror has been added to the number of horrors to which railway travellers are exposed') and the subject for several dramatic illustrations. Thirty-three people had been killed. A week later the *Illustrated London News* was still covering Abergele, this time providing illustrations of the mass funeral. As L. T. C. Rolt notes, 'other accidents have claimed a heavier toll in human life, but never in railway history has disaster struck more swiftly or in so hideous a form' (*Red for Danger*, 181). The accident occurred when the Irish mail from Euston collided with runaway wagons from a goods train, containing seven and three-quarter tons of paraffin. In the conflagration that ensued, all of the passengers in the first carriages were turned into charred fragments of flesh and bone. What struck one witness to the disaster, the Marquis of Hamilton, was the *rapidity* with which life was extinguished:

We were startled by a collision and a shock . . . I immediately jumped out of the carriage, when a fearful sight met my view. Already the three passenger carriages in front of ours, the vans and the engine were enveloped in dense sheets of flame and smoke, rising fully 20 feet . . . it was the work of an instant. No words can convey the instantaneous nature of the explosion and conflagration. I had actually got out almost before the shock of the collision was over, and this was the spectacle which already presented itself. Not a sound, not a scream, not a struggle to escape, or a movement of any sort was apparent in the doomed carriages. It was as though an electric flash had at once paralyzed and stricken every one of their occupants. So complete was the absence of any presence of living or struggling life in them that . . . it was imagined that the burning carriages were destitute of passengers . . . [51]

As the *News* phrased it in its lead story, 'Not a cry escaped them – not a struggle was observed – not a chance of rescue was given.'[52]

While we might speculate that the special infernal horror of the Abergele disaster was fresh in the minds of *After Dark*'s audiences, what I wish to emphasize is the typicality of this accident. The reiterations in the contemporary accounts of the instantaneous nature of the crash, point to a popular perception of something qualitatively different in all industrial-technology accidents: they occur in 'machine time', not human time. Human agency cannot usually move rapidly enough to intervene, so rescues are few and far between. In fact such accidents are often too quick for the eye, perception taking place after the event: if you see it, you are still alive. It was this dimension of the industrial accident that Dickens registered as the uncanny in his Christmas ghost story of 1865, 'The Signalman' (written after his own railway accident in June 1865 at Staplehurst): the signalman sees an accident happen *before* it takes place. Response precedes stimulus; that is the only way a 'railway rescue' would be very likely.

We can understand the appeal of Boucicault's *After Dark* and the other 'railway rescue' plays in this light: they envision scenarios in which a human agent can beat a mechanical agent; the human for a moment comes to enter and master the temporal world of the machine. The third act of *After Dark* contains Boucicault's version of this contest of man versus machine. The villains have thrown the hero, the sandwich-board man, Old Tom, into a wine vault beneath a gambling den. This vault is adjacent to the new underground railway tunnel and a narrow opening connects the two. Old Tom's former army comrade, Captain Gordon Chumley, has crossed the villains and they have left him unconscious on the railway line to meet his death. In Act 3.1 Old Tom is trying to escape by digging his way out of the vault and into the tunnel when he sees his old friend on the rails:

OLD TOM: About 4 courses of bricks will leave one room to pass. What is that on the line? There is something, surely, there. [*A distant telegraph alarm rings. The semaphore levers play, and the lamps revolve.*] Great Heaven! 'tis Gordon. I'm here. He does not answer me. [*A whistle is heard, and distant train passes.*] Ah! murderers. I see their plan. They have dragged his insensible body to that place, and left him there to be killed by a passing train. Demons! Wretches! [*He works madly at the orifice. The bricks fall under his blows. The orifice increases. He tries to struggle through it.*] Not yet. [*The alarm rings again. The levers in the front play. The red light burns, and a white light is turned to Left Hand tunnel. The wheels of an approaching train are heard.*] Oh, heaven! give me strength – down – down. One moment! [*A large piece of wall falls in, and Old Tom comes with it.*] See, it comes, the monster comes. [*A loud rumbling and crashing sound is heard. He tries to move Gordon, but seeing the locomotive close*

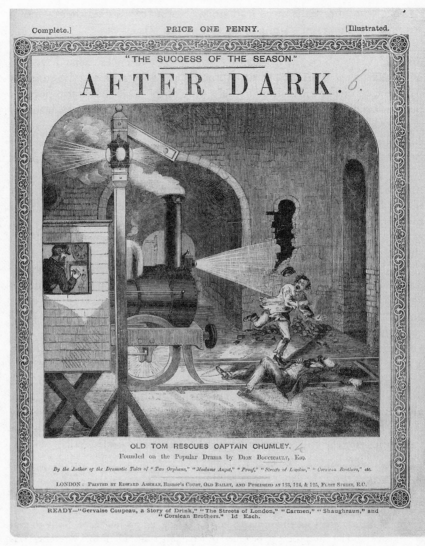

1 Cover illustration for H. L. Williams's adaptation of *After Dark* (1880?) showing the railway rescue

on him, he flings himself on the body, and, clasping it in his arms, rolls over with it forward. A locomotive, followed by a train of carriages, rushes over the place, and, as it disappears, Old Tom frees himself from Chumley, and gazes after the train.][53]

Old Tom precipitates himself into the dark world of the train, a world whose alien nature is dramatized through its 'inhuman' languages (semaphore, telegraph alarms, lights and whistles), and he beats it on its own ground. While the hero of *The Poor of New York* defeats an old threat to humanity – fire – Tom defeats a force that might stand in for modernity itself. And if the train iconically represents a threatening modernity, night after night at the Princess's, Old Tom, like his equivalents in the other railway rescues, shows that that threat can be mastered. Modernity is made visible – it is embodied on stage in the express train – and thus made beatable, and the pastoral is reaffirmed.[54]

There is, of course, an irony here. As Jonathan Crary has shown, a discourse of attention, dealing with such topics as the possibility of creating attentive subjects, of measuring attention, and of guarding against distraction and fatigue, emerges from almost complete silence in the 1850s to scientific respectability from the 1870s on.[55] Crary traces the shadows of this preoccupation with the unstable perceptions of the modern subject through the visual arts, but it is tempting to see the emergence of popular 'sensation drama', with its mesmerizing sensation scenes, as also taking place against this grander backdrop of the problems generated by the collision of modernization with the (resistant but presumably expandable) limits of the human sensorium. What we see at the Princess's Theatre and elsewhere, is an audience seeking escape from the wear and tear of industrial culture with its demands for attentiveness, alertness, and concentration, only to find that attentiveness is also the price to be paid for the pleasures of the popular theatre. The members of the audience are drawn to the edges of their seats, and their attention focused on an industrial scenario, but now this is meant to be fun: they are meant to be thrilled rather than traumatized.[56]

THE DARK FACE OF MODERNITY

In outrunning the train, Old Tom also thwarts the villains – the Jewish moneylender and gambling-house proprietor, Dicey Morris, and the *chevalier d'industrie*, Chandos Bellingham (alias Richard Knatchbull) – who have hatched a complicated scheme to blackmail a young aristocrat, Sir George Medhurst. A synopsis of the plot may be useful at this point. Medhurst has become penniless through youthful extravagance, and is now living under

an alias as the driver of a London night-cab. Dicey Morris holds a note of
hand upon which Medhurst has forged his father's signature to pay a gambling debt, and uses this to blackmail him. The young aristocrat is married
to the long-lost daughter of Old Tom (formerly, Frank Dalton, officer of
dragoons), Fanny (now known as Eliza), who has worked as a barmaid
for Morris. George's inheritance of his father's fortune is contingent upon
his marrying his cousin, Rose Egerton, who in turn loves, and is loved by,
Captain Gordon Chumley, Old Tom's former fellow-officer. The villains
get Eliza out of the way in order to facilitate Medhurst's marriage to Rose,
when they hope to be able to extract most of his inheritance from him.
Old Tom saves Eliza from drowning in the Thames in the first of the play's
rescue scenes (also a feature of *Les Bohémiens de Paris*, Moncrieff's *Scamps
of London*, and *Under the Gaslight*). When Chumley discovers the plot
against Medhurst, he goes to Morris's den to secure the return of the forged
signature. Recognizing Bellingham/Knatchbull as an escaped convict, he
hopes to use this information to bring Morris and Bellingham to terms.
Old Tom is present in the den when Chumley is drugged and carried into
the cellar (and ultimately to the underground railway line), but ends up in
the cellar himself when he tries to intervene. As we have seen, he risks his
life to rescue Chumley, and the villains are ultimately brought to justice.
Old Tom reveals his true identity to his daughter, and the two couples are
brought together.

  In outline, this tale of a military man who loses his manhood, only to
find it again by rescuing first his daughter and then his former comrade,
seems commonplace enough except for the appeal of the up-to-date railway
element. I want to suggest, though, that the villains of the piece, and the
threats that they represent, shed some further light on what is distinctive
about Boucicault's railway play. *After Dark* is not just a railway sensation
scene wrapped up in indifferent plot materials: while in Daly's *Under the
Gaslight* the railway rescue seems to have little to do with the main concerns of the play, Boucicault puts the railway to elaborate thematic use.
Specifically, the play identifies a certain form of modern urban evil with
the railway from the very first scene of the play, where Morris (accompanied by a band of 'Girls and Men') and Bellingham are seen arriving at a
bustling Victoria station after a day at the races. As in Boucicault's models,
Les Bohémiens de Paris and *The Scamps of London*, this is a crowded scene
with passengers, railway porters, umbrella and match-sellers, a 'boardman',
or sandwich-board man (Old Tom), and a policeman. What this opening scene establishes is that the form of modernity that the train brings
and symbolizes also provides a suitable matrix for people like Morris and
Bellingham, upstarts and criminals: they are railway-age scoundrels, and

men of the crowd. If modernity comes, Boucicault seems to ask, can villainy be far behind?

Bellingham, we learn, is a convicted felon who has earlier seduced Old Tom's wife and entrusted Tom's daughter, Eliza, to the care of Morris; he has escaped from transportation in Australia, been a bushranger and officer in the Confederate army, and now hides behind his rather grand name and the manners of a gentleman.[57] He is the type of all that is heartless and modern (*Bellingham*: 'Science has done away with all that ancient delicateness. You must not think of remorse; it is simply nausea' (Act 2.2)).

If Bellingham is more ruthless, it is Morris, the Jewish gambling-house proprietor (though also, he tells us, 'a payer of rates and taxes and a member of the westry' (sic)), who appears to be the main agent of the London underworld in the play. He owns a gambling club, the 'Silver Hell',[58] in Rupert Street, near Leicester Square, and the Elysium Music Hall across the river in Broadway, Westminster. That Morris is identified in the play as a Jew is significant, as it marks him as an agent of a dangerous form of modernity. As both Bryan Cheyette and Michael Ragussis have argued, in the nineteenth century 'the Jew' becomes a crucial figure for the imagining of modern British identity.[59] Matthew Arnold's *Culture and Anarchy* (1869), with its analysis of the 'Hebraic' and 'Hellenic' strains of British life, is a well-known example, in which Arnold ultimately associates the bad, uncultured, modernity of the Victorian bourgeoisie with the 'Hebraic' (as Ragussis shows, Arnold was very much responding to the claims that Disraeli had earlier made in his novels for the influence of Judaism on British culture). By the end of the century, in *The Modern Jew* (1899), Arnold White would describe Britain's Jewish population in terms of 'cosmopolitan and materialist influences fatal to the existence of the English nation'.[60] But long before this, occupational restrictions in pre-Emancipation Britain meant that Jews tended to be over-represented in business and finance, and this in turn shaped the image of British Jews as 'the personification of capitalism'.[61] At any rate, 'the Jew' as a figure for the dark side of progress was already available to Boucicault in 1868 and, as we shall see, the play pairs this figure with that other icon of the modern, the railway.

Pairs of villains like Bellingham and Morris date back at least to Montorgueil and Digonard in *Les Bohémiens de Paris*, who become an-glicized as Devereux (alias Fox Skinner) and Hawksworth Shabner in Moncrieff's *Scamps of London*. In 1863 Tom Taylor had deployed a similar pair, James Dalton and Melter Moss it *The Ticket-of-Leave Man* (Olympia, May 1863). Morris certainly owes some of his traits to these predecessors – Moss in particular was played according to one reviewer as 'an old shuffling, shambling, snuffy scoundrel of the Fagin breed'.[62] But Morris's ethnicity

is made far more explicit. The play announces Morris's Jewishness in part
through his 'un-English' accent (e.g. in Act 1.1 he says 'shentlemans' for gentleman and 'prinshiples' for principles), but just in case the audience misses
the point, Chumley also describes him as looking like 'a Jew horse dealer'.[63]
The narrativized, penny-pamphlet version of the play by Henry Llewellyn
Williams (Figure 1), though published some years later than the play, gives
us some idea of how Morris's Jewishness might have been concretized in a
stage production ('His curly black hair was lustrous with oil; and so were
his whiskers, which almost came round to his nose – a nose that revealed
the Israelite a mile off, though Mr Dicey Morris has the impudence to deny
he was born one of 'the peoplesh').[64] In fact, the actor who played Morris,
Dominick Murray, was better known for his stage-Irishmen, which appears
to have led to a certain confusion of types, the *Daily Telegraph*'s reviewer
complaining that: 'When Mr Dominick Murray has completely effaced the
remembrance of his Hibernian impersonations, his coarse and crafty Jew
will be an excellent embodiment.'[65]

'The Jew' is marked by occupation as well as by accent and appearance.
Morris's gambling dens and his bill-discounting associate him with 'dirty'
money; his music-hall with the demi-monde – the play making it fairly
clear that Morris's premises are used by prostitutes.[66] His place within a
vulgar new commercial culture is further signalled in the first scene of
the play by his use of advertising to promote his shady enterprises (Old
Tom, the hero of the piece, is degraded as one of his 'boardmen'). In
effect, all that middle-class Victorians disliked about the urban, commercial
culture that sustained British prosperity is condensed in the 'un-English'
Morris.[67]

Morris's demonized commercialism focuses anxieties about the power
of new money to disrupt traditional status hierarchies. The play represents
this through Morris's desire to be seen as a rate-payer and a 'member of the
westry'. The narrativized version of the play lingers longer on Morris's (un-
successful) attempts to push himself across class boundaries by adopting an
expensive but garish mode of dress. Morris is 'resplendent as a gingerbread
general . . . He [wears] a grey overcoat lined with blue silk, fancy socks, low
shoes . . . primrose gloves, with a diamond ring or two, heavy seals of a
chain representing hounds chasing a fox, and a gossamer green veil around
a white silk hat' (Williams, *After Dark*, 2). In Williams's version the train
quite literally becomes the vehicle for the counter-jumping of Morris and
his followers: they have 'run up in a first-class [train compartment], though
holding "second" tickets, by sheer force of "cheek," and a little bribery of
the guards' (2). Morris and his friends do not know their station, as it were.

If the railway and the bustling railway station seem to augur a disruptive, vulgar, and 'un-English' modernity, the underground railway provides an image of the overlap of modernity and alien criminality. The Metropolitan underground railway opened its first section, from Paddington to Farrington Street, on 10 January 1863. Victoria station, where Act 1.1 is set, opened in 1860 as a mainline railway station, but it shortly afterwards also became one of the early underground stations on the Metropolitan District line.[68] While the new system was publicly hailed as a remarkable piece of technological progress, Boucicault presents it as an agent of darkness, combining the bad modernity of the railway and the bad modernity of Morris and his associates. In effect, in *After Dark* the London underground offers a direct line to London's underworld. Dicey Morris's seedy gambling den also accommodates drinking, moneylending, prostitution, and two 'negro minstrels', Jem and Josey. That its cellars open onto the underground railway line is more than a handy coincidence for the villains of the play: underworld and underground, the play seems to suggest, belong together – they both allow evil to well up into the streets of London.

Darkness in the play takes on a moral character, as in melodrama more generally. The drugging and robbery of Chumley in Morris's den is for Old Tom 'one of the crimes so frequent now; not the open robbery in the day, but done in some hidden den, after dark' (Act 2.1). The underground represents this 'after dark' London – to Old Tom the railway line even 'looks like a long, dark street, with green and red lights in the distance' (Act 3.1). The tunnel itself as much as the actual train appears to be a threat, and the law can scarcely penetrate its gloom. But crucially the play also associates this darkness with race, specifically with Morris's Jewishness. For nineteenth-century racial science, Sander Gilman has argued, Jews are black; not only are they perceived as dark-skinned, but Robert Knox even writes at mid-century of the 'African character' of Jewish physiognomy.[69] The reviews give little idea of how exactly the character of Dicey Morris was filled out on stage, whether or not, for example, he was played as the swarthy-skinned Fagin of Dickens and Cruikshank, still very familiar to the readers of the 1860s.[70] However, the text of the play itself also marks Morris's putative racial difference, albeit indirectly. In effect, Morris's 'blackness' is associated with the blackness of the 'negro minstrels', Jem and Josey, who play in his music hall/gambling den.[71] More than local colour, the minstrels metonymically announce Morris's racial separateness; the minstrels carry his blackness for him, as it were. Morris may wish to appear as an English gentleman and a member of the vestry, but the play brands him as a fundamentally and *visibly* alien presence. If anything, the play suggests that popular anti-Semitism continued unabated between Jewish Emancipation in 1858 and the influx of Ashkenazi Jews in 1881, and bears out Michael Ragussis's contention that 'the Judaization of England was a perennial fear in the eighteenth and nineteenth centuries'.[72]

In the medical and scientific discourses of the nineteenth century, the putative darkness of Jews connotes disease.[73] Pseudo-scientific accretions to traditional prejudices associated this colouring with a whole range of afflictions, from syphilis to hysteria, the last coming to signify the debilitating effects of modern, urban life.[74] Modernity, cities, Jews, and disease all jostle together in the nineteenth-century imaginary, and the associations between them grow closer as the explanatory power of biology is accorded more and more credence in the late nineteenth century. There is a danger here, of course, of reading later continental anti-Semitism into Boucicault's mid-Victorian play, and we cannot assume that all of these associations were as current in the London of the 1860s as they would be in the Vienna of the fin de siècle. And yet, the play seems to depend on the audience's ability to recognize Morris's baleful influence (extending from the seamy quarters of Westminster to the West End) and the underground railway as aspects of a *common* darkness, and I would suggest, of a diseased modernity. If, then, the underground resembles a dark street, symbolically it is more like a sewer, from which the rats of modernity, Morris and Bellingham, have crawled. Just as he has earlier plunged into the Thames to save his daughter, Old Tom has to enter this sewer/tunnel to save his friend Chumley.

By reading the underground as a sewer I may appear to be going beyond the bounds of critical discretion in my pursuit of the veiled connections among Morris's Jewishness, an unhealthy modernity, and the railway. After all, the play nowhere explicitly refers to the underground in such terms. But the underground/sewer connection was already very much there in the popular discourse of the 1860s, perhaps in part because the building of the underground coincided with the expansion of London's drainage system between 1859 and 1865, both processes occasioning extensive excavations, and both part of the emergence of the modern, 'networked' city.[75] For its first passengers the underground was 'the drain' (a similarly phobic language would be used to describe the tube system when it opened in 1890).[76] In an article of 30 November 1861, *The Times* mobilizes a similar set of cloacal associations in acknowledging public anxieties about the new transport system then under construction.

A subterranean railway under London was awfully suggestive of dank, noisome tunnels buried many fathoms deep beyond the reach of light or life; passages inhabited by rats, soaked with sewer drippings, and poisoned by the escape of gas mains. It seemed an insult to common sense to suppose that people who could travel as cheaply on the outside of a Paddington 'bus would prefer, as a merely quicker medium, to be driven amid palpable darkness through the foul subsoil of London.[77]

For Boucicault, evidently, the 'palpable darkness', and 'the foul subsoil of London' were metaphorical rather than literal dangers. The Bellinghams, but especially the Dicey Morrises, of London, would breed in the 'noisome tunnels' created by modernity. Implicitly drawing upon a long tradition of anti-Semitic conceptions of the 'dirty Jew', and articulating this with the smelly modernity of the underground railway, Boucicault produces a powerfully phobic image of the forces of change at work in Britain.[78] We are not so very far here from T. S. Eliot's 'The rats are underneath the piles / The Jew is underneath the lot / Money in Furs.'[79]

When Old Tom risks his own life to rescue Gordon Chumley from the path of the underground train, then, he is not simply beating technology and the clock – for Boucicault's audience he is also asserting the traditional values of an aristo-military caste, against the bad and foreign modernity of a Dicey Morris. This is a fantasy about gender as well as about national identity, of course. To defeat the forces of bad modernity, English masculinity must be regenerated. If Old Tom is put on the road to recovery by his rescue of his daughter from the Thames, it is from his second baptism in the sewer of modernity that he emerges fully restored to his former heroic self. In this crucial second rescue scene, it is a man who saves another man. Daly in *Under the Gaslight* has Laura, the resilient and resourceful heroine, save a one-armed army veteran, Snorkey, who has befriended her. Boucicault, in effect, makes his damaged ex-soldier whole again by having him rescue another man; Daly's relatively progressive gendered spectacle becomes in Boucicault's play a fantasy of homosociality and traditional male heroism in a disturbingly modern world.

There is, then, more than one fantasy at work in *After Dark*, and we might speculate that the play's enormous popularity derived from its giving shape to these different anxieties from the Victorian social imaginary. In common with Augustin Daly's *Under the Gaslight*, and a whole series of other 'railway rescue' plays, Boucicault's play drew audiences with a sensation scene that pitted human against machine, each time giving victory to the human. But coupled to the locomotive terrors of industrial technology, *After Dark* imagines another threat – an alien, commercial, and criminal modernity personified by Dicey Morris. Ultimately, though, just as Old Tom wins his race with the express, 'traditional' English values triumph over this dangerous, racialized modernity. In staging the confrontation of human and machine, Boucicault and his rivals gave a visible form to something invisible: the difference between machine time and human time that gives the industrial accident its specific quality. But the play uses Morris as an icon of modernity just as it uses the express. The dangers condensed in the figure of Dicey Morris are also in the end exorcized from the world of the play – like the express train, Morris can be thwarted on stage by individual heroism.

If behind the more obvious fears evoked by the express train we can discern a constellation of anxieties around the figure of Morris, there is also a sense in which Morris himself represents a screen-threat – it is not so much Morris as the milieu from which he emerges that is the real source of darkness in the play. Moreover, the underground/sewer to which Morris is linked suggests a threat that will expand as the city itself expands, a darkness that is inseparable from the very fabric of the city network, part of the very DNA of modernity. By locating the 'drain' – the underground railway tunnel – at the very heart of his London after dark, making it the local habitation of a demonic modernity, Boucicault puts in play fears that cannot be dispelled by limelight: the underground/sewer does not easily lend itself to the visual logic of melodrama. *After Dark* provides one of the most spectacular sensation scenes of Victorian drama, but it also pushes at the representational limits of this theatre of spectacle. (One of the ironies, here, of course, is that Boucicault's representation of the rotten, 'networked' city depends on the fact that the Victorian stage was itself increasingly 'networked' – its visible representational space concealing a complicated array of trapdoors, treadmills, and pulleys. The stage, that is to say, worked by the same logic of appearance and reality as the modern street, or the department store.[80])

To conclude, sensation melodrama placed the metropolis on stage, inventing a Bohemia to both fascinate and frighten the Victorian audience, and feeding and whetting the Victorian appetite for visual pleasure. Modernity is the precondition for this drama, but modernity also takes to the boards in it as technology, as the crowd, as urban setting – the 'locomotives and steamboats, racecourses and chimney-pots' regretted by the critic in *The Mask*. Yet perhaps the same frenzy of the visible of which sensation drama was a part, rendered those shapeless threats that were less articulable in the visual language of the Victorian stage all the more frightening.

By the end of the century the two-dimensional painted train had lost its power to inspire anything but laughter, the amused reviewer of a 1900 railway rescue at the Grand Theatre, Fulham, commenting that 'we tremble to think what would have happened to that train if the body of Gordon Chumley had remained to block its way'.[81] While the city continued to appear across genres as a site of menace, the railway terror had lost its frisson, and it would require the new representational apparatus of the cinema to breathe life back into it.[82] But if the railway terror had lost some of its power to shock, this was at least in part because the Victorians had been retrained to accommodate the shocks of mechanical modernity. In the next chapter we look at the sensation novel, which I will argue, helped to accomplish that retraining by naturalizing the modern nervous subject.

CHAPTER 2

Sensation fiction and the modernization of the senses

> Even these metallic problems have their melodramatic side
> (Oscar Wilde, *The Importance of Being Earnest*)[1]

First, two episodes of Victorian nerves. On 10 June 1865 the London *Times* reported a 'Dreadful Railway Accident at Staplehurst: 10 Persons Killed – Upwards of 20 Wounded'. One of the passengers, who had 'a narrow escape... fortunately for himself and for the interests of literature', was Charles Dickens.[2] The previous day the 2:38 tidal train from Folkestone had come off the rails at the viaduct just outside Staplehurst. The track was being repaired at the time of the accident, and a section of it had been taken up. Having read the wrong timetable, the foreman in charge of the repairs did not expect the train for another two hours, and by the time the train driver saw the flagman – who was in the wrong place – it was much too late to brake. The front of the train cleared the gap in the tracks, but the rest of the carriages plunged down into the river-bed. Only one of the seven first-class carriages escaped the fall, through being securely coupled to the second-class carriage in front, and in that lucky carriage were Charles Dickens, his mistress, Ellen Ternan, and her mother. Also present was the manuscript of *Our Mutual Friend*, which, famously, Dickens rescued from the precariously balanced carriage, after first extricating the Ternans and offering what assistance he could to the injured and dying. (*Our Mutual Friend* seems to have survived the accident unscathed, and bears no traces of its misadventure except for the Preface in which Dickens mentions the accident. Dickens did not fail to put his railway experience to literary work, though: it is scarcely a coincidence that 'Mugby Junction', featuring Dickens's railway-accident ghost story, 'The Signalman' was the Christmas Number of *All the Year Round* that year.) Ellen Ternan appears to have been hurt in the crash, but Dickens felt no ill-effects until he was back in London, when he describes himself as being 'quite shattered and broken up'.[3] 'Shaken' is the word that Dickens consistently uses to describe his nervous condition in letter after letter. On 10 June he apologizes to Charles Lever that he 'can't sign [his] flourish, being nervously shaken'.[4] On 13 June his body was still reliving the original impact: 'In writing these scanty words of recollection I feel the shake and I am obliged to stop' (*Letters*, III, 138). On 21 June he still feels 'a little shaken in [his] nervous system by the terrible and affecting incidents of the late railway accident'.[5]

And the effects lingered long after, as Peter Ackroyd describes:

The effect of the Staplehurst accident 'tells more and more,' [Dickens] noted in 1867, and then a year later he confessed that '. . . I have sudden vague rushes of terror, even when riding in a hansom cab, which are perfectly unreasonable but quite insurmountable.' His son, Henry, recalled that 'I have seen him sometimes in a railway carriage when there was a slight jolt. When this happened he was almost in a state of panic and gripped the seat with both hands.' And Mamie remembered that '. . . my father's nerves never really were the same again . . . we have often seen him, when travelling home from London, suddenly fall into a paroxysm of fear, tremble all over, clutch the arms of the railway carriage, large beads of perspiration standing on his face, and suffer agonies of terror. We . . . would touch his hand gently now and then. He had, however, . . . no idea of our presence . . .' (*Dickens*, 963)

Although Dickens got off lightly in the accident itself, then, the original jolt seems to have left its mark on his body, to have filed itself away in his nervous system; he relived the event over and over, experiencing all the anxiety that he didn't feel at the time. He died on the anniversary of the crash five years later. As Wolfgang Schivelbusch notes, we can identify Dickens as one of the most famous victims of a peculiarly modern form of nervous after-effect: shock.[6]

A rather different accident transforms the life of Walter Hartright, the hero of *The Woman in White* (1859–60), the work of Dickens's friend and literary collaborator, Wilkie Collins. Walking back to London one night after a visit to his mother and sister in Hampstead, the young art teacher encounters a woman dressed all in white, an event which sets the wheels of the novel's complicated plot in motion:

in one moment every drop of blood in my body was brought to a stop by the touch of a hand laid lightly and suddenly on my shoulder from behind me. There, in the middle of the broad, bright high-road – there, as if it had that moment sprung out of the earth or dropped from the heaven – stood the figure of a solitary Woman, dressed from head to foot in white garments; her face bent in grave inquiry on mine, her hand pointing to the dark cloud over London, as I faced her.[7]

As in Dickens's case, this single collision reverberates through Hartright's life. He relives the shock of the original encounter when he first sees Laura Fairlie, the heiress with whom he falls in love, and recognizes her as the double of Anne Catherick, the original Woman in White: 'I started up from the ottoman . . . A thrill of the same feeling which ran through me when the touch was laid on my shoulder on the lonely high road, chilled me again' (*W*, 51). Hartright even feels all the shock of the original incident in *describing* it many years later ('I tremble, now, when I write it' (*W*, 17)): history becomes embodied; the body-made-nervous acts as a recording surface for the protagonist's experience. But where Dickens's shattered nerves separated him from others, Hartright's tremors make him part of a community of the nervous in the novel, rather like the playgoers who watched the sensational railway rescues of the last chapter. That is to say, his is not the only body in the novel whose tics record shocks experienced – or anticipate those yet to be received. For example, this body language connects Laura Fairlie and Anne Catherick, Laura's half-sister, and the pawn in a plot to impersonate her: Anne's 'nervous, uncertain lips' (*W*, 15) double Laura's 'sensitive lips . . . subject to a slight nervous contraction' (*W*, 41). Laura's guardian, the self-centred Mr Fairlie, repeatedly complains of 'the wretched state of [his] nerves' (*W*, 33, 34). Nor are the villains of the piece immune from anxiety: Sir Percival Glyde has a fit of trembling before he is sure of Laura's hand in marriage, and there is 'suppressed anxiety and agitation in every line of his face' (*W*, 149); the nerves of the criminal genius, Count Fosco, 'are so finely strung that he starts at chance noises' (*W*, 199). Even the minor characters enter this nervous freemasonry: the 'light-haired man with the scar on his cheek' who belongs to the same mysterious 'Brotherhood' as Count Fosco (and Walter's friend Pesca) has at least one 'long, delicate, nervous hand' (*W*, 579). I will not belabour the point: as a number of critics have demonstrated, nerves are everywhere aquiver in this novel. Moreover, the effect of the novel seems to be to set the reader's nerves jangling in sympathetic vibration. In an early review of the novel, novelist and critic Mrs Oliphant described the effect on the reader of the scene in which Walter first sees Laura: 'The reader's nerves are affected like the hero's. He [sic] feels the thrill of the untoward resemblance and an ominous, painful mystery.'[8]

What links these trembling bodies, fictional and actual? How do we connect sensation novels such as *The Woman in White* and Charles Dickens's experiences on the 2:38 from Folkestone? The railway, I will argue, provides the missing link. Unlike the railway rescue plays we saw in chapter 1, *The Woman in White* is not in any obvious way about the railway, though it did become a 'railway novel' (cf. the airport novel) or 'yellowback'. (As it happens, Walter's accidental encounter *is* followed by a railway accident – his train breaks down between Lancaster and Carlisle – but he suffers no more than a few hours' delay.) To make the connection, the railway must again be understood as more than a simple mode of transport: as I argued in the last chapter, for the Victorians it stood as both agent and icon of the acceleration of the pace of everyday life, annihilating an older experience of time and space, and making new demands on the sensorium of the traveller. Like the modern city and the factory floor, then, the railway required a reorientation of the subject towards modernity.[9] As Dickens's case suggests, this vehicle of modernization also brought with it a new potential for harm; the early encounters between the human body and the discipline of the railway were not always happy ones. The sensation drama, as we have seen, attempted to put modernity on stage in an attempt to localize it and thus escape it, though I have also suggested that the paradoxical side-effect of this was that the sensation scene came to demand the same sort of attentiveness as the industrial task. But in the sensation novel there is not only an attempt to describe the speeded-up railway age, but also a much more thoroughgoing attempt to *accommodate* that world. The sensation novel, I want to argue, provides a species of temporal training: through its deployment of suspense and nervousness the sensation novel synchronizes its readers with industrial modernity. Characters and readers alike experience a feeling of being relentlessly driven along that maps not just the human/machine encounter, but also the broader experience of modernity's iron cage. To read the sensation novel this way is to suggest that it runs counter to the main tendency of Victorian fiction, which, after a brief flirtation with machine culture in the industrial novels of the 1840s, pays scant attention to it. Even in the industrial novel, the transformations wrought by industrial technology tend to be *over*-assimilated into Victorian culture to the point that the new forces at work are not seen to change anything fundamental: in the marriage of North and South there was little question which was thought to be the more important partner.[10] The sensation novel itself does not escape this neo-pastoralist impulse: at the end of *The Woman in White*, for example, Walter, Laura, and Marian leave London for the rural world of Limmeridge House. But as the shaking hands of its principal narrator, Walter, testify, the repercussions of modernity are felt even there, in the very fibres of the body.

In the final section of this chapter I turn to a later moment in Victorian culture, and to a rather different country house: The Manor House, Woolton, Hertfordshire, where Jack Worthing discovers that his origin is not after all a terminus, and learns the vital Importance of Being Earnest. Oscar Wilde's most famous comedy pokes considerable fun at mid-Victorian sensibilities, not just the cult of earnestness, but also its fanciful double, the mid-Victorian novel, and behind both of these, the railway as icon of progresss. In *The Importance of Being Earnest*, Wilde is, in effect, playfully signalling that the end of the Victorian line has been reached. However, as the epigraph to this chapter suggests, I also consider Wilde's play to be, like the sensation novel, concerned with the subject's response to modernity. Wilde mocks the anxious accommodation with modernity that the sensation novel essays, instead embracing the modern as a heady source of experience.

A word first about modern nervousness, and the related topic of shock. In a general sense we identify anxiety and nervousness with *modernism*, and with the twentieth century rather than the nineteenth.[11] Central modernist artifacts, from Edvard Munch's *The Scream* (1893) to T. S. Eliot's *The Wasteland* (1922), seem to depend on the representation of, and appeal to, a specifically anxious modern subject. Critical thought sometimes takes this alignment of modernism and nervousness as axiomatic. For example, Fredric Jameson's influential account of the postmodern chronicles the displacement of a modernist thematics of angst and anomie, anxiety and alienation, by a postmodernist 'waning of affect'; in this 'shift in the dynamics of cultural pathology', the neurotic subject of modernism yields to the schizophrenic subject of postmodernism, removed equally from history and anxiety.[12] Modernism, of course, is also associated with shock, though as technique as much as theme: Buñuel/Dali's *Un Chien Andalou* (1928), or Picasso's *Guernica* (1937), for example, depend on the judicious use of shock to destabilize the audience's relation to the art object. In this particular sense, shock may be thought of as *the* technique of the historical avant garde.[13] Here, though, I will be taking up Walter Benjamin's argument that the hyperstimulation of the nerves is itself a component of historical *modernization*, and enters the fabric of everyday life in the great nineteenth-century metropolises before it makes itself available as artistic technique or as subject matter. In 'On Some Motifs in Baudelaire', Benjamin points to shock as the defining experience of modern life in the nineteenth century, whether it be the disturbance felt by the pedestrian jostled by the city crowd (one might think of Walter Hartright's solitary experience as a sort of stylized version of such anonymous encounters) or the mechanical jolts endured by the industrial worker.[14] Drawing on Georg Simmel's essay, 'The Metropolis and Mental Life' (1903), Benjamin's account of Baudelaire enables us to distinguish more precisely between nervousness and shock, and to conceptualize the relations between the two.[15] Benjamin suggests that, somewhat paradoxically, heightened consciousness – low-level anxiety, that is – is the subject's *defence-mechanism* against shock ('The greater the share of the shock factor in particular impressions, the more constantly consciousness has to be alert as a screen against stimuli' (*Illuminations*, 163)). The subject protects itself against modernity by secreting a layer of consciousness, as it were. Where nervousness or anxiety is, then, shock is not: by living on his/her nerves, the modern subject seeks to actually cocoon him or herself from the impact of modernization. It is in this emphasis on the uses of anxiety that Benjamin's account most significantly departs from the more familiar Romantic lament over the stultifying impact of modernity on the sensorium. The corollary of such laments is that the stultified subject craves more and more sensational entertainment.[16] That anxiety may shield the subject rather than cause harm is something that I will return to again when I discuss the effects of the sensation novel – and indeed the railway – on the British middle classes. For now it will suffice to keep in mind that anxiety may have its uses.

PREACHING TO THE NERVES

The vogue of the sensation novel followed closely on the heels of that of the sensation drama. Collins's novel provided the basic formula: a fast-paced narrative of domestic crime/mystery with a contemporary setting. By the mid-1860s, it seemed to some that sensation was poised to take over the entire genre, a reviewer in the *Westminster Gazette* in 1866 warning of a 'Sensational Mania'. By 1867, Mrs Oliphant was complaining that 'all our minor novelists, almost without exception, are of the school called Sensational'.[17] *Punch* had given its official recognition as early as 1863 to the vogue that followed the phenomenal success of such novels as *The Woman in White* and *Lady Audley's Secret*, producing its own sensational serial, 'Mokeanna; or, The White Witness: A Tale of the Times'. The sensation novel repaid its debt to the stage in adaptations of the most successful novels, but the new novels also lent themselves to stage parody, a burlesque based on Collins's novel, Watts Phillips's *The Woman in Mauve*, appearing at the Haymarket in 1865.[18] There were spin-offs of other kinds too, *The Woman in White* inspiring two new dances, a Woman in White Waltz and a Fosco Galop, though I have been unable to discover whether these were any more frantic than their predecessors. While the sensation drama was characterized primarily by its use of stage spectacle, and only secondarily by its use of suspense, in the case of the sensation novel it was suspense, or the appeal to the nerves, that was seen as the signature of the genre. As D. A. Miller describes: 'The genre offers us one of the first instances of modern literature to address itself primarily to the sympathetic nervous system, where it grounds its characteristic adrenalin effects: accelerated heart rate and respiration, increased blood pressure, the pallor resulting from vasoconstriction, and so on.'[19] Certainly this veritable assault on the reader's body was the aspect of the new fiction most frequently noted by contemporary reviewers. Mrs Oliphant, whom I have already cited, described *The Woman in White* as producing a 'simple physical effect' that linked character and reader.[20] H. L. Mansel, in his much-quoted attack on the sensationalists, describes them as 'preaching to the nerves'.[21] The rule of the new school of fiction, he suggests, might well be '*les nerfs, voilà tout l'homme*' ('Sensation Novels', 482). In a trope typical of attacks on popular culture, then as now, he charges the sensation novel with being numbingly dull (as lacking in all variety) at the same time that he describes it as hyper-stimulating. Thus the only differences among such novels, he suggests, lie in the species of sensation at which they aim: 'There are novels of the warming-pan type, and others of the galvanic-battery type – some which gently stimulate a particular feeling, and others which carry the whole nervous system *by steam*' (487, emphasis added). Like pornography, or like its more innocent twin, melodrama, then, the sensation novel was thought to conjure up a corporeal rather than a cerebral response in the reader. Nor did the pornographic connection go unmade: Mrs Oliphant, for one, thought that representing the appetite for 'sensuous raptures' among the female protagonists of these novels 'as the natural sentiment of English girls' was a decidedly unhealthy practice ('Novels', 259).

The most influential account of the sensation novel retains the original view of the genre as 'preaching to the nerves' but reads the sermon very differently. Far from thinking that the sensation novel released a tide of dangerous nervous energy, D. A. Miller historicizes the induced trepidations of sensation fiction in terms of the disciplinary function of the novel, specifically in terms of its construction of a proper model of the family through the simultaneous entertainment and violent rejection of same-sex desire. For Miller, the nervousness of the novel is coded as feminine and feminizing. Developing Mrs Oliphant's early insight into the effects on the reader of *The Woman in White*, he argues that through 'his' stand-in (or stunt-man, as it were) in the text, Walter Hartright, the reader 'catches' this nervousness from the very touch of the Woman in White when Walter meets her on the road to London. Miller reads the masculine experience of feminine nervousness as a species of homosexual panic, as a fantasy of '*anima muliebris in corpore virili inclusa*', nineteenth-century sexology's (Karl Ulrich's) definition of male homosexuality. The trajectory of the novel is, then, to employ this nervousness, to transform Hartright's fears – and by extension, the reader's – into heterosexual desire, and to secure by the end of the novel the unchecked dominance of the nuclear family, with its own delicate balance of heterosexual and homosocial forces. For Miller, the 'positive personal shocks' and paranoid plots of *The Woman in White* amount to a novelistic disciplinary machine, a die with which a certain form of modern subjectivity is stamped, and with which the reader is quite literally impressed.[22]

D. A. Miller is undoubtedly correct in claiming that nervousness is pandemic in *The Woman in White*, but he overestimates the part that Anne Catherick, the Woman in White herself, plays in circulating this affect. *Before* his fateful meeting with Anne Catherick on the road to London, Walter Hartright is already, like many of the novel's other characters, in a 'restless frame of mind and body' (*W*, 14; compare the 'restless habit' (126) that Laura's hands have) – in fact that is why he takes the longer route back to London that brings him into contact with her. Nor is this original nervousness unique to *The Woman in White*. The scheming anti-heroine of Collins's *Armadale*, Lydia Gwilt, also suffers in this way, asking her shady accomplice, Mother Oldershaw, to send her laudanum to stop her grinding her teeth in her sleep – and she has nerves of steel compared to that novel's curious hero, Ozias Midwinter, alias Allan Armadale. Lady Audley, in M. E. Braddon's *Lady Audley's Secret*, is highly strung to the point of madness, and ends her days in a private 'maison de santé'. The nervousness that pervades these novels, in other words, does not spring from any one centre. It seems to be in excess of any actual narrative motivation; it is an affect looking for a cause. The shady Doctor Downward in *Armadale* at one point expresses a view that is amply borne out by the sensation novel in general, that they 'live in an age when nervous derangement (parent of insanity) is steadily on the increase'.[23] Certainly, the sheer number of private asylums we encounter in these novels would seem to bear out such a theory: *Armadale*, *The Woman in White*, *Lady Audley's Secret*, Charles Reade's *Hard Cash*, and Joseph Sheridan Le Fanu's *The Rose and the Key*, all feature such institutions.

To explain these nerves-without-a-cause, and their readerly attractions, we have to look outside the novel. Miller's account is properly attentive to the nervous palpitations at the heart of the railway novel, but it cuts the latter off too abruptly from the railway. Hysteria, which Miller reads in terms of homosexual panic, also recalls the experience of automatism, of involuntary motion, associated with the body in machine culture, and I want to argue that the specifically modern nervousness which Miller identifies in the sensation novel is bound up with that modernization of the senses effected by the technological revolutions of the nineteenth century.[24] In this situation, the body is experienced as the interface between the new technology and nature, as both a potential machine itself, and as a resistance to the modernizing effects of the machine.[25] The defensive gait of the city dweller, the mechanical movements of the factory worker, the compulsive dice-throwing of the gambler – for Walter Benjamin these are the somatic indices of a new experience of space and time. And it is such bodies we find in the sensation novel, bodies 'feminized', but also galvanized.

RAILWAY SPINE

The 1860s also saw a widespread concern with what at first seems like a very different and considerably less pleasant sort of sensation – that of the railway accident. For a time, the railway, rather than the city street or the factory floor, represented *the* site of confrontation of the body and the forces of modernization, and a whole pathology of the railway developed.

In medical literature the new subject appeared for the first time in 1866. *The Lancet* published a three-part article by Thomas Buzzard entitled 'On Cases of Injury from Railway Accidents.' In the same year William Camps, an author who had previously published papers on epilepsy and hysteria, published his 'Railway Accidents or Collisions: Their Effects, Immediate and Remote, Upon the Brain and Spinal Cord and other Portions of the Nervous System.' Finally, that year also saw the publication of an epoch-making book by John Eric Erichsen, *On Railway and Other Injuries of the Nervous System* . . . After the near-absence of material dealing with such accidents in *The Lancet* of previous years, this sudden onset of a literature was remarkable – as was the fact that not one of the three authors makes any reference either to any of the others or to previous publications.[26]

What emerges in these and subsequent publications is a conception of the unique quality of the railway accident. This uniqueness lay in the fact that even those passengers who appeared to suffer little or no injury as a result of a collision frequently experienced profound psychological distress *afterwards* (as we saw in the case of Charles Dickens). Initial medical assumptions that the cause of such distress lay in some actual injury to the spine – what became known as 'railway spine' – gradually yielded to the view that the injury was psychic rather than physical, 'that the "mental shock" resulted not from a mechanical but from a psychic blow' (Schivelbusch, *The Railway Journey*, 143). Towards the end of the century this new category of psychic shock, 'railway brain', came to be termed 'traumatic neurosis'. When the First World War sent home the first cases of 'shell shock', there was already an abundant medical literature of shock stemming from the railways.

Let us not get side-tracked, however. To return to the 1860s, there was also a new concern with the deleterious effects of railway travel *even in the absence* of accidents. In the early days of railway transport, as Schivelbusch has noted, medical interest in the effects of railway travel was focused on the engine drivers and firemen, but by the 1860s the passengers had become the centre of attention. In the *Report of the Commission on the Influence of Railway Travel on Public Health*, published in the *Lancet* in 1862, Lord Shaftesbury is quoted to the effect that 'the very power of locomotion keeps persons in a state of great nervous excitement', so much so that many who travel by rail 'have been obliged to give it up in consequence of the effect on the nervous system'.[27] Evidently, Mrs Merridew's remark in Collins's later popular success, *The Moonstone*, that 'Railway travel always makes [her] nervous',[28] would have been readily understood by contemporary readers. The rapid series of jolts experienced by the railway traveller were seen to have damaging physical effects, as the traveller's body was forced to absorb the 'small regular concussions' (*Report*, 4 January 1862, 17) produced by the friction between the rapidly moving train and the tracks. Since the railway carriage was envisaged as 'a framework of bones without muscles' (19), the traveller's body was imagined as supplying the missing shock-absorbing connective tissue. There were even less tangible threats associated with the new mode of transport. The report refers to 'an often experienced condition of uneasiness, scarcely amounting to actual fear' on the part of railway travellers.[29] This trepidation was thought to be caused by fears of lateness and of collision. The report also dwells on the potentially harmful effects of the visual aspect of the railway journey: the traveller is swamped with sensory stimuli; he or she is 'forced into subjective states of mental activity' (*Report*, 11 January 1862, 51), and the optical nerve is strained by the rapid and unassimilable succession of impressions. Nor does reading offer any respite from visual overload; instead, the 'shifting characters of his book or newspaper . . . impose yet further labour on the eye' (51).

Not all of the accounts of the physical effects of railway travel are quite so damning. The jolts of the railway were also thought to produce a specifically sexual response. The sexual possibilities of the train are documented in a variety of Victorian sources. For example, 'Walter', the pseudonymous author of the infamous *My Secret Life*, describes several sexual encounters on the railway (vol. II, chapter 11; vol. IX, chapter 13).[30] Indeed, the putative aphrodisiac effects of trains have remained part of our popular culture, both as a narrative component of films as different as *North By Northwest* and *Risky Business*, and in the romantic potential ascribed to such fairground attractions as the 'ghost train' and the rollercoaster.[31] But in the 1860s the sexual potential of the railway also entrained certain anxieties, though these were ascribed not to the movement of train travel, but to the isolation involved. Indeed, the isolation of the carriages became a source of anxiety to railway travellers and authorities alike, some railways providing separate ladies' compartments to prevent 'outrages'. Among male travellers there were anxieties about wrongful accusation.[32] In a letter to his mother, Wilkie Collins wrote that 'Danger from virtuous single ladies whose character is "dearer to them than their lives" is serious. I won't travel alone with a woman – I promise you that.'[33] The train, as harbinger of modernity, appeared to threaten not just to shake up the individual body, but to erode the social barriers between the sexes in a way that was both tantalizing and frightening. The same threat/promise would later be taken up by other technologies, such as the cinema and the automobile.

In general, the railway journey is described as a constant assault on the fragile nervous system of the traveller, which recalls the way in which reading the sensation novel was characterized. The traveller, like the reader of sensation fiction (and perhaps the audience for sensation drama), is thought to be harnessed into a particular apparatus. The novel threatened to couple the reader to its mechanism, the reader being 'compelled to go on to the end, whether he likes it or not', as Mansel puts it, by its powerful narrative motor (cf. Walter's equation of his mission with the impulse of the narrative itself: 'the course of this narrative, steadily flowing on . . . carries me forward to the End' [*W*, 523]). The train incorporates the traveller as a sort of human cushion or shock-absorber. In both cases, the subject is thought to be reduced to a position of passive reception, but also to be over-stimulated by this experience, to be rendered uneasy, even fearful. Nor, indeed, was the reader the only one to suffer where fiction was concerned. The demands of serial publication meant that the writer, too, was quite literally harnessed to the text. Wilkie Collins, who was subject to a variety of nervous disorders, was described by Dickens as completely exhausted by 'the battle against the infernal periodical system' in composing *The Woman in White*.[34] To write, as to read sensation fiction was to risk being carried away.

The heated response to both the railway and the sensation novel suggests difficulties in accommodating a specifically modern form of sensory experience, though also a more general feeling of powerlessness in the face of rapid change. Travellers, characters, and readers alike seemed to emblematize the subject of modernity, locked in an iron cage. As Jenny Bourne Taylor has noted, the critical reaction to the sensation novel partly derived from the fact that reviewers saw it as condensing the zeitgeist. 'Sensation' came to act as a sort of cultural-critical shorthand: 'When critics self-consciously referred to the 1860s as an "age of sensation," they meant . . . that the word encapsulated the experience of modernity itself – the sense of continuous and rapid change, of shocks, thrills, intensity, excitement.'[35] As we saw in chapter 1, sensation became, in effect, a keyword of modernity. In reviews of the novels themselves, divisions between individual readers' bodies and the social body were frequently erased, and the fictions of Collins, Braddon, Wood, and their peers were perceived as 'a collective nervous disorder, a morbid addiction within the middle class that worked directly on the body of the reader and as an infection from outside'.[36] The American nerve specialist, George Miller Beard, made explicit the assumptions about connections among new technologies, new literature, and physio-cultural change when he attributed the 'development and very rapid increase of nervousness' to 'modern civilization' itself, which he saw as having five characteristics: 'steam power, the periodical press, the telegraph, the sciences, and the mental activity of women'.[37] In the case of the railway, Schivelbusch argues that it excited such deep feelings among the middle classes because it gave them their most direct experience of the powerful forces of industrial modernity, the same forces that the working class encountered on the factory floor.[38] Thus the Victorians took to the new mode of travel with apparent alacrity, but their over-hastily repressed anxieties were quick to resurface; by the 1860s, railway travel had been almost completely assimilated into everyday life, but accidents brought back all the original affect. While one might expect the railway accident to be a cause of concern in the early years of the railway, there is a lag of twenty years or so before this happens. The flurry of medical publications of the 1860s about the shocks attending train travel represents a forced acknowledgment of the transformation of the human sensorium by modernization.

However, it is not so much the phenomenon of shock per se – the return of the repressed of modernization – that provides our connection to the sensation novel as what, in human consciousness, acts as a buffer *against* shock. Following Benjamin, this buffer is a form of heightened consciousness, and specifically heightened consciousness of time – something that the pamphlets of the 1860s saw as a harmful consequence of train travel. That the railways transformed the Victorian experience of time as well as space is no mere hyperbole: the train brought with it standard time. Before the railway's advent, numerous local times flourished: 'London time ran four minutes ahead of time in Reading, seven minutes and thirty seconds ahead of Cirencester time, fourteen minutes ahead of Bridgwater time.'[39] The railway depended on standardized time and strict timetabling, and these ushered in a new time consciousness (a time consciousness that the factory worker had already learnt in a different way). The modern traveller needed to have a watch, and anxiety about missing trains became a recognizable medical complaint, as the title of a contemporary monograph, *Hurried to Death*, suggests. The railway traveller was even perceived to age more quickly, as if he or she were getting an overdose of time – season-ticket holders 'especially on the Brighton line' were seen to be particularly at risk.[40] For the railway – one might say for the entry of industrial modernity in general into everyday life – to be literally a less shocking experience, the traveller had to be brought up to speed. Rather than being a lesser variety of shock, then, the nervousness that the *Lancet* reports of the 1860s comment on was actually a shield against shock, and the passengers who felt 'Hurried to Death' were undergoing, however uncomfortably, a species of temporal training. That training would be continued by the sensation novel. Far from being a simple reaction to an age of sensory overload, sensation could have its uses.

RAILWAY NOVELS

The sensation novel is not *about* the railway in any simple sense, but there are indications that the latter is something like a determining absence for these novels, as the crowd, and the experience of urban modernity *tout court* are for the sensation drama. Sometimes, of course, the railway is more directly evoked in the text. In M. E. Braddon's *Lady Audley's Secret* and Wilkie Collins's *No Name*, for example, the protagonists lose their parents in off-stage railway accidents, linking the metaphorical isolation of these characters with processes of modernization. Rather exceptionally in the sensation novel, Mrs Wood's *East Lynne* incorporates the railway into the novel's own judicial mechanism: Isabel is punished by the novel for her flight from her husband when she is disfigured in a railway accident, her illegitimate child being killed (cf. Dickens's *Dombey and Son*, where the would-be adulterer, Carker, is killed by a train, or indeed the fate of that other nineteenth-century sinner against domesticity, Anna Karenina). Even though the railway accident keeps a rather low profile in the sensation novel – there are almost as many accidents in such domestic novels as *Cranford* – contemporary readers clearly associated the two.[41] So much so, that when Bret Harte wrote his 'Condensed Novels' spoof on the novels of M. E.

Braddon and Mrs Henry Wood, 'Selina Sedilia', he felt obliged to include a railway accident, in which 'Burke the Slogger', the working-class husband of the conniving Lady Selina, is conveniently killed.[42])

It is not these cameo appearances by the railway that principally concern us, though, but rather how the sensation novel reinforced the transformation of human experience of time and space being effected by the railways (and of course by the telegraph and the cheap postal system, the principal elements of the communications revolution that accompanied the railways). In part what the novels aimed at was bringing the present to life. H. L. Mansel notes that the particular effects attempted in the sensation novel require a contemporary setting, since 'a tale that aims at electrifying the reader is never thoroughly effective unless the scene be laid in our own day, and among the people we are in the habit of meeting' ('Sensation Novels', 499–9). Or, as he more dramatically puts it, 'It is necessary to be near a mine to be blown up by its explosion' (488). This was the quality that Henry James also recognized as marking off the sensation novel from the gothic: 'What are the Appenines to us or we to the Appenines? Instead of the terrors of Udolpho, we were treated to the terrors of the cheerful country house, or the busy London lodgings. And there is no doubt that these were infinitely the more terrible.'[43] But even more essential to the sensation novel than being contemporary is being on time: like its descendant, the thriller, this is a *punctual* form, depending on accurate time-keeping and scrupulous attention to the calendar. Time is as important to the sensation novel as it is to a modernist novel of temporality like *A la recherche du temps perdu*, but it is external, 'objective' time and not Bergsonian *durée* that it places centre stage.

The sensation novel is a novel of suspense, and is the first subgenre in which a Bradshaw's railway schedule and a watch become necessary to the principal characters. (As if to alert us to the centrality of time, watches pop up in unlikely places in *The Woman in White*: Sir Percival's burnt body is identified by his; earlier he bribes Anne Catherick with a gold watch to alter the parish marriage register and conceal his illegitimacy.) The novels depend on the rapid succession of diverse locations, at the same time that the distance between these locations is erased. Alternating locations are not of course *unique* to these novels, but only in the world of sensational crime do they become essential. Stephen Knight notes that the social and physical mobility of a modernizing society are essential ingredients of the first detective novels in the 1820s, where 'the recurrent mechanism . . . is travel to resolve mysterious crimes: up the road to York, out to the towns of the Thames valley, in and around the swelling villages that were rapidly becoming London'.[44] The sensation novel sees this mobility become even more pronounced, and closely bound to the expanding railway network. In the case of *The Woman in White*, Knight points out that the movements of the characters have in some cases only just become possible in 1849–51, the period in which the action of the novel takes place. Thus Carlisle had only been linked to the capital since 1844, Euston railway station opened in 1846, and Waterloo, where Laura arrives from Blackwater Park, opened in 1848. In the equally briskly paced *Lady Audley's Secret*, amateur detective Robert Audley shuttles between London, Audley Place, Southampton, Portsmouth, Liverpool, Dorsetshire, and Yorkshire in search of clues, taking expresses wherever possible, and fretting when he has to take a slower train. The temporal armature of the story is filled out with references to the 10:50 (express), the 3:00, 3:30, and 6:15 trains to London from the neighbourhood of Audley Court, the early express to Southampton from London, (arriving rather vaguely between eleven and twelve o'clock), and an express from Wildernsea to London leaving at 'a quarter past one',[45] to name just a few. In *The Woman in White*, Walter flits by rail between London and Blackwater Park (Hampshire), Wellingham (also Hampshire), and Limmeridge (Cumberland). This use of 'location shooting' placed new demands on the author too. While writing *Armadale*, Wilkie Collins visited, among other places, the Isle of Man, Great Yarmouth, and Naples in search of local colour. (Like Dickens, Collins was not a keen rail traveller. As Catherine Peters notes, 'the man who so often used trains in the plots of his novels hated travel by them'.[46])

The time consciousness of the sensation novel is emblematized by the role that 'telegraphic messages' (an offshoot of the railway) play. Thanks to the new networks of communication, not a moment is lost:

Robert Audley had requested Clara Talboys to telegraph an answer to his question, in order to avoid the loss of a day in the accomplishment of the investigation he had promised to perform. The telegraphic answer reached Fig-tree Court before twelve o'clock the next day . . . Within an hour of the receipt of this message Mr Audley arrived at the King's Cross station, and took his ticket for Wildernsea by an express train that started at a quarter before two. (*Lady Audley's Secret*, 241)

His quarry, Lady Audley, is equally adept at exploiting the resources of the new transportation and communication system, making good use of 'telegraphic messages' as well as trains in her attempt to keep her secret. New technologies are not a simple backdrop to these stories, then – victory goes to whoever masters them. Timing is all-important to the plots of both *Lady Audley's Secret* and Collins's *The Woman in White*, which both turn on accurate date-keeping. In *The Woman in White*, for example, the plot to replace Laura with her dying double turns on the date of Laura's rail journey to London, since Anne Catherick's death in London before Laura's arrival there is the one weak spot in Fosco's plan (famously, Collins got the dates wrong in the first version of the novel).

The Woman in White utilizes, perhaps even introduces, a temporal trope that will later become a staple of the suspense plot: what we might call the dramatic time limit, or deadline. In the form that this takes in Collins's tale, Walter Hartright insures himself against foul play when he goes to visit Count Fosco by leaving a letter with his friend Pesca, to be opened if Hartright has not returned by nine o'clock the next morning. The sealed letter will reveal Fosco's identity, leading to his certain death at the hands of the 'Brotherhood', the shadowy European secret society in the novel. To extract a date from Fosco, one might say, Hartright uses a time. Fosco's hand trembles as he asks how long he has 'before the clock strikes and the seal is broken' (*W*, 548); time itself, rather than Hartright, has become his enemy. It is perhaps not over-fanciful to recognize in this scene a secularized version of Dr Faustus's appointment with damnation, or to speculate that the ensuing scene, in which Fosco writes against the clock to cover sheet after sheet of paper with the details of the plot against Laura, also perhaps represents a nightmare vision of Collins's own writing to deadline. (One also thinks of the countless 'working to deadline' scenes in modern screen thrillers, where the fingers of the hero or heroine fumble over colour-coded wires to defuse a time-bomb.) Fosco, though, rises to the occasion, and seems relatively unperturbed at the way the temporal discipline of the railway or factory timetable has entered the home:

Four o'clock has just struck. Good! Arrangement, revision, reading from four to five. Short snooze of restoration for myself, from five to six. Final preparations, from six to seven. Affair of agent and sealed letter from seven to eight. At eight, *en route*. Behold the programme! (*W*, 553)

This highlighting of clock time, location, and motion is not incidental to the suspense for which these novels are famous, but its precondition. The pleasures of fictional suspense and the anxieties of clock-watching appear as part of the same historical moment. What the sensation novel was preaching to the nerves was a new time-discipline: to be immersed in the plot of a sensation novel, to have one's nerves quiver with those of the hero or heroine, was to be wired into a new mode of temporality. Time-consciousness would be recast as pleasurable suspense. Just as the cinema would later 'train' people in the mode of distracted perception necessary to navigate the modern metropolis, in the 1860s the sensation novel trained its readers to live within the temporality of the railway age.

However, there is evidence to suggest that the novels view the new 'punctual' subject that they are helping to shape with some degree of trepidation. More than *The Woman in White* or *Lady Audley's Secret*, Collins's *Armadale* suggests that the modern, nervous, and punctual body has itself become a facet of technology; and at the same time it suggests that fiction has become as mechanical as its characters. One of the most memorable – and most peculiar – features of the novel is the detailed description of the clock constructed by Major Milroy on the example of a famous Strasbourg clock and 'the extraordinary automaton figures which that clock puts in motion' (*Armadale*, 213), which appear and disappear as the chimes sound. The Major, describing the workings of his elaborate timepiece, might well be Collins himself explaining the inner workings of this most plotted of plot-driven novels: 'The machinery is a little complicated, and there are defects in it which I am ashamed to say I have not yet succeeded in remedying as I could wish. Sometimes the figures go all wrong, and sometimes they go all right' (215). In fact, the mechanical hitches that ruin the performance of the Major's automata (a door that won't open to allow the automata through) comically prefigure the snags in the plot to murder Allan Armadale at the nervous sanatorium; it is these snags that result in the deaths of Ozias Midwinter and Lydia Gwilt. But the mechanical motion of the figures points beyond the demands of serial-plotting to the nature of the characters themselves. Encouraging the reader to equate the clock's figures with those of the narrative, 'mechanical' and 'mechanically' are two of the terms most often used to describe Ozias in motion: for example, 'He rose mechanically to kindle a light' (260), '"Miss Gwilt!" he exclaimed, and mechanically held out his hand' (370), and 'Midwinter mechanically checked himself before he turned the corner of the house' (379). If the clock can act as a *mise-en-abîme* of the novel's action, this is in part because the characters themselves have become automata. But as in the case of the railway passenger, to become part of a mechanical apparatus is not to be freed from human nervousness; rather it is to be all the more subject to it. As if to highlight this idea that mechanical motion and nervousness are complements rather than opposites, Midwinter is just as often described as 'hysterical', and reaches a sort of hysterical peak during the scene in which he is shown the clock by Major Milroy.

Armadale shows that if the sensation novel takes part in the production of the modern nervous body, it can also manifest considerable pessimism about the future of that body. The most vivid example of this dystopian vision of the modernized body – at once mechanical and nervous – appears not in *Armadale*, though, but in Collins's *The Law and the Lady*. Miserrimus Dexter is an extreme version of Midwinter, and Collins's other nervous and feminized men. What in them is borderline hysteria is in him almost madness; similarly, if Ozias has a 'sensitive feminine organization', Miserrimus is literally not a 'whole' man – he has no legs. Ozias Midwinter appears at times like a clockwork figure, but the wheelchair-bound Dexter is a human locomotive in an infernal setting. In one scene he appears as a 'fantastic and frightful apparition, man and machinery blended in one', frenetically wheeling himself around his firelit room 'with floating hair, and arms furiously raised and lowered . . . through the field of red light'.[47] Departing from the verisimilitudes of the sensation novel to produce a more fantastic mode, Collins produces in Dexter one of the most memorable figures of Victorian technological nightmare. Dexter is animated by an almost superhuman energy, and possessed of considerable creative powers, but he also represents for Collins a falling-off from the human. While he is described above as half-man, half-machine, 'the new Centaur' (*Law and the Lady*, 206), later he appears in a Darwinian light as 'half-monkey, half-man' (347). Dexter seems to demonstrate that the human/machine hybrid is unstable, and like some other hybrids, sterile.[48]

SHEDDING VICTORIAN BAGGAGE

By the end of the century, as we saw in the previous chapter, the on-stage railway rescue had become available for debunking. The sensation novel had to endure a similar fate. When Oscar Wilde comes to write his determinedly anti-Victorian *The Importance of Being Earnest* in 1894–5, he fixes on the sensation novel and the railway, as emblems of the mid-Victorianism to which he is determinedly waving goodbye from the platform, with tears of mirth rolling down his cheeks. However, there is more at stake here than the use of the sensation novel and the railway as a convenient shorthand for mid-Victorian Britain. Wilde is rejecting the entire problematic of modernity implicit in the railway/sensation nexus. For him, modernity is not a dangerous new force with which the subject has to come to terms, or a new form of discipline; rather it is a potent source of experience, and experience is a good in itself.

Wilde's philosophy of modernity can be seen as a strategic reworking of the work of Walter Pater, most obviously the infamous 'Conclusion' to *The Renaissance*. While Pater's essays on Botticelli, Michelangelo, Da Vinci, and others seem to studiously avoid the Victorian present and cling to past glories, the world that Pater evokes in the 'Conclusion', where 'at first sight experience seems to bury us under a flood of external objects, pressing upon us with a sharp and importunate reality, calling us out of ourselves in a thousand forms of action', recalls the world of nineteenth-century modernity – the world of the railway and of shock – and not some timeless experiential reality.[49] Pater's injunction to 'be present always at the focus where the greatest number of vital forces unite in their purest energy' (*The Renaissance*, 236) is a prescription for a world in which 'all melts under our feet' (237), a phrase that seems to echo Karl Marx's description of Victorian modernity: 'all that is solid melts into air'. We have seen how the popular fiction of the 1860s attempts to produce an appropriate subject for this experiential world by preaching to the nerves. The sensation novel, I have argued, is a suspense-machine, and that suspense works to retool the subject of modernity, who without some such training risks being overwhelmed by modernity – of melting along with the ground under his or her feet. This is not at all Pater's view of the subject's confrontation with modernity. Rather than growing a protective carapace of consciousness, the subject, he suggests, should embrace the experiential possibilities on offer:

While all melts under our feet, we may well grasp at any exquisite passion, or any contribution to knowledge that seems by a lifted horizon to set the spirit free for a moment, or any stirring of the senses, strange dyes, strange colours, and curious odours, or work of the artist's hands, or the face of one's friend . . . What we have to do is to be forever testing new opinions and courting new impressions. (237)

It might at first glance seem from this that the proper response to a world of flux, then, is to dive into the flow, to make experience an end in itself. Pater is not quite saying this, though others decided that he was, famously leading Pater to suppress the 'Conclusion' from the second edition of *The Renaissance*. In the end, for Pater, art and timeless form provide an idealist escape route from the bustle of modernity. The world that at first seems to threaten to overwhelm the subject, becomes itself available for aesthetic consumption. The hysterically unstable machine-self that Collins imagines at the end of *The Law and the Lady* yields to a self that is pure energy and yet outside the flux, burning with a hard, gem-like flame, and yet not consumed.

   Pater's advocacy of experience is taken up by Wilde and reworked along decidedly less idealist lines, most obviously in *The Picture of Dorian Gray* (1890), which transforms Pater's doctrine through a liberal admixture of the materialist decadence of Huysmanns's *A Rebours*. But *The Importance of Being Earnest* also owes something to the railway. In the play, Dorian's appetite for experience as an end in itself has been comically transformed into Algernon's passion for cucumber sandwiches, and into his practice of 'Bunburyism'. He may seem to glow with the warmth of buttered muffins rather than burn with a hard, gem-like flame, but Algernon's imaginary visits to his imaginary hypochondriac friend, Bunbury, provide him with the excuses necessary for an elaborate double life, just as his magical portrait makes it possible for Dorian to expand the range of *his* experiences, and live a double life without consequences. Jack, likewise, has created a dual existence for himself to avoid his responsibilities in the country by inventing a scapegrace younger brother, Ernest, whom he has to keep on the straight and narrow by regular visits to the fleshpots of the town. As Christopher Craft has shown, we get a better sense of the submerged illicit nature of those London visits in the four-act version of the play, in which Jack's extravagant dining at the Savoy (in the character of Ernest) almost lands Algernon (in the character of Ernest) in jail for debt.[50] Craft points out that the Savoy was also one of the venues for Wilde's own assignations with male prostitutes, and that one form of appetite systematically displaces another in the play. Dorian's debauchery becomes Algernon's gluttony, gothic excesses become comic ones. Algernon and – despite occasional lip-service – Jack, as much as Dorian, take Pater's dictum that 'what is only conventional has no real claim upon us' (*The Renaissance*, 238) at face value.

However, Wilde's play spends less time on the celebration of experience than on elaborate jokes at the expense of an outdated Victorianism, and a conception of the subject that we might take to be mid-Victorian. This earlier version of the self Wilde associates with the cult of earnestness, with the railway, and with the mid-Victorian novel, especially in its sensational form. Wilde grasps the fact that all three of these travel on the one ticket: the railway, the cult of earnestness, and the frissons of the sensation novel are alike essential to the formation of the Victorian self; muscular Christians like Tom Brown can never quite escape from the noise of the railroad, or the nervousness of a Walter Hartright.

It will be remembered that Ernest, alias Jack Worthing, is very much a railway child, found in a handbag left at the cloakroom in Victoria station (opened in 1860) by Miss Prism, and named for the destination marked on his finder's first-class ticket. The choice of stations is hardly fortuitous: Wilde is at some pains to tell us that Ernest/Jack is a *Victorian* railway child. It is Jack's dubious past life as a parcel that prompts Lady Bracknell to satirically inquire in Act 3 as to the antecedents of his ward, Cecily Cardew: 'is Miss Cardew at all connected with any of the larger railway stations in London? I ask merely for information. Until yesterday I had no idea that there were any families or persons whose origin was a terminus.'⁵¹ Not the least of the joke is that Lady Bracknell herself is also a railway child, insofar as the Victorian culture that she represents, with its particular problematics of modernization, was a railway culture. Lady Bracknell's reluctance to allow her only daughter to 'marry into a cloak room, and form an alliance with a parcel' (*The Importance of Being Earnest*, 172–3) echoes some of the more hostile early accounts of the railway that saw it as transforming people into so many packages, shuttled around the country (Ruskin, for example, describes the railway as changing 'the traveller from a man into a living parcel').⁵² In a more prosaic way, Lady Bracknell herself becomes such a parcel – one might even say an old bag – when she has to take a luggage train to pursue Gwendolen into the country (313).

But if Jack's luggage connections show that his roots lie in an earlier Victorian culture, he is also close kin to the mid-Victorian novel. This is a play in which books can be mistaken for people, and the changeling left by Miss Prism in Jack's perambulator turns out to be none other than 'the manuscript of a three-volume novel of more than usually revolting sentimentality' (336). The pram, as far as Wilde is concerned, of course, is the right place for this species of fiction. That the sensation novel as much as, if not more than, the sentimental novel is the target of Wilde's wit is suggested by a comment of Cecily's on the novels she receives from Mudie's Circulating Library, which, like memory, '[chronicle] the things that have never happened, and couldn't possibly have happened' (204). But there is a more serious criticism of the Victorian three-decker involved, I think. If Wilde's own literary children have outgrown such mid-Victorian pleasures, this is because they have also outgrown mid-Victorian anxieties. Miss Prism's 'railway novel', like the railway itself, was once an index of Victorian up-to-date-ness; now it is a form that has outlived its function. The sensation novel can scarcely have any further role in a world where Gwendolen can say 'I never travel without my diary. One should always have something sensational to read in a train' (272). The body-made-nervous addressed by the sensation novel has no place in Wilde's sophisticated world. When Lady Bracknell pulls out her watch and worries that they 'have already missed five, if not six trains', it is not because she feels hurried to death but only because 'to miss any more might expose [them] to comment on the platform' (331).

For Wilde, the railway/sensation phase of modernity is over. With Gwendolen's terse anatomy of the technique of sensation fiction – 'This suspense is terrible. I hope it will last' (343) – the play consigns the sensation novel to the past, and with it the problem that it responded to, the accommodation of the self and mechanized modernity. Wilde sees no need for any such reconciliation, and accordingly the sensation novel has become a piece of old rolling-stock, interesting to take apart, but irrelevant to the concerns of the present. With hindsight, of course, it is easy to see that Wilde was altogether too optimistic about the disappearance of the antinomies of modernization.

Wilde's romantic comedy of double lives, fictive brothers, and lost luggage, premiered on 14 February (St Valentine's Day) 1895, and has often been seen as marking the end of a certain type of Victorianism. But *Earnest* was far from being the only sign that month of seismic change in a familiar nineteenth-century landscape. The previous day two actual brothers, Louis and Auguste Lumière, Lyon-based manufacturers of photographic equipment, had patented a device that captured moving pictures (it was actually a combined camera, printer, and projector). Inspired by Thomas Edison's moving-picture peep-hole machine, the kinetoscope, their machine could project larger-than-life moving images for an audience. They called their new machine the *cinématographe*, and staged their first public screening in December of that year in the basement lounge of the Grand Café on the Boulevard de Capucines in Paris. When early the following year London audiences had their first chance to see the flickering images conjured up by the *cinématographe* and its competitors, one of the first images they saw was a train arriving at a station platform. In our next chapter we will look at the reception of this last Victorian machine, which came to act as agent and emblem of another phase of modernity, and which would change again the way in which people thought about bodies and technology.

CHAPTER 3

The Boerograph

> In the late summer, I think, of 1913, I was invited to Manoeuvres
> round Frensham Ponds at Aldershot... When the sham fight was
> developing, the day turned blue-hazy, the sky lowered, and the heat
> struck like the Karroo, as one scuttled among the heaths listening
> to the uncontrolled clang of the musketry fire. It came over me that
> anything might be afoot in such weather, pom-poms for instance,
> half-heard on a flank, or the glint of a helio[graph] through a cloud-
> drift. In short I conceived of the whole pressure of our dead of the
> Boer War flickering and re-forming as the horizon flickered in the
> heat.
>
> (Rudyard Kipling, *Something of Myself*)[1]

We have been discussing the ways in which Victorian drama and fiction
mediate and meditate on the industrialization of everyday life. As we have
seen, the railway and railway time come to stand for that transformation,
while also acting as important participants in it. The body that is posited
as taking part in this process is the sensational body, the body nervous, an
organism speeded-up to meet the demands of a new space/time regime, or
even, as in the 'railway rescue' scenario, an organism whose acceleration is
paradoxically imagined as enabling an escape from the very modernity that
requires such acceleration.

The railway was the iconic technology of Victorian modernity, but that
is in part, of course, because it was an early arrival on the Victorian scene,
a product of the first industrial revolution built on iron, coal, and steam.
A second industrial revolution – involving advances in the chemical in-
dustries and in the use of electricity, and the development of the internal
combustion engine, inter alia – occurs in the last decades of the nineteenth
century. It introduces new technologies that alter the fabric of everyday life
in as dramatic a fashion as the railway: the telephone, the automobile, and
electric lighting, for example. Here, though, it is on the cinematograph,
the last great Victorian machine, that I wish to concentrate, focusing in

particular on early attempts to understand and map its particular effects on the subject. As Lynne Kirby and Anne Friedberg, among others, have shown, the initial response to the cinematograph is continuous in many respects with the response to the railway, not least because the latter offered an experiential paradigm that helped the first spectators to accommodate the new medium.[2] At a more literal level, the panoramic commodity experience of the railway excursion yielded to cinematic 'phantom rides' like Hale's Tours, in which long tracking shots were used to give the viewer the experience of virtual mobility.[3] However, despite such continuities there is an obvious difference between the two machines: unlike the railway, the cinema is a technology of the image. This means that it is a self-reflexive machine – it can represent itself and its spectators, as in such films as *The Countryman's First Sight of the Animated Pictures* (1901). But it also means that when we move from the railway machine to the cinema machine as icon and agent of modernization we have to consider two different human/machine collisions. One involves the body of the spectator, the other the body that has been filmed – de-realized but also made magically present through its capture by the cinema machine. While the former body comes to be imagined in ways that are consistent with the nervous, over-stimulated railway body, the latter is something for which the cultural imaginary of the railway has no equivalent.

In this chapter I want to consider some of the early responses to the cinematograph, including a short story, Rudyard Kipling's 'Mrs Bathurst' (1904), that explore the effects of the new medium's industrial magic on the viewer and the viewed. Resisting as best I can the temptations of teleology, I am not proposing that we may discover the essence of film by looking at this early moment. Rather, I want to argue that the experience of the cinematograph's first audiences was in many respects unique, and it is this uniqueness that I wish to attempt to illuminate.

SHADOWLAND

There appears to be something devilish about mechanical reproduction. One of the clichés about 'primitive' cultures is that they believe that the camera can steal one's soul, but the most sophisticated of Euro-American cultural theorists have long harboured similar suspicions. Walter Benjamin argued that mechanical reproduction destroyed the aura of unique objects, though he did not regard this as such a bad thing. Fredric Jameson has more recently charged postmodern cinema with killing off history and substituting its own glossy changelings. For Jean Baudrillard and Paul Virilio it is reality itself that has been replaced by the chimeras conjured up by the media. Even Roland Barthes's poignant tribute to photography, *Camera Lucida*, ends with a jeremiad about the present moment in which 'the photograph crushes all other images by its tyranny . . . de-realiz[ing] the human world of conflict and desires'.[4]

One might climb to higher theoretical ground and endorse Guy Debord's argument in *The Society of the Spectacle* that the de-realization wrought by the mechanical image is in fact a secondary effect, and that it is capitalism itself, with its privileging of the commodity form, that has sucked the life out of reality: the phantasmagoria of the society of the spectacle, then, like Marx's dancing tables, are not so much about visuality as about commodi-fication. All the camera does is to help to make reality available as portable merchandise.

Alternatively, while Freud does not explore it, one might argue that there is a much larger category of the technological uncanny,[5] and that the ghostliness of mechanical image-reproduction stands in synecdochi-cally for that of machine culture in general. Mechanization, the develop-ment, in effect, of a second nature, introduces its own spectres – ghosts in the machine, though scarcely in Arthur Koestler's sense. In this light we might speculate that perhaps the gothic novel, which also appears towards the end of the eighteenth century, owes as much to the in-dustrial revolution as to the French. Certainly, Mary Shelley's epochal science fiction/horror novel, *Frankenstein* (1818), might also be consid-ered an industrial novel (cf. the exploration of the uncanniness of indus-trial time in such residual Victorian gothic as Dickens's 'The Signalman' (1865)).

Yet the mechanical reproduction of the image seems to be a special case, with its own discrete history. Assumptions about the uncanny effects of photo-reproduction perhaps owe something to the history of the applica-tions of such technologies, and earlier technologies of the image. The first commercially successful deployment of the magic lantern, for example, was Étienne Gaspar Robert's *Fantasmagorie* (cf. the name Thomas Armat would much later give to his 1895 moving-picture projector, the 'Phantoscope'). At the turn of the eighteenth century, Parisian audiences flocked to see this elaborate slide show in which the spirits of Robespierre, Voltaire, Lavoisier, and Rousseau, among others, were conjured up to produce a pleasurable frisson.[6] When the Daguerrotype appeared at the end of the 1830s, trick photographs producing ghostly images were not long in following, and, as Tom Gunning has shown, spirit photography enjoyed a considerable vogue throughout the nineteenth century.[7]

But even when photographic technology was used more straightforwardly there was something uncanny about it: the camera that supposedly never lied may have offered a new support to positivism, but it also created what Gunning terms a 'parallel world of phantasmatic doubles'. To this extent, arguments for the peculiar uncanniness of photography may derive not from its dubious ancestry but from its indexical quality. As Roland Barthes observes, what we see in the photographic image is not simply a copy of its referent 'but an emanation of past reality' that pursues its own career independently of its original. Light reflected from the object creates a chemical reaction in the sensitive photographic plate, leaving visible traces. The positive print developed from this negative is more removed from the absent original, but it is still something more (or less) than a representation. For Barthes, this connection to the absent referent makes of photography 'a magic, not an art'.[8] Even in mass-reproduced photo-images something of the original is still there, preserved, as it were, in high-tech amber.

How do we square the lexis of enchantment that attaches to photo-reproduction with the idea that the latter takes part in the modernization of the senses? After all, while Barthes may wish to make a case for the ontological distinctness of the still photograph, recent cultural histories have tended to position photography within a continuum of nineteenth-century visual assemblages – with the stereoscope, the panorama, the diorama, and, of course, the cinematograph – all of them playing some part in the modernization of the visual field. This modernization, like that effected by the railway, has been seen to entail a retraining or disciplining of the subject, the interpellation of progressively more sedentarized, cellularized, and privatized versions of the viewing self, in effect the retooling of that self for industrial tasks, as Jonathan Crary has described. None of that sounds very magical. But as he and others have also noted, this is only one side of the modernization of visuality. There is also a less carceral, more oneiric aspect to the modern visual field, from the creation of a phantasmagoria of commodified images in consumer culture, especially through advertising (Benjamin), to the installation of a virtual and mobilized gaze (Friedberg), to the creation of states of reverie (Crary). It is, perhaps, this aspect of the modernization of visuality that finds expression in the language of magic, even of necromancy, that follows the cinematograph from its inception.

'Mrs Bathurst' is not the only literary text from the turn of the century to comment on the cultural impact of the cinematograph. H. G. Wells had earlier imagined a future world where moving pictures form part of the fabric of everyday life in *When the Sleeper Awakes* (1899), and G. E. Farrow's children's story, 'The Cinematograph Train' (1904) also incorporates the

new medium. But while Wells dwells on the cinema's potential for surveil-
lance, and Farrow explores its kinship with the world of dreams, Kipling explores its uncanny aspect, its creation of images that are more than images.[9]
'Mrs Bathurst', then, owes kin to that extensive set of late Victorian tales
that dwell on the existence of 'dead' things that have a life of their own –
vampires, mummies, portraits (it is tempting to speculate that the appearance of those tales in or around 1895 is not a coincidence). Set in South
Africa just after the Anglo-Boer War, it tells the story of a warrant officer,
Vickery, who goes to see an early film show, 'Home and Friends for a Tickey'
(viz. threepence) while on shore leave in Cape Town. There he recognizes
in one of the actualités a woman he was once romantically involved with,
the Mrs Bathurst of the title, as she alights from the Western Mail train
at Paddington station in London. Haunted by her image, he goes to see
the show night after night, before eventually losing his wits and deserting
while supposedly on an official mission inland. Later, it appears (though
we can be certain of little in this most elliptical of Kipling stories), his body
is found in the South African interior. He and a companion have been
burnt to charcoal after being caught in an electrical storm in a teak forest.
Kipling's story explores the magical capacity of the new image technology
to transmit the force of personality across thousands of miles, but also seems
to suggest an annihilating power inherent in the camera's look.

'Mrs Bathurst', then, appears to be a precocious instance of the the-
orization of the peculiar magic of the cinema. I want to argue, though,
that there are also more local reasons for the eerie light in which the new
technology of the image first appears in the early 1900s. In particular,
I will suggest that the capacity of the camera to conjure up Gunning's
'parallel world of phantasmatic doubles' took on a special resonance in
a Britain that had to simultaneously assimilate the new medium of motion pictures and a particular national trauma, the military catastrophe of
the distant Anglo-Boer War (1899–1902). While 'Mrs Bathurst' takes stock
of a revolution of the image, then, it is also a story about industrialized
warfare.

THE WARGRAPH

By the turn of the century, moving pictures – also known as living pictures
and animated pictures, inter alia – were still a novelty in Britain, but an
increasingly familiar one. They had become a regular feature on music-hall
programmes, and were also to be seen at fairs, town halls, and a variety of
other venues. Considerations of content were beginning to intrude upon

film as a novel medium: audiences were losing interest in moving pictures for their own sake, and their drifting attention had to be focused with new subject matter. By 1898, British film pioneer R. W. Paul was already claiming that 'the day is past when anything in the way of animated pictures will do for an audience'.[10]

As it happens, this phase of transition coincided with a national event that would provide an almost endless supply of topical content – the Anglo-Boer War, or the War in South Africa, as it was more often termed. Lured by the gold mines of the Rand, prodded by the High Commissioner for South Africa, Sir Alfred Milner, and 'gold bugs' like Cecil Rhodes and Alfred Beit, and motivated by its rivalry in the region with Germany, Britain sought to break the power of the Boers, and add the Transvaal and Orange Free State to its existing territories, the Cape Colony and Natal. An excuse to initiate hostilities appeared in the form of the Transvaal government's treatment of the largely British 'Uitlander' majority, the numerous miners, engineers, and managers who had flocked to the lucrative mines of the Rand. Britain pressed the Transvaal to enfranchise the 'Uitlanders', but the Boers feared that the balance of power would tip against them if they did so. In October 1899 the Transvaal government was manipulated into starting a war that Britain would eventually win, but at a high price: 22,000 colonial and imperial troops lost their lives, most of them to disease and inadequately treated wounds.[11] As Thomas Pakenham notes, at a cost to the exchequer of £200 million, it was the most expensive military expedition since the Napoleonic wars (*The Boer War*, 512). Losses on the Boer side were probably higher still – they lost fewer troops (some 7,000), but between 18,000 and 28,000 men, women, and children died in the infamous 'concentration camps' run by the British forces. Records of deaths among the many black Africans who took part in, or who were overtaken by, this putative 'white man's war' are much less accurate, but it is unlikely that they fared *better* than the Boers or the British. 20,000 are thought to have died in the camps alone.[12]

What was supposed to have been a 'small war' against a nation of backward settlers without a professional army grew into a military disaster for Britain, which suffered the additional ignominy of being portrayed as the villain of the piece in the international press.[13] The war has been described as Britain's Vietnam.[14] Reports of the high numbers of casualties and, equally shocking at the time, of British surrenders, stunned the newspaper-reading public, more accustomed to conflicts that pitted Britain's own heavily armed troops against the spear-bearing armies of non-industrialized nations. This was also one of the first modern media wars, and responses to the war were shaped by the newspapers to a greater extent than earlier conflicts had been. This was a period of expansion for the British popular press: Harmsworth's *Daily Mail* first appeared in 1896, the *Daily Express* in 1900. Sir George White's defeat at Ladysmith thus quickly became 'Mournful Monday'; the week in December 1899 that saw reverses at Stormberg, Magersfontein, and Colenso became the 'Black Week'.[15] If the press made British failures part of a sort of national calendar, the successes of the war were inscribed just as indelibly in the national consciousness, the relief of Mafeking famously adding a new verb to the English language: 'to maffick', meaning to celebrate exuberantly.

The cinema played its own part in mediating the war to the British public. Since the war came only three years after the first commercial display of the cinematograph in England, unsurprisingly the first motion pictures that many Britons saw were Boer War actualités, which held considerable appeal for the jingoist audiences of fin-de-siècle musical halls in which early films were often shown.[16] So closely associated were the new medium and the war that some exhibitors even referred in their advertisements to the 'Boerograph' or the 'Wargraph' rather than the cinematograph.[17] Indeed, whatever its importance for British imperial history, the war acted as a stimulus to the still very fragile emergent film industry, just as the Spanish–American war had done in the United States in 1898.[18]

The war in South Africa was also closely connected to shifts in the older image medium, the still camera. The first user-friendly camera, the Kodak, had come on the market some ten years earlier, ushering in the era of the mass amateur photographer, and during the war the much cheaper Kodak Brownie, retailing at five shillings (including two rolls of film) became available. As a result, thousands of snapshots of the South African conflict were taken, making it the first major historical event of any sort to be captured in this fashion by amateurs, and putting into popular circulation a series of images of the distant conflict that, together with newspaper lithographs and actualité footage, gave the South African war an unprecedented visual presence in Britain.[19]

As film historian John Barnes has recorded in detail, almost everyone involved in British film production took advantage of the ready market for images of the overseas war. There was a popular desire to 'see' the war, to make it somehow more present or to quite literally bring it home. But perhaps the most striking aspect of the Boer War in terms of its visuality was that for a variety of reasons there was not so very much to see. The Boers inflicted heavy casualties on the British forces by refusing to confront them in pitched battles, relying to a large extent on guerilla tactics. As a war, the South African conflict was decidedly *unspectacular*, a far cry from the deadly pageantry of earlier conflicts. For the first time the British army came up against an enemy armed with long-range, high velocity magazine rifles using smokeless cartridges. Accurate and concentrated fire from such weapons – German-made Mausers for the most part – rendered the traditional cavalry charge and close-formation infantry advance almost suicidal. At Magersfontein, the *Times* correspondent describes how a force of 3,000 British troops was cut to shreds by 'the most devastating volley that has probably been poured into any body of men'.[20] Boer marksmen ended another aspect of traditional military practice – the use of readily visible insignia of rank. As the same correspondent put it in December 1899: 'It is not too much to say that as the Zulu war stopped once for all the carrying of colours into action, so the present war will finally have forbidden officers to be in any way marked or distinguished from their men.'[21] The long-range rifle stretched the battlefield over miles, the use of smokeless cartridges rendering the enemy positions almost invisible. 'The enemy', as Thomas Pakenham puts it, 'were an army of ghosts' (*The Boer War*, 179).[22] Months into the war, many of the British troops had yet to see any Boers, alive or dead (360). If the industrialized transport medium of the railway altered the experience of time and space in peacetime, industrialized warfare annihilated an older experience of battle time and battle space. Just when the image-reproductive technology of the cinematograph could have properly captured it, the era of the pitched battle was over, making a totalizing view impossible for cameraman and general alike.[23]

Rudyard Kipling quickly grasped the way in which the Boer War simply did not make itself available as a spectacle either to those present in South Africa or to their friends at home. While working at Lord Roberts's request on the British propaganda paper, the Bloemfontein *Friend*, he witnessed the Battle of Karee Siding:

The enormous pale landscape swallowed up seven thousand troops without a sign . . . We went on into a vacant world full of sunshine and distances, where now and again a single bullet sang to himself. [Kipling and his companion are mistaken for combatants and come under fire.] I prayed that the [British combatants] would go elsewhere, which they presently did, for the aimed fire slackened and a wandering colonial, bored to extinction, turned up with news from a far flank. 'No; nothing doing and *no one to see.*' Then more cracklings and a most cautious move forward to the lip of a large hollow where sheep were grazing. Some of them began to drop and kick. 'That's both sides trying sighting-shots,' said my companion. 'What range do you make it?' I asked. 'Eight hundred [yards], at the nearest. That's close quarters nowadays. *You'll never see anything closer than this. Modern rifles make it impossible'* . . . We waited, *seeing nothing* in the emptiness, and hearing only a faint murmur as of wind along gas-jets, running in and out of the unconcerned hills [my emphasis].[24]

If the war itself could not easily be captured on camera, at least its effects could, and Kipling became involved in this side of the war, sending a Kodak camera to a Mr Brooks, and asking him 'to take photos of graves to send home to relatives' in England; such visual evidence would, he believed, 'ease the minds' of those at home.[25]

The earliest cinematograph footage of the war consisted of actualité scenes of British troops embarking for South Africa, e.g. British Mutoscope and Biograph's *General Buller Embarking at Southampton* (1899), or Robert William Paul's *Scots: Embarkation of the Scots' Guards* (1899). These army crowd scenes in fact mimic the non-military crowd scenes that were already a staple of film shows in this period.[26] A few film-makers did take their cameras to South Africa, but given the battlefield's resistance to the camera, much of the footage sent back showed troop arrivals and deployment, armoured trains, and other sometimes spectacular but scarcely dramatic scenes. Some audiences would already have been familiar with such footage from an extremely popular British film from the Sudan campaign, John Benett-Stanford's *Alarming Queen's Company of Grenadier Guards at Omdurman* (1898), which showed British troops just before the actual battle (Benett-Stanford would also film the Boer War).[27] British Mutoscope and Biograph's William Kennedy-Laurie Dickson, who had earlier worked with Thomas Edison in the United States, and who had in fact been a key figure in the development of Edison's kinetoscope, succeeded better than most in filming actual battle scenes, as he records in his memoir, *The Biograph in Battle*.[28] But even he was largely restricted to showing what came before or after battles, or shots of long-range bombardment.

Troop departures and arrivals were, then, the staples of most film shows. Whatever appeal these scenes may have held, they possessed little narrative interest. Small wonder 'then' that British film-makers who wished to meet the public demand for South African material began to stage their own pro-filmic and more 'traditional' Boer War back in England: long before Jean Baudrillard saw the Gulf War on television, the first simulacral battles took place. For example, one of the most prolific of the film pioneers, R. W. Paul, used English locations and the military expertise of Sir Robert Ashe to make *Glencoe: Battle of Glencoe* and *Mafeking: Bombardment of Mafeking*.[29] Other films made in England, such as *The Sneaky Boer*, demonstrate a more obvious propaganda element, highlighting the ungentlemanly tactics of the Boers (in a similar, untitled, piece they attack a field hospital, beat up the nurses, and are about to shoot them when British troops arrive to save the day). The immediate inspiration for these 'faked' battle scenes was probably the work of Georges Méliès, magician turned film-maker. Méliès had pioneered the war 'docudrama' with his *Combat Naval en Grèce* (1897) and *Quais de la Havane* (based on the explosion of the U.S. warship, the *Maine*, in Havana harbour). However, it was more likely his hugely successful *L'Affaire Dreyfus* (1899), a fictionalized account of the political scandal of the year, that suggested a way to render the 'unfilmable war' filmable.[30] Indeed it is scarcely an exaggeration to say that Méliès's work was to point the way for the subsequent development of the narrative fictional feature.[31] At the time, some critics were ambivalent about the implications of such trends: 'where is this new kind of photo-faking to stop?' asked the *Photographic Times*.[32] If real events could be convincingly faked, how could one distinguish actualités from fiction? The indexical quality of the photo-image was placed under suspicion.

Photo-faking would not stop, of course. In its unfilmable aspect, as in many others, the Boer War appears to have been a dress rehearsal for the First World War. When the great pioneer of American cinema, D. W. Griffith, arrived in France in 1918 to make a propaganda film about the war, like his Boer War, predecessors he found the reality of the battle-field a bit of a disappointment. To an even greater extent than during the Boer War, military technology in 1914–18 transformed the rules of engagement and the spatio-temporal world of combat, annihilating the recognizable contours of the landscape itself. Like his counterparts in the South African war, Griffith sensibly took himself off to Salisbury Plain, and later back to the Lasky Ranch in Hollywood, to stage a more satisfactory, pro-filmic war. The resulting feature, *Hearts of the World* (1918), was a great success.[33]

MORITURI TE SALUTANT

In 1901, though, what most audiences saw on screen were not photo-faked episodes, still less full-length features, but programmes of short actualités. John Barnes has suggested that the sheer numbers of such actualités may indicate that audiences went not so much to see the arrivals and departures themselves as news items, but in the hope of seeing someone they *knew*.[34] Thus in Manchester in June 1901, Thomas-Edison's Animated Pictures (which had in fact no relation to Thomas Edison himself) were advertising, under the caption 'War in Manchester', moving pictures of such episodes as the 'Grand Entry into Ladysmith', but they also hoped to pique local interest in the war with 'The Return of the Brave Manchester Volunteers Just from the Front' and 'General Buller's Visit to Manchester'.[35] The other films on offer included racing footage from the Manchester Cup, and scenes from the recent Whit Monday schools' procession.

It was in fact this footage from the 'scholars' procession' that would come to attract most press attention. In their daily round-up of items of local interest, 'Manchester Mems.', the Manchester *Daily Dispatch* of 18 June described a moving episode at one performance:

A pathetic incident occurred the other night during the performance of Edison's animated photography at the Great St James's Hall. A child who took part in the scholars' procession was accidentally killed the next day, and her mother on seeing her portrait on the screen swooned away. On her recovery she declared that the likeness was so vivid that for the moment she thought that she had seen a vision, and was in consequence utterly overcome.[36]

Shorter accounts of the same incident appeared that evening in the *Manchester Evening Chronicle*, the sister-publication of the *Dispatch*, and also in the *Manchester Evening Mail*. The fact that all three articles describe the incident in almost the same words suggests that their accounts may have been based on a press release from the Thomas-Edison company rather than on local informants.

Whatever its source, the 'pathetic incident' seems to have taken on a life of its own. As Simon Popple has noted in a different context, almost two months later the same story appears in the *Photographic Chronicle* in its regular 'Snapshots' column. There, the originally rather thin account from the provincial papers is fleshed out a little:

A Pathetic incident – A pathetic incident recently occurred in the St James's Hall, Manchester. Messrs Edison were showing some scenes of the Whit Monday Sunday School processions in Manchester. Suddenly a woman's voice in the audience was heard to proclaim hysterically, 'There's my Annie!' And it was, but alas! in the interval between the photograph being taken and the day on which the poor mother saw the picture the child had been killed. To the mother the illusion was too real but too transient, and for the time being she simply saw her little one walking serenely behind the banner of her Sunday School in the most natural way imaginable. After this incident hundreds of people from the neighbourhood in which the little girl lived came to see the almost living image of their departed friend.[37]

The capacity of the new medium (an interesting term in itself) to conjure up phantasms of the dead, or at least departed, was also touched on in another 'Snapshots' piece in the same issue:

'Hello Bill!' – When showing animated pictures it is said to be no unusual thing for
a girl to cry out 'Dad!' on seeing the figure of her father, who is perhaps a soldier
in South Africa, walking on the screen, whilst old pals of soldiers can barely resist
the impulse to call out to their pictures in the old terms, 'Hello, Bill!'

Popple notes that such recognition scenes occurred frequently.[38]

But did early audiences actually confuse image and reality? This idea that
the filmic image is so real that the naive audience cannot distinguish it from
reality is pervasive in the early folklore of the cinema, perhaps too much so
for it to be taken entirely at face value. Indeed, a number of films from this
period dramatize this very confusion. Both the British *The Countryman's
First Sight of the Animated Pictures* (1901) and the American *Uncle Josh at the
Moving Picture Show* (1902) centre on the response of a 'naive' spectator to
film, with which the actual audience can contrast their own more knowing
attitude.[39] What we have in the 'Dad' and the ('barely resisted') 'Hello Bill'
incidents is more likely an early instance of the interactive nature of 'silent'
cinema, where the audience, unlike that of sound cinema, but similar to
that of music-hall or vaudeville, would often respond directly and vocally
to what was on screen. Kipling incorporates this aspect of the early shows
into 'Mrs Bathurst' – one of Vickery's fellow audience members who also
recognizes Mrs Bathurst comments immediately: 'Christ! there's Mrs B.!'[40]
The 'Annie' episode, if it happened at all, would also belong to this pattern
of interaction.

More interesting, though, is the circulation of the 'Annie' story during
the Boer War. I want to argue that in fact the two 'snapshots' in the form
that they appear in the *Photographic Chronicle* have to be read together and
read symptomatically to be understood properly. The embellished, and
indeed possibly apocryphal, Sunday school story and the 'Dad' and 'Hello
Bill' pieces testify to the impact of the Boer War as a media event involving
the articulation of the two terms of the film-show that Kipling describes in
'Mrs Bathurst' – 'Home and Friends' – and a third term, death, and they
point to a significant aspect of fin-de-siècle cinematograph spectatorship.
The little girl who sees her soldier father on screen, and the little girl who is
seen on screen by her mother, are strangely twinned. The British troops –
'Bill' and his fellow soldiers – who die off screen in their thousands are
melodramatically condensed as the little Sunday-school girl, Annie. The
audience viewing the pictures of these troops may, on the other hand,
sentimentally identify itself with the little girl crying 'Dad'. For if, as John
Barnes argues, audiences went to see actualités of troop departures and

arrivals, not for their news value, but in the hope of seeing familiar faces, we have to consider that many of the originals of those familiar faces never returned from South Africa. Their 'animated pictures', though, carried on their independent wraith-like existence long after the originals were dead. Roland Barthes likens all photography to a species of embalming, but he argues that through a sort of dramatic irony, photographs of those about to die have a specially affecting quality.[41] In late Victorian and Edwardian Britain, this occasional quality of the still photo became characteristic of a whole new medium. Thanks to the convergence of that medium with one of the first industrialized wars, for many people their first experience of the new reproductive technology must have been doubly uncanny: the 'living pictures' were so many ghosts of the recently dead, or those soon to die.

HOME AND FRIENDS FOR A TICKEY

Kipling's 'Mrs Bathurst' has long enjoyed a reputation as a 'problem' story, Angus Wilson claiming that 'Mrs Bathurst' 'has aroused as much puzzle-solving among [Kipling's] devotees as the unfinished *Edwin Drood* has among Dickensians'.[42] Another biographer, Lord Birkenhead, quotes C. S. Lewis on the story's impenetrable quality: 'I still do not know exactly what happened in Mrs Bathurst'.[43] J. M. S. Tompkins tries to throw some light into the story's darker corners by arguing that it is 'one of the earliest and most extreme of [Kipling's] experiments in suppressed narrative', and goes on to suggest that it may even be an example of mimetic form, that is to say that it is cinematic in style as well as content. The account of the Biograph that we hear in the story may thus be seen to be also a description of Kipling's method: 'This is not a continuous narrative; but neither is it confusion. Rather it is like the early biograph, "just like life . . . only when any one came down too far towards us that was watchin', they walked right out o' the picture, so to speak".'[44] For Wilson, at least, this impenetrability generates more annoyance than interest. He describes the story as 'pretentious' (*The Strange Ride*, 222) and sees it as a failure. 'Mr [Kingsley] Amis', he notes, 'has suggested that it fails because Kipling, in his passion for paring down his work, has rendered it unintelligible. He may well be right, but I think it is more likely that it never had much meaning' (222). 'The "difficulty" of "Mrs Bathurst" is of little interest,' he adds, 'for in the last resort, the story is empty' (223). Moreover, 'we don't care what happens because we don't know the characters' (223). But perhaps Wilson may find the story empty because he is looking for the wrong things. If we do not know the characters, this can scarcely be separated from the fact that this is a story that deals with the possibility of ever knowing others, or 'seeing' them. To this extent the story's structure, with its internal narrators and self-reflexive story-telling situation, recalls other fin-de-siècle tales of epistemology and the visual: for example, *The Turn of the Screw*, or *Heart of Darkness*. More clearly than those, though, it suggests that such narratives were written against the background of the emergence of new ways of seeing, such as that provided by the cinematograph, which would come to be a rival form of entertainment to prose fiction.

Kipling's enthusiasm for the world of technology, but also more generally for the realm of men, work, efficiency, and imperial power, is readily apparent in much of his writing. The admiration for technology and efficiency in particular produces something like a species of armchair futurism in such stories as 'Steam Tactics', 'The Ship that Found Herself', and '.007'. At times, though, it exists alongside a much less strident interest in the technological uncanny. Even within *Traffics and Discoveries* itself there are two other stories that resonate with 'Mrs Bathurst'.[45] In 'They', the narrator is a keen motorist. On one of his country drives he comes across a country house haunted by the ghosts of dead children, and is vouchsafed a moment of contact with his own lost child. Somehow the activity of driving, rather than being seen as antithetical to the world of spiritual experience, seems to be conducive to this ghostly encounter. In 'Wireless', a consumptive assistant pharmacist is inspired to write Keats's 'The Eve of St Agnes', a poem which he has never heard of, while in the next room an early wireless experiment takes place. As in 'Mrs Bathurst', the most up-to-date technology appears to coincide with, or even generate, less tangible but equally powerful forces. Kipling's vision of modernization, then, does not always imagine the progressive disenchantment of the world through the brave march of technology; rather, new technologies bring with them their own mysteries.

The first reference to 'Mrs Bathurst' is in a letter from Kipling to Leslie Cope Cornford dated 24 February 1904, when Kipling was wintering with his family at their house in Capetown, 'The Woolsack'. 'I've done 2 Pyecroft stories – one pure farce and the other . . . [a] rather ghostly tragedy', the latter 'a thing that had been lying at the back of my head to [sic] these last 3 years [i.e. placing its genesis somewhere in the middle of the Boer War]. Mrs Bathurst is its simple and engaging name.'[46] However, in the autobiographical *Something of Myself*, Kipling dates the origins of the story to a visit to New Zealand in 1891: 'all I carried away from the magic town of Auckland was the face and voice of a woman who sold me beer at a little hotel there'. Years later in South Africa he recalled her when he heard the phrase that he uses to describe Mrs Bathurst: that she 'never scrupled to help a lame duck or step on a scorpion'.[47] In 1891, of course, there was no Biograph or cinematograph, so we may surmise that Kipling's memories of New Zealand were reactivated by seeing an early film show of the kind that he describes in the story: 'pictures of prize-fights and steamers . . . London Bridge with the omnibuses – a troopship goin' to the war – marines on parade at Portsmouth, an' the Plymouth Express arrivin' at Paddin'ton' (*Traffics and Discoveries*, 278).

'Mrs Bathurst' is a story within a story and is set in South Africa, shortly after the war. It is prefaced by an 'excerpt' from a mock-Elizabethan play, 'Lyden's *Irenius*', the point of which appears to be that a woman's love can unintentionally destroy a man: 'She that damned him to death knew not that she did it, or would have died ere she had done it' (266). Our primary narrator is, we surmise, a man like Kipling himself, a naval aficionado, comfortable with the slang and technical jargon of seamen. While visiting Simon's Cove to see a British naval ship, he meets an old friend, Inspector Hooper of the Cape Government Railways, and the two take a train down the coast to have lunch in cooler surroundings. Mr Hooper is about to show our narrator a 'curiosity' found inland when they are joined in their brake-van by another friend of the narrator, Mr Pyecroft, a petty-officer in the navy, and Sergeant Pritchard, a marine. After several famous episodes of naval and marine desertion are recalled, Pyecroft tells the story (already familiar to Pritchard) of a warrant officer, Vickery, and the Mrs Bathurst of the title. Vickery is a recently widowed man with a fifteen-year-old daughter, and with only eighteen months to serve before qualifying for his navy pension; Mrs Bathurst is the proprietor of a small hotel near Auckland. Pyecroft himself knows her a little, and describes her as a woman with a strangely impressive presence: "Tisn't beauty, so to speak, nor good talk necessarily. It's just It. Some women'll stay in a man's memory if they once walk down a street' (277). But Vickery, who seems to have had some sort of intimate relationship to Mrs Bathurst in Auckland, is overwhelmed by the sight of her on-screen image when he goes to see an early film show put on by Phyllis's Circus in Cape Town:

Then the Western Mail came in to Paddin'ton on the big magic lantern sheet. First we saw the platform empty an' the porters standin' by. Then the engine come in, head on, an' the women in the front row jumped: she headed so straight. Then the doors opened and the passengers came out and the porters got the luggage – just like life. Only – only when anyone came down too far towards us that was watchin', they walked right out o' the picture, so to speak. I was 'ighly interested, I can tell you. So were all of us . . . I watched an old man with a rug 'oo'd dropped a book . . . when quite slowly be'ind two porters – carryin' a little reticule an' lookin' from side to side – comes out Mrs Bathurst . . . She walked on and on till she melted out of the picture. (279)

For Pyecroft 'it's like meetin' old friends', but Vickery becomes obsessed, telling Pyecroft 'it will be four-and-twenty hours less four minutes before I see her again' (280), and dragging him along to see the show for five consecutive nights until the circus leaves town. Vickery somehow obtains permission to go inland to take charge of some naval ammunition left over from the war at Bloemfontein, whereupon he disappears. At the end of Pyecroft's narrative, Hooper tells the group that the bodies of two tramps have been found by the railway tracks beyond Bulawayo. The two have been turned to charcoal, either by lightning or by a forest fire started by the lightning. They fall to pieces when an attempt is made to move them, but Hooper notices that a tattoo resembling Vickery's is still visible on one of them.

It is difficult in a summary to do justice to the elliptical nature of the story (though the elliptical nature of Kipling's reported Cockney speech will be apparent from the above passage). We are never sure of the exact nature of the relationship between Vickery and Mrs Bathurst, though we assume there is some former intimacy. Nor are we sure why she is in London, though Vickery thinks that she is looking for him. We are not even sure what it is about her appearance on screen that obsesses Vickery, though we are given quite a clear idea of the effect of her image on him, and even the contagious impact of this upon Pyecroft. The warrant officer brings Pyecroft along one night to confirm that it is indeed Mrs Bathurst, and Pyecroft describes the look of horrified anticipation on Vickery's face before the show in an unusually graphic image:

I caught 'is face under a lamp just then, an' the appearance of it quite cured me of my thirsts. Don't mistake. It didn't frighten me. It made me anxious. I can't tell you what it was like, but that was the effect which it 'ad on me. If you want to know, it reminded me of those things in bottles in those herbalistic shops at Plymouth – preserved in spirits of wine. White an' crumply things – previous to birth as you might say. (279)

The striking image shows us the powerful effect of the cinema on Vickery, but it also prepares us for the fact that he will indeed be found curiously preserved, though not pickled, at the story's end.

'Mrs Bathurst', then, posits film as a form of mechanical reproduction that has powerful effects on its audience, or rather a section of it, but the story also explores the effect of film on those whose images are reproduced. The response to the railway in the 1860s was framed in the psycho-physiological language of nerves, anxiety, and suspense, as we have seen, and this partly extended to the body of the cinema spectator, but the effects of the last machine were also described in the language of magic. Where the body (including the brain) was the interface between subject and modernity in the 1860s, here the soul also seems to be at stake. Mrs Bathurst herself is described as having a peculiar degree of what the story itself calls 'It' – what we might call sex appeal, or presence, or charisma – but her screen image is even more powerful, or more accurately, her effect on the character of Vickery suggests that it is. Far from depriving her of her natural aura, the cinematograph seems to magnify it. In this respect Kipling looks forward to the period when the film industry would draw on the unique reproductive power of the cinema to create a whole series of powerful female icons, veritable screen goddesses. This is something to which I will return in chapter 4. But Mrs Bathurst's ghostly power also has a more local origin, I believe. What I want to focus on for the remainder of this chapter is the extent to which Kipling's story connects the cinema to the war and to the Wargraph. For if Mrs Bathurst comes to haunt Vickery and drive him to his peculiar end, this has something to do with the way the story's film show mimics in inverted form the effects of the Boerograph back home in England.

It is instructive in this respect to contrast 'Mrs Bathurst' with the more mainstream representations of imperial reverie. A popular sentimental topos that occurs across a variety of mass media at the end of the nineteenth century is the 'Soldier's Dream'. The highly successful American illustrator, Howard Chandler Christy, first came to popular attention with his illustrations for a Richard Harding Davis magazine story, 'The Soldier's Dream' (1898), in which an American soldier during the Spanish–American war daydreams of his ideal woman. As Martha Banta records, so evocative was Christy's 'pipedream' picture, in which the woman's image appears in the soldier's pipe-smoke, that readers of *Scribner's Magazine* sent marriage proposals to this imaginary woman, and she was even used to market hats, shoes, and gowns.[48] Similarly affective dream-visions had appeared in stereopticon slides, and the idea would go on to appear in postcards and in film.[49] Nor was the motif confined to soldiers, or even the visual – one of the most popular songs of the 1890s was 'The Miner's Dream of Home'.[50] The military version, though, seems to have enjoyed a certain pre-eminence. A filmic example exists from the Boer War, R. W. Paul's *His Mother's Portrait* (1900), where trick photography is used to show a wounded British soldier in South Africa and his vision of his mother at home.[51] And even as late as the first World War a British postcard uses the same topos to illustrate a popular song, 'For Killarney and You'. This depicts a British soldier looking pensively into the distance, while inset above him we see his distant love, the 'fair colleen whose heart is the truest'.[52]

One can read this topos is various ways, not least as part of the sentimentalization of empire and of the armed forces in a period of dramatic imperial expansion. 'Home' takes on a mythic significance in this melodramatic mapping of Britain's global territory. When film takes up this topos it acquires a self-reflexive dimension, thematizing the cinema's ability to make the absent home/family/sweetheart present to those overseas, or more often to virtually bring home to his family the absent soldier, as much actualité footage did, as we have seen. But Kipling departs from other treatments of the dream theme in a number of respects. For one thing it is not 'home' and his wife that Vickery glimpses through the magic of the cinematograph; rather it is (we presume) his lover. And far from being comforted by the sight of his distant love, Vickery appears to be driven mad by it: this is more the 'Soldier's Nightmare' than the 'Soldier's Dream'. In effect, rather than rehearsing the familiar materials of imperial reverie, what Kipling seems to have done is to evoke the memento mori aspect of the 'Wargraph' actualités that we earlier saw condensed in the 'Hello Bill' and Manchester scholars' procession stories. In 'Mrs Bathurst' these materials reappear, but in a curious chiasmus. Thus the audience in this case is not a domestic and civilian one looking at potentially doomed loved ones departing for South Africa, as in the 'Hello Bill' reports, but military personnel in South Africa looking at pictures of home. And unlike the soldiers in the actualités, there is no suggestion that Mrs Bathurst is anything but alive, albeit far away: Vickery is haunted by the living. It is London that has become the flickering, ghostly city, and the live civilians who have become so many phantasmatic doubles.

Vickery's torment ends with his almost excessive annihilation by lightning at the end of the internal narrative. Here the story is anything but straightforward, but we are invited to match our knowledge of Vickery's disappearance, gleaned from Pyecroft's account, with Inspector Hooper's description of two bodies found outside Bulawayo. Vickery and an unidentified companion are found next to the railway tracks in the middle of a forest, 'both stone dead and as black as charcoal' (285), after 'a bit of a thunderstorm in the teak' (285). At first this may recall those allegories of the destruction of the subject before the forces of turn-of-the-century modernity that close such narratives as *Dr Jekyll and Mr Hyde*, *The Picture of Dorian Gray*, *The Invisible Man*, and even *Dracula*. But while Vickery appears to be a man destroyed by the effects of technology, the story also complicates any straightforward opposition between Vickery and the cinema. Vickery, like the nervy Walter Hartright of *The Woman in White*, seems in fact to be an ideal subject for the technologies of modernity even before his encounter with the cinematograph. More Miserrimus Dexter than Walter Hartright, his nickname, 'Click', derives from the peculiar clicking noise he makes with his false teeth, a noise evidently meant to remind the reader of that made by a projector. It is through these same clicking teeth and his crumbling tattoo that his charred body will tentatively be identified later in the story: his most machine-like attribute survives intact.

It is not an encounter with machine culture per se that petrifies Vickery, I would suggest, but an encounter with the specific nature of the Boerograph or Wargraph, and his excessive annihilation at the story's end is a symptom of what the story has elided: the war dead. At times the links to the experience of the war are so tenuous as to be almost invisible. The question of 'seeing' Mrs Bathurst at first appears to be part of a more purely aesthetic thematics of impressionistic narration, recalling Joseph Conrad or Henry James, perhaps. Marlow's anxiety as to whether or not his audience can 'see' the mysterious figure of Kurtz, is echoed by the comments of Inspector Hooper on Mrs Bathurst: 'I don't *see* her yet somehow' (276).[53] This same motif appears in the references to Mrs Bathurst's 'blindish look' (279), or even Sergeant Pritchard's toast to Inspector Hooper: 'I'm lookin' at you!' (277). Pyecroft gives a more comprehensive, though by no means self-explanatory expression to the epistemological aspect of his story: 'I used to think seein' and hearin' was the only regulation aids to ascertainin' facts, but as we get older we get more accommodatin' (277). But this aspect of the story also evokes the issues of visibility raised by the war – for those actually there in South Africa who found that their experience of other wars was no preparation for warfare with an invisible enemy, but also for those at home who longed desperately to 'see' the war, and who had to make do with actualités of marching troops, and 'photo-faked' battle scenes from Salisbury Plain.

The repressed material returns in a somewhat more direct fashion at the story's close. If Mrs Bathurst appears before Vickery as a living picture, Vickery himself ultimately becomes a 'still'. Found with him are his trademark clicking false teeth, but Vickery is also recognizable by his tattoo, which shows up just as 'writing shows up on a burned letter' (285): he has, in effect, become a human negative. Having watched the not-quite-human image of the living Mrs Bathurst, Vickery himself ends by becoming a sort of quasi-human object, almost a mummy, the ultimate in indexical representation.[54] In the end, if he has symbolically joined Mrs Bathurst's screen image, he has literally joined the army of the war dead.

The experience of the Boer War brings Kipling to dust off a familiar enough thematics of art versus life, immortality versus death, in order to transfer it to mechanical reproduction. While the story's displacements at first make it difficult to even see that it is a war story, the ending reminds us of the other 22,000 British soldiers (to mention only the British casualties) who disappeared in the South African interior. Just as Vickery has been turned into a three-dimensional negative by an electrical storm, the war dead survived, by the industrial light and magic of cinema, as so many shaky on-screen images, not so much signs whose referents have disappeared as mummies. If 'Mrs Bathurst' is one of Kipling's most inscrutable tales, then, it is in part because we sense in it the 'whole pressure of [the] dead of the Boer War flickering and re-forming' as he puts it in the epigraph to this chapter: Kipling's story is just as much of a Wargraph in its own way as the early cinematograph. Mrs Bathurst's 'It' is something that we will encounter again in chapter 4, but Kipling's prose Wargraph brings together the cinema and the dead in a way that we will not see again until the final chapter, in the death cult of J. G. Ballard's *Crash*.

'It': the last machine and the invention of sex appeal

Every nice boy, it is said, falls in love with Mary, Queen of Scots . . .
Every man with a sixpence to spend on his amusement falls in love with
Miss Mary Pickford . . . Centuries were necessary to raise Queen Mary
to her pinnacle of devotion; by the alchemy of a machine, centuries
have been shortened into days and nights.

(*Times* editorial, June 1920)[1]

There is something about Mrs Bathurst. Long before her on-screen appearance she is said to possess, or be possessed by, a certain magic – 'It'. Elsewhere in *Traffics and Discoveries*, in 'Wireless', Kipling uses the same term, 'It', as a synonym for electricity, which is also described as magical. The narrator asks young Mr Cashell about the wireless experiment he is conducting: '"But what *is* it? . . . Electricity is out of my beat altogether." "Ah, if you knew *that* you'd know something nobody knows. It's just It – what we call Electricity, but the magic – the manifestations – the Hertzian waves – are all revealed by *this*. The coherer we call it."'[2] 'Wireless' turns on the way in which Mr Cashell's assistant, Mr Shaynor, comes to act as a sort of human 'coherer' for messages out there in the ether, semi-consciously transcribing a version of Keats's 'Eve of St Agnes', though he has never heard of the poem. As in 'Mrs Bathurst', technological modernization makes the world more rather than less mysterious. Mrs Bathurst's 'It', then, might be thought of as a sort of personal electro-magnetism, but this renaming scarcely makes her powers of attraction any more intelligible. Moreover, the cinema apparatus magnifies Mrs Bathurst's 'It' to the point that her on-screen representation does not simply attract Vickery – it obsesses him. Curiously, the flickering image of a woman produced by the alchemy of a machine seems to exert more power over him than the woman herself. Kipling's story thus anticipates two overlapping aspects of twentieth-century modernity. One is the development of a concept and vocabulary of sexual attractiveness independent of beauty per se – 'It', or 'sex appeal', or even 'S.A.' as it comes to be

76

called in the 1920s; the other, the power of the cinema to create powerful icons. The first of these can be seen as part of a more general attempt to rethink modern subjectivity along new lines. If the body was imagined as being somehow modernized through its encounters with various technologies, there was a counter-tendency to see the body as a repository of more primitive animal forces, even though these forces were paradoxically described at times in the language of electricity.[3] Kipling also anticipates the apparent capacity of the cinema to turn mortals, even flawed ones, into powerful screen icons, generally attributed with this same quality of sex appeal. When he wrote 'Mrs Bathurst', audiences had not yet begun to pick out their favourite actors from the largely anonymous early silent casts of fiction films (though as we discussed in the last chapter, they went to see individuals in actualités). But by 1910 that process was already under way, and by the 1920s the star system was fully developed in the film industry in the United States. Kipling does not, of course, anticipate all: the cinema machine of the 1920s is not that of 1904, and while Mrs Bathurst's screen image has the power to enchant Vickery alone, the gods and goddesses of the film industry exert a more democratic appeal. Further, at the historical moment I will be looking at here, the powers of attraction that they possess come to be curiously intertwined with the appeal of the commodity form.

Such colloquialisms as 'screen goddess' are illuminating.[4] Indeed, cinema quite literally creates a new pantheon, but one in which all the deities are deities of love. The stage had its bright and particular stars long before the rise of the cinema – 'matinée idol' is, after all, a theatrical term – but film allowed the viewing subject to be all alone in the dark with the star in quite a new way, combining the illusion of intimacy with a larger-than-life quality for which the stage had no equivalent. No stage special effects could replicate the cinematic close-up, in which the flawless face of the star could fill the whole screen, an effect which early audiences sometimes found disconcerting as well as fascinating. As film-maker Chris Marker describes his first cinema experience in the 1920s in *Immemory* (1999): 'Nothing had prepared me for the shock of seeing a face enlarged to the dimensions of a house.'[5] Alexander Walker argues that the close-up 'was to be the decisive break with stage convention, the most potent means of establishing an actor's uniqueness and the beginning of the psychological interplay of the filmgoers' and the film actors' emotions'.[6] A significant part of this emotional involvement was sexual – the cinema in effect made possible a form of hyper-intimacy, or hyper-eroticism, that we have in the meantime come to take for granted.[7] From a different perspective to that of Walker, Jean-Louis Baudry, Laura Mulvey, and others have theorized the relationship between the viewing subject and the screen in terms of psychic regression and unconscious desire.[8] But whether or not one subscribes to 'apparatus theories', psychoanalytical or otherwise, it is possible to see that in the United States, and to a lesser extent in Europe, the cinema colonized the sphere of intimacy from the early years of the twentieth century on. It is scarcely an exaggeration to say that twentieth-century sexuality was routed through the cinema, the last machine, though this machine almost from the start functioned alongside another, the publicity machine. In this chapter I want to look at a particular moment in this remodelling of the sexual self, a moment in which the concept of 'It' meets the full iconogenic power of the cinema. This involved a number of collisions: between elements of fin-de-siècle, middle-class British culture – including the concept of 'It' – and the nascent power of the less class-specific film industry, which by the 1920s was already dominated by the United States; and, as we shall see, between two very different women, the popular late Victorian and Edwardian novelist, Elinor Glyn, and the Brooklyn-born actress, Clara Bow. Out of those collisions in 1926 a key figure of modern sexuality, the '"It" Girl', was born.

There have been many attempts to describe the species of 'training' that the cinema performs. For Walter Benjamin, what the cinema provided was a sort of crash-course in modernity itself, the cinema being for him the form in which the shock-effects of modernity were internalized as a formal principal, though he remained in some doubt as to whether this was part of the problem of the decline of experience under modernity or a possible solution.[9] The left has had no monopoly on functionalist theories of the cinema, of course. As Miriam Hansen has argued, almost since its inception the cinema of the United States in particular has been credited with an integrative function. According to such accounts, the 'universal language' of the silent cinema worked to acculturate recently arrived working-class immigrants, to acclimatize them to urban American life. This view of the role of early cinema was later reinforced by Lewis Jacobs in his classic *Rise of the American Film* (New York, 1939), though Jacobs also lamented what he saw as a subsequent gentrification of the cinema after 1914. As the film industry grew, so the story goes, the cinema of attractions was replaced by the fictional feature film, and the middle class rather than the working class came to fill the increasingly plush cinema seats, as nickelodeons yielded to cinema palaces. But as Hansen points out, it is not so much that working-class immigrants were excluded from cinema after 1914 as that the cinema industry was working to assimilate them into a more homogeneous national consumer culture, where ethnic and class identities were to be bracketed.[10] Rarely, if ever, had national identity and national prosperity come to be so closely identified as they were in the United States in the post-war years. The business of America, as President Coolidge told the Society of American Newspaper Editors in 1925, was business. A fundamental aspect of the appeal of this newly integrative national consumer culture was its linkage of commodity-based happiness with the 'modern' sexuality of the American Girl. The nervous, accelerated body-in-motion of the nineteenth century comes to be replaced with the more positive icon of the 'fast' flapper, the dancing daughter of modernity. (The flapper was an important figure of modernity in Britain too in the post-war years, as Billie Melman has described, but was largely portrayed in more negative terms.[11]) To Benjamin's account of the cinema as a crash-course in distracted perception, we need, then, to add that the cinema also provided a school for pleasure. As we shall see, in the 1920s, 'It' was a key mediating term in this process, and in the film that we shall be looking at most closely, a modern Cinderella story also entitled *It* (1927), sexual and consumer satisfaction, and kineticism, are inseparable. But before the feature, as it were, let us consider the two female leads in the story of 'It', and their historical moment.

NELLIE SUTHERLAND/ELINOR GLYN/MADAME GLYN

Elinor Glyn's life was an unusual one by any standards.[12] Born on the island of Jersey in 1864 to Canadian parents, Elinor Sutherland ('Nellie') grew up in Guelph, Ontario, and later back on Jersey, in surroundings that were solidly middle-class if not particularly affluent. Her stepfather had some titled connections in Scotland, while on her mother's side she had some wealthy French cousins, and young Nellie grew up with very decided views on the importance of good breeding, and a weakness for ancien régime style. When her sister Lucy (the couturière, 'Lucile', later Lady Duff Gordon, who played her own part in the shaping of modern consumer culture) married well, it gave Elinor access to English county society, and her own marriage in 1892 to an impoverished country squire, Clayton Glyn, further secured her position in that society, which was to provide the setting for most of her novels, beginning with the highly successful comedy of manners, *The Visits of Elizabeth* (1900).

Glyn was shrewd enough to turn her minor fame to good account, and she made a number of influential friends, including Alfred, Lord Milner (encountered in the last chapter as High Commissioner for the Cape Colony), George Nathaniel, Lord Curzon, with whom she had an affair for a number of years, F. H. Bradley, the philosopher, and the Grand Duchess Kiril of Russia, who invited her to St Petersburg to write a novel set at the Russian court (published as *His Hour* in 1910). But it was the publication of *Three Weeks* in 1907 that turned Elinor Glyn, the society novelist with a talent for befriending the rich and famous, into Elinor Glyn, the household name, and led her from Europe to Hollywood. The novel itself resembles a spicier version of *The Prisoner of Zenda*, and describes the romance between a young Englishman, Paul Verdayne, and the mysterious older woman whom he first encounters while they are both staying at a Swiss hotel. What scandalized readers in 1907 is that it is she who takes the more active part in the three-week affair that follows. Lush passages describe her seduction of Paul on a tiger-skin before a blazing fire, and in a moonlit loggia on a couch strewn with rose petals. (It would be fair to say that a number of the twentieth century's sexual clichés derive from *Three Weeks*.) Ultimately we discover that the mysterious seductress is the wronged Queen of a Ruritanian kingdom; she gives birth to Paul's child, who will be heir to the throne, but is herself murdered at her husband's command.

Few novels become the subject of anonymous popular verse, but *Three Weeks* is one of them:

> Would you like to sin
> With Elinor Glyn
> On a tiger-skin?
> Or would you prefer
> To err
> With her
> On some other fur?[13]

The novel made Glyn a byword for raciness, which did little for her position in English society, but ensured her a welcome in wider and more lucrative circles. Tiger-skin became her signature fabric, the official flag, as it were, of primitive animal passion with a hint of luxury. Without *Three Weeks* it is unlikely that she would have attracted the interest of Hollywood's biggest film production company, Famous Players-Lasky, later Paramount, who after the war began to hire well-known European writers to write for the screen, and lend some of their cultural cachet to the still rather declassé film industry. Interest in Glyn may also have been driven by a more general Hollywood campaign to buy European 'passion' in this period, leading to its acquisition of such diverse talents as Vilma Banky, Greta Garbo and Mauritz Stiller, and Pola Negri.[14] After initial advances were made through her agent, Hughes Massie, in June 1920, Glyn met in Paris with a Miss Mayo, a representative of the production company, and settled the details of a contract under which she would be paid $10,000 to come to Hollywood and learn about film, and then write a scenario and supervise its production. In Hollywood that autumn, she joined a British expatriate group at the Hollywood Hotel that included Sir Gilbert Parker, Edward Knoblock, and even for a period W. Somerset Maugham, (though not, *pace* a Paramount advertisement of 1921 (Figure 2) – 'The Greatest Living Authors Now Working With Paramount' – Joseph Conrad and Arnold Bennett).[15]

According to studio founder and head of production, Jesse Lasky, he himself came up with the Glyn-esque title, *The Great Moment* (the rights to *Three Weeks* were already owned by another company), and put Glyn to work fashioning a story out of it tailored to one of Famous Players-Lasky's actresses, Gloria Swanson. Swanson had started in slapstick comedy and 'bathing beauty' parts with Triangle and Mack Sennett's Keystone studio, and had even appeared in a railway-rescue film, *Teddy at the Throttle* (1917), one of the many cinematic descendants of the railway rescues we encountered in chapter 1. But realizing her potential, Cecil B. DeMille had made her one of his principal players in the series of high-society sex dramas he was then making at Famous Players-Lasky, beginning with *Don't Change Your Husband* (1919). By the early 1920s, Swanson was as famous for her sophisticated taste in clothes as for her acting, with her own nationally syndicated column, 'The Well-Dressed Woman', which according to one wry newspaper report, inspired 'innocent virgins in Decatur and Pawtucket [to] imitate her with astounding results'.[16] Now she was to be a major star.[17] Glyn's task, accordingly, was to provide Swanson with a role in keeping with her reputation as the personification of upper-class glamour and sexual sophistication.[18] A major studio publicity campaign for *The Great Moment* made the most of the fact that this was Swanson's first starring role (with her name above the film title in promotional material), and Glyn's first ever screen story (Figure 3).[19] Swanson was reported as saying that she used to 'thrill' over *Three Weeks*, and Glyn was supposed to have been lured to Hollywood partly on the strength of seeing Swanson's performance in *Male and Female* (1919), this having inspired her to write a part for her.[20] The two were frequently photographed together, Glyn wearing her trademark tiger-skin accessories, while Swanson appears in the high fashion that her fans had

2 Advertisement for Paramount Pictures from *Shadowland*, May 1921

3 Advertisement for *The Great Moment* from *Moving Picture World*, 18 June 1921

4 Elinor Glyn and Gloria Swanson in a publicity shot used to illustrate a Swanson
bio-sketch, 'My Glorious Career', from *Movie Weekly* (n.d. 1921)

come to expect (Figure 4). Swanson obligingly described Glyn as the third
major influence on her career after Mack Sennett and Cecil B. DeMille.[21]

Glyn soon realized that her presence in the movie colony had more to
do with her publicity value than any contribution she might make to film
production, and she had to struggle to get any hearing for her suggestions:
'No one wanted our advice or assistance, nor did they intend to take it.'[22]

She received writing credits on *The Great Moment*, and her name above the title, but the actual scenario was written by a regular studio writer, Monte Katterjohn. Nonetheless, she quickly and effectively established herself as a Hollywood presence, abetted by the studio publicity campaign for Famous Players-Lasky as the most literary of studios. She was to be seen at every Hollywood event of note: *Photoplay*, the *New York Telegraph*, and other papers and magazines reported her appearances at the gala opening of the Ambassador Theatre in March 1921; at the Pageant Ball for charity at the Ambassador Hotel in April (she appeared as the Empress Josephine); at the Washington Day Races in June, and at the premiere of *The Three Musketeers* in September.[23] She became part of the social circle around William Randolph Hearst and Marion Davies, and a regular visitor at 'Pickfair', Douglas Fairbanks and Mary Pickford's regal home. Anecdotes about her are scattered through the memoirs of the period, though it is often difficult to disentangle fact from Hollywood legend. Most sources agree, though, that her appearance and manner made her stand out even in a community where eccentricity was the norm. Anita Loos gives a thumbnail sketch: 'Her appearance was bizarre; the make-up she wore might have been scraped off the white cliffs of Dover, and it provided a startling contrast to her dyed red hair, green eyes, and mouth of vivid crimson. She jangled with long ear-rings, economically set with second-rate gems.'[24] One Hollywood wit described her as looking like Western star William S. Hart in drag.[25] Even Gloria Swanson, who was to become a friend, recalls her as looking like 'something from another world'.[26] But Glyn's peculiar appearance was largely an attempt to artificially generate the youthfulness so highly valued in the film industry, and increasingly in the United States in general: 'She was the first woman I'd ever seen wearing false eyelashes . . . Her teeth were too even and white to be real.'[27] Eventually this quest for youth would lead her to undertake an early and painful variety of cosmetic surgery.

As 'Madame Glyn' she appears to have considered that it was her mission to bestow her own sense of style and her particular brand of European sophistication on the rather rough-and-ready Hollywood colony (it was not that many years, after all, since film-makers had moved from New York to California in search of perennial sunlight, low humidity, varied locations, and cheap labour).[28] According to Loos:

Elinor's first move in Hollywood was to establish a 'salon', and on Sunday after-noons she invited us all to her suite in the hotel for tea (tea!), during which she lay on a tiger-skin rug, wearing Persian pajamas in the pastel shades made famous by her sister Lucille [sic], and recited poems of Shelley and Swinburne, to which, for good measure, she added Ella Wheeler Wilcox. Quoting from the latter, Elinor would declaim, 'Smile and the world smiles with you, weep and you weep alone', doing so in lugubrious tones that precluded any attempt at smiling . . . We all knew that Elinor's salons were merely her own particular form of publicity.[29]

Jesse Lasky likewise describes her being 'as adept as Salvador Dali at drawing attention to herself. She was "good copy".'[30] It seems to have worked. Glyn became a Hollywood grande dame. Swanson evokes Glyn's reign of style-terror: 'She went everywhere and passed her fearsome verdicts on everything. This is glamorous, she would say. That is hideous, she would say . . . people moved aside for her as if she were a sorceress on fire or a giant sting ray.'[31] Leatrice Gilbert Fountain, daughter and biographer of silent star, John Gilbert, claims that every Hollywood home had all of Glyn's work on prominent display.[32] One measure of her ubiquity in 1920s Hollywood is the frequency with which she is to be seen peering out at the camera from the back row of group photographs from the social gatherings of the period, and her occasional cameo appearances (also useful publicity material) – as a bridge player in DeMille's 1921, *The Affairs of Anatol*, as herself in two promotional films, MGM's 1925 untitled 'studio tour' film and the 1926 *Screen Snapshots*, and in King Vidor's *Show People* (1928). As we shall see, she also makes a cameo appearance as herself in *It*.[33]

That Glyn as grande dame is, in retrospect, a figure more amusing than intimidating, should not lead us to underestimate her influence on the cinema of the 1920s. While other foreign writers tended to bridle at their treatment in Hollywood and rarely lingered, Glyn created a niche for herself and stayed for seven years. Leatrice Gilbert Fountain succinctly explained part of the secret of her success: 'elegance and style became Elinor's stock in trade'.[34] Constantly upbraiding the studios for their weakness in art direction, Glyn relied on her reputation as a 'society' writer, but also on her aristocratic connections, just as Gloria Swanson's marriage to the Marquis de la Falaise de la Coudraye enhanced *her* on-screen image as the epitome of style. To use the more sociological vocabulary of Pierre Bourdieu, Glyn had cultural capital that the studios wished to exploit by hiring her. But Glyn herself made the most of her opportunities and profited handsomely.[35] Though having little economic capital, Glyn manoeuvred herself into a position as a minor Hollywood player. While we might treat with some degree of scepticism the list of stars Glyn claims to have 'discovered' – John Gilbert, Gary Cooper, and Clara Bow[36] – she had a significant impact on the careers of many figures whose names have become far more familiar than hers.[37] It was not just a sense of European style that Glyn purveyed, though. While we may treat with caution Samuel Goldwyn's claim that 'Elinor was the first person to put sex appeal into the cinema', we shall

see that she played an important part in defining sexuality for the 1920s, and thus had her part to play in the modernization of subjectivity we have been following. As she pointed out to Swanson: 'If motion picture producers knew what sex appeal was, they'd have no need of me, now, would they?'[38] While marketing herself as embodying 'traditional' European style, then, she also associated herself with the latest trend in European thought, psychology.

In Glyn's first film, *The Great Moment* (1920), directed by Sam Wood, formerly Cecil B. DeMille's assistant, Swanson plays the part of an aristocratic young English woman, Nadine Pelham, though in a typical Glyn touch of primitivism, she is also half-Gypsy, accounting for her passionate temperament. While visiting America with her father and fiancé, Nadine falls for the democratic manly vigour of a rugged American engineer, Bayard Delaval (Milton Sills), who manages her father's Nevada gold-mine. Bolstered by a major publicity drive, featuring plenty of location shots, and giving Swanson ample opportunities to wear extravagant costumes (she plays the Tartar Gypsy mother as well as the daughter), the film did well, and Glyn's contract was renewed for a second film – another lush romantic spectacle, *Beyond the Rocks* (1921) – this time based on one of her earlier novels. Also directed by Wood, this paired Swanson with the actor who was then emerging as Hollywood's greatest male sex symbol, Rudolph Valentino (Glyn describes Swanson and Valentino with delightful understatement as 'two really able artistes and remarkably attractive personalities').[39] Again, publicity was lavished on the project, with a similar emphasis to the previous film. 'A pulsating love story – by one of the world's greatest writers of love tales – with the screen's two greatest lovers in the leading roles', trumpeted one promotional tag.[40] The success of *Beyond the Rocks* consolidated her reputation for making risqué, but not too risqué, high-society drama – 'Elinor's latest is sex-stuff but it's toned down', confided the *Washington Press*.[41]

In this respect she could not have come to Hollywood, and especially to Famous Players-Lasky, at a better time, since, as Sumiko Higashi has described, in these same years the studio's major director, Cecil B. DeMille, was reshaping the dreams of American consumers with a series of films that married commodity spectacle to erotic display (e.g. *Old Wives for New* (1918), *Why Change Your Wife?* (1920), and *The Affairs of Anatol* (1921)). The equation of conspicuous consumption with sexual liberation was meant to appeal to the female audiences that Hollywood increasingly coveted.[42] Glyn's own talent for writing sensual high-society romance dovetailed with what DeMille was trying to achieve, and together with him and Swanson, she became synonymous with glamorous costume drama, and with daring on-screen representations of love among the rich.

Glyn moved to the Goldwyn Company (later Metro-Goldwyn and MGM) to make six more films, including a version of her best-known work, *Three Weeks* (1923), with Aileen Pringle, and *His Hour* (1924), which featured John Gilbert. Around this time her family, worried about her limited business sense and the fact that she could spend money even more quickly than she could earn it, decided to make Elinor Glyn into a corporate entity, Elinor Glyn Limited. She herself was not given a seat on the board.[43] There were consolations, though: the legendary Cedric Gibbons was resident art director at MGM, and she found the studio more open to her suggestions for costumes and settings than Famous Players-Lasky had been. Nonetheless, in 1927 she returned to her old studio to make three more films, including *It*, the film that would enshrine a new term for sexual attractiveness, and transform its star, Clara Bow, from 'movie star to historic symbol'.[44]

THE LOVE MAGNET

Early in 1926 Glyn published a novella-length piece, *It*, in *Hearst's International Combined with Cosmopolitan*. (*Cosmopolitan* would in its later avatars play no small part in shaping twentieth-century conceptions of sexuality, though in this period it was best known as a vehicle for the short stories and serialized novels of such popular writers as Mary Roberts Rinehart, Ring Lardner, Robert Hichens, and W. Somerset Maugham.) There she spelled out the meaning of 'It' as a 'nameless charm with a strong magnetism'.[45] Not to be confused with beauty, 'It' is a sort of 'sex magnetism' (*It*, 20). It is 'that magic quality . . . that strange physical magnetism which emanates unconsciously from certain beings, and which they lose once self-consciousness sets in' (104). As with Kipling, Glyn's version of 'It' appears to be somewhere between a personal field of gravity and a magic spell.

The story itself concerns the relationship that develops between a beautiful but impoverished society girl, Ava Cleveland, and a charismatic self-made man, John Gaunt. They are immediately attracted to each other, since they both have 'It' in abundance. In dire need of money, Ava comes to work for Gaunt in his department store, but she is too proud to surrender herself to the masterful Gaunt, and repulses his advances. Eventually, of course, they are both powerless to resist the 'primitive force' (126) that draws them together. Visiting his apartment, she is overcome by his sexual magnetism: 'all the chains of civilization – all the conventions of the world of society

[fall] from her' (175), and she is prepared to sleep with him without marry-ing him. But of course he wants to marry her anyway, and both primitive passion and the proprieties are satisfied in the end.

But whence 'It'? Long before writing *It* Glyn had been interested in the concept. She first airs it in her novel of 1915, *The Man and the Moment*: '"It" does not depend upon looks . . . it does not depend upon intelligence or character or – anything – as you say, it is just "It".'[46] When she arrived in Hollywood, she had for a time put forward Gloria Swanson as the pos-sessor of this mysterious quality: 'Elinor Glyn, the high priestess of words describing the feminine complex, says [Swanson] possesses "it" – and that is as closely as she can indicate Gloria's intangible personality.'[47] Elsewhere she describes the 'magnetism' of Swanson's eyes. While she might have claimed otherwise, Glyn's use of 'It' is clearly not entirely her own – the echoes of Kipling seem clear enough for one thing. It is possible, though, that they were both drawing on a common late Victorian source, since there are a number of pre- or non-Freudian, popular fin-de-siècle accounts of attractiveness that anticipate their use of the term. As Daniel Pick has recounted, theories of mesmeric influence were advanced throughout the nineteenth century, but towards the end of the century older theories of fascination began to assimilate the language of the second industrial revo-lution. For example, a pamphlet of 1890, *Soul-Subtlety: or, How to Fascinate*, describes 'those wondrous, far-reaching occult powers, electric or magnetic, which have some influence over every atom in existence, whether mineral, vegetable, or animal.'[48] Glyn's 'sex magnetism' also echoes the 'mysteri-ous psycho-physical quality of personal magnetism' or 'soul-beauty' that H. Ellen Browning describes in her *Beauty Culture* (1898).[49] (The recur-rence of the term 'soul' here also suggests the influence of theosophy and spiritualism, part of the mystical backlash against the increasing dominance of science.)

But there is also a rawer edge to 'It', something of animal passion on a tiger-skin rather than soul calling to soul – something sexual as we would now understand that term. Glyn's earlier fiction was part of a general shift in the representation of sex in the 1900s, a discursive shift from the Victorian interest in the 'problem' of various marginal, deviant, and transgressive sexualities to focus on the 'normal' couple. But if sex is more openly part of turn-of-the-century fiction, it is often described in 'scientific' terms – the language of primitivism, in Glyn as much as in a very different writer like D. H. Lawrence, merges with the language of sexual science. The end of the nineteenth century abounds in hyphenated 'sex' terms, including 'sex-novel', and Glyn's term may owe something to the theories of eugenics advanced by such writers as H. G. Wells, Karl Pearson, and Olive Schreiner, who thought that Victorian prudery was dangerous to the health of the race, and sought to put the discussion of 'sex-feeling', marriage, and child-rearing on a more scientific basis. For the eugenicists, sexual attraction and sexual pleasure were positive forces that could be harnessed for the good of the race.[50] As Angelique Richardson has shown, among more conservative writers too the language of love became more high-tech in the 1890s, as in this piece of sexual-scientific pastiche from one of the 'New Woman' novels, Sarah Grand's *The Heavenly Twins* (1893): 'An electric current passing through a coil of wire makes a magnet of a bar of iron lying within it, but not touching it. So a woman is turned into a love-magnet by a tingling current of life running round her.'[51]

The concept of 'It', then, is rooted in various late Victorian and Edwardian discourses – from diluted aesthetic theory, to spiritualism, to popular science – all of them aspects of a more general attempt to re-imagine the human subject as a sexual being. Of course the most successful product of this cultural moment was psychoanalysis, which managed to separate itself out from the general field and lay claim to a more scientific rigour. The language of 'sex-feeling' and animal passion, came to be outflanked by theories of the unconscious, of drives and cathexes.[52] There is a certain irony, then, to the fact that the immediate context for Glyn's *succès fou* in the United States was the efflorescence of popular sexology after Freud's 1909 visit to the United States, and that *It*'s hodgepodge of magnetism and primitivism looked like a popular analogue to Freud's drives and instincts.[53] On her first visit to the United States, Glyn herself had attempted to harness the prestige then beginning to accrue to psychology: 'One must study psychology to understand [*Three Weeks*] . . . Psychology answers everything.'[54] In 1908 America may not have been quite ready for this, but by the 1920s, psychology – which almost invariably meant sex – was the topic of the moment. As Frederick Lewis Allen records, 'new words and phrases began to be bandied about the cocktail-tray and the Mah Jong table – inferiority complex, sadism, masochism, Oedipus complex'.[55] Science in general was enjoying unprecedented prestige, but 'psychology was king'.[56]

Glyn's particular insight was to blend the 'scientific' conception of sexual attraction as a powerful irrational force with the more familiar materials of love and romance. Readers were happier to be treated to the potentially disturbing revelations of psychology when they were properly dressed up. The animal passion connoted by the tiger-skin was always to be offset by romantic rose petals in Glyn's world; the radical estrangement from the self connoted by the concept of the 'id' could be evoked in the more domesticated 'It'. Through her books and screenplays, but also through lectures and essays on love (e.g. *The Philosophy of Love* (1923), which sold a quarter of a million copies in the first six months after publication)[57], Glyn established herself as a psychology expert as well as a style expert, and in the process contributed to the post-war redefinition of popular ideas about sexuality, romance and gender. As Marjorie Rosen puts it, 'by 1920 . . . Glyn . . . had become the nation's arbiter of love'.[58] Her syndicated column, 'In Filmdom with Elinor Glyn', which featured in 100 newspapers in the United States, gave her another pulpit from which to expound her views on the 'psychology of human nature'.[59] Her astuteness with the concept of 'It' was to dangle it before readers only to jerk it away again. Even after *It* the novella and *It* the film she kept redefining the term. At times 'It' seemed to promise a certain earthiness, but Glyn also wished it to have its feet off the ground. Where psychology traced human motivation back to drives, instincts, cathexes, and to certain biological givens, Glyn's 'It' seemed to hint at the ineffable, some *je ne sais quoi*, little short of the sublime. But when 'It,' became anchored to a particular star's body, that of Clara Bow, the term would take on a new set of meanings, and soar beyond Glyn's attempts to maintain it as her own trademark concept.

FLAMING YOUTH

While it is difficult to understand Glyn's success without some sense of Freud's impact, the willingness with which Freud had been embraced was itself the result of shifts in attitudes over a longer *durée*. One such shift concerned the new prominence of 'youth'. Historically, this was also rooted in the more general modernization of subjectivity, as increased specialization in the work-place gave education a greater role, and extended the duration of adolescence. Greater affluence, and more widespread acceptance among married couples of contraception, helped to create smaller, closer family units, but also meant that love and sex could be seen as at least partly separate from procreation. The disconnection of women's sexuality from motherhood was especially significant.[60] By the 1920s, Victorian sexual mores were in eclipse, as 'new sexual norms spread from bohemian circles to the rest of America'.[61] The relative independence of sexuality from reproduction, and the extension of the educational period entailed the 'cultural invention of adolescence and youth as a prolonged – and potentially dangerous – period for education and social interaction'.[62] Youth was highly desirable, but it also became a problem worried over by social commentators of all political hues. But as Paula S. Fass has argued, 1920s debates about 'flaming youth' can be read as part of a more general attempt to assimilate cultural change, the 'problem' of youth standing in for the problem of rapid social transformation.[63]

Young women in particular were seen to be at the cutting edge of the modernization of social and sexual mores. Women had finally secured the right to vote through the nineteenth amendment to the Constitution in 1919, and this new political independence was perceived to carry over into other areas. Thus the embodiment of American fears and desires about youth came to be not so much the young male as the 'flapper', who was to the 1920s what the 'New Woman' had been to the 1880s and 90s. For a progressive social commentator like Ben B. Lindsey, the Denver judge and author of *The Revolt of Modern Youth* (1925) and a controversial book about modern sexual practice, *The Companionate Marriage* (1927), the 'derided flapper' was the 'major determining factor' in the creation of more liberal attitudes to sex.[64] For more conservative commentators, on the other hand, the smoking, drinking, dancing flapper with her rouge and lipstick, bobbed hair, rolled stockings, and knee-length dresses, seemed to announce the advent of a post-war sexual libertinism, as well as a more general social malaise.[65]

While evidence of changes in actual sexual behaviour is notoriously difficult to obtain, there are indications that there were real as well as perceived changes. At least among the children of the middle classes, older patterns of courtship gave way to the new idea of 'dating'. A young woman could see different young men on different nights without any of them being her suitor in the traditional sense. Changes in courtship practices were inseparable from changes in patterns of leisure consumption: home-based 'keeping company' yielded to the cash-dependent night out. In part thanks to the greater mobility provided by the automobile, dating couples went out to the cinema, or to restaurants and dance halls.[66] With looser clothing for women came looser morals, or so it appeared to commentators who were appalled and fascinated in equal measure at the phenomenon of 'petting' (even Glyn voiced her discomfort with it).[67] More relaxed physical relations between the sexes probably *were* enabled by such factors as the closed automobile, the darkened cinema auditorium, the greater acceptance of unchaperoned parties, and the expansion of coed colleges. The authors of the influential survey of middle-American life, *Middletown*, also attribute behavioural changes to popular cultural factors – 'the constant public watching of lovemaking on the screen', and the treatment of romance in *True Story* and other popular magazines.[68]

Youth-themed fiction, notably the campus novel, enjoyed an unprecedented vogue as a window onto this shocking new world: F. Scott Fitzgerald's *This Side of Paradise* (1920), Lynn and Lois Montross's *Town and Gown* (1923), and Percy Marks's *The Plastic Age* (1924), led the trend. Marks, a Dartmouth professor, depicts the young scapegraces of the fictional Sanford College as rather innocent villains, as one discerns from this confession by the hero's room-mate, Carl Peters: 'You see, I'm a bad egg. I drink and gamble and pet. I haven't gone the limit yet [sc. had sex] on – on account of my old lady [sc. mother] – but I will.'[69]

Hollywood was not slow to exploit the vogue of 'flaming youth'. By the 1920s, American audiences were familiar with both the almost sexless girl-next-door appeal of Mary Pickford, 'America's Sweetheart', and exotic 'vamps' and femme fatales after the fashion of Theda Bara, Nita Naldi, or Pola Negri. While Pickford's young heroines were popular long after Pickford herself tired of such parts, creating opportunities for younger ingenues like Mary Miles Minter, the vamp had become too much of a cliché. The athletic and home-grown young 'flapper' was a natural replacement, and a string of youth-exploitation films followed. The film advertisements cited in *Middletown* give some idea of the version of youth on offer. *Flaming Youth* supposedly revealed 'neckers, petters, white kisses, red kisses, pleasure-mad daughters, sensation-craving mothers . . . the truth bold, naked, sensational'. Another youth film, *Alimony*, offered 'brilliant men, jazz babies, champagne baths, midnight revels, petting parties in the purple dawn, all ending in one terrific smashing climax that makes you gasp'.[70]

To conservative commentators, such films only served to confirm what they already believed – that the movies were damaging the nation's health. At the beginning of the 1920s, the Chicago Motion Picture Commission heard grim testimony about the physical effects of the last machine. The extent to which the rhetoric employed echoes that of the early responses to the railway suggests that, like the railway, or indeed like the flapper, the cinema focused more general anxieties about historical transformation. Frequent cinema attendance was said to result in nervousness, Saint Vitus's dance, myopia, and sleeplessness. Even the less hostile accounts dwelt on the physical effects of frequent film attendance. Artist Henry Clive, for example, was widely reported as arguing that movies had changed American facial expressions, that the previously stern and set national visage had become 'more mobile [and] more plastic' as audiences mimicked their favourite stars (as Rae Beth Gordon has shown, this mimetic theory had considerable currency in France).[71] However, in a shift that also recalls the nineteenth-century accommodation of the railway, by the end of the decade there was a greater focus on the psychological and moral effects of the movies. The prestige of the social sciences was harnessed to produce studies with such titles as *Motion Pictures and Youth* (1933), and *Our Movie-Made Children* (1933). To Edward Alsworth Ross in *World Drift* (1928), Hollywood had created a 'sex-wise, sex-excited, and sex-absorbed' generation. For many, the '"love chase" has come to be the master interest in life'.[72]

By this time too, Hollywood, worried about its image after the Roscoe 'Fatty' Arbuckle and William Desmond Taylor scandals, had hired former Postmaster-General Will Hays from President Warren Harding's cabinet as a sort of in-house censor and public relations man.[73] Hays administered the production code adopted by the Association of Motion Picture Producers and Distributors, helping to deflect some of the hostility of those commentators on the Christian right who associated Hollywood with the decline of the morals of America's youth. His WASP-ish image also reassured those who worried that the country's entertainment industry was coming to be dominated by Jewish immigrants.[74] Some of Glyn's material was perceived as rather too racy for this new, respectable Hollywood. Screen kisses in *Beyond the Rocks* were shot in two versions: extended versions for European audiences, and shorter, more chaste, versions for the U.S. market. This was indeed industrialized entertainment – as Swanson puts it, 'American fevers were now controlled by the stopwatch.'[75]

The film *It*, then, emerged into a series of debates, not just about the nature of American youth, but also about the effects of cinema as industrial entertainment. The film's kinship to the youth-exploitation film would have been clear enough. Not only does it announce 'It' or 'sex appeal' as its very theme, but its star, Clara Bow, had already played flapper roles in the 1925 film version of *The Plastic Age* and in Herbert Brenon's *Dancing Mothers* (1926). At the centre of *It*, as at the centre of those other films, is the body of the new American girl, a body that seems to act as shorthand for modernization itself. But *It*, as we shall see, also develops a commentary on its own nature as industrial entertainment, and suggests the positive effects of machinic pleasure.

CLARA BOW/CLARA BEAUX

Our other female lead, Clara Bow, the '"It" Girl'-to-be, started her vertiginous ascent to the pantheon of screen goddesses from the lowest point possible. Born in Brooklyn in 1905 into grinding poverty, she was the child of a hard-drinking and possibly abusive father and a mentally unstable mother. As a teenager she won the Brewster Publications' (publishers of

Motion Picture, Shadowland, and *Motion Picture Classic*) Fame and Fortune Award, a beauty contest for which the first prize was a screen test. Her first screen part in William Christy Cabanne's *Beyond the Rainbow* (1922) ended up on the cutting-room floor (the film was later re-edited to include her, and rereleased after Bow became famous), but small parts in other east-coast productions, *Down to the Sea in Ships* (1922) and *Enemies of Women* (1923), followed. Through actress-agent Maxine Alton, Bow came to the attention of Preferred Pictures executive B. P. Schulberg, who put her under contract. Still in her teens, she took the train across the country to Los Angeles.

Schulberg, Bow's 'mentor', was an astute manipulator of the publicity machine as it had developed in the 1920s, the great age of advertising, but it took him a while to find an appropriate persona for his new protegée. Initially, he exploited his new screen property by lending her out to other studios to make cheap, programme-filling pictures, but seeing her potential to fit the contours of the new flapper type pioneered by Colleen Moore, he eventually gave her a leading role in the *The Plastic Age* (1925) in which she plays the part of Cynthia, the 'fast' coed at Prescott College (her billing was as 'The hottest jazz-baby in films'). When Schulberg's Preferred Pictures was absorbed by Famous Players-Lasky/Paramount (Schulberg retaining semi-independent producer status), Bow was put to work in similar parts, as the flapper daughter, 'Kittens', in *Dancing Mothers* (1926), and as the resilient manicurist heroine, Alverna, in *Mantrap* (1926). To reinforce her on-screen flapper persona, the public was fed a steady diet of tidbits about the star's off-screen romances, with such figures as Gilbert Roland (a co-star in *The Plastic Age*), Victor Fleming (director of *Mantrap*) and Gary Cooper (who had small parts in *Wings* (1927) and *It*) – one of the few men described as having 'It' by Glyn.[76] (Bow's romances appear to have been plentiful enough, but it seems unlikely they were quite as colourful as one might assume from subsequent Hollywood memoirs, and exposés of dubious accuracy, such as Kenneth Anger's infamous *Hollywood Babylon* of 1959.)

According to one account, Glyn had written her novella with the encouragement of Walter Wanger, head of production at Paramount's East Coast studios.[77] But it seems more likely that it was in fact Schulberg who read Glyn's story when it was published in *Hearst's International Combined with Cosmopolitan*, and arranged the match of Glyn's concept and prestige to Bow's screen presence.[78] When he bought the rights to the *Cosmopolitan* story he also paid $50,000 to Glyn to promote Bow as the embodiment of 'It'. 'Of all the lovely young ladies I've met in Hollywood, Clara Bow has "It", Glyn pronounced on cue.[79] (Elsewhere she reportedly discerned 'It' in Bow's co-star, Antonio Moreno, the doorman of the

Ambassador Hotel, and Rex, King of the Wild Horses, equine star of *Wild Blood* (1928).[80]) As part of Schulberg's campaign, the young star and the ageing novelist were frequently to be seen together, in a reprise of the Glyn and Swanson promotion.[81] It is difficult to imagine a less likely pair than the literary grande dame and the relatively unschooled and plain-spoken Bow. As David Stenn records, when Madame Glyn attempted to shape her into something approaching her own ideal of seductive womanhood, Bow tired of her interference, calling her 'that shithead' (*Clara Bow*, 86). But their collaboration, however forced and uneasy, would reshape the way Americans thought about sex, and in the process, Clara Bow, formerly dubbed the 'The Brooklyn Bonfire' for her auburn hair, would become *the* '"It" Girl'.

IT

One could be forgiven for thinking that *It* the film is simply a vehicle for Glyn's psychology of sex, and that Bow merely helps to put Glyn's message across. Certainly Madame Glyn did her best literally to leave her mark on the picture. The film opens with a title above Glyn's signature: '"It" is that quality possessed by some which draws all others with its magnetic force. With "It" you win all men if you are a woman – and all women if you are a man. "It" can be a quality of mind as well as a physical attraction.' In one of the film's opening shots, the hero's rather foppish friend, Monty, is showing reading from *Cosmopolitan*. The intertitle again quotes Glyn: '"It" is that peculiar quality which some persons possess, which attracts others of the opposite sex. The possessor of "It" must be absolutely un-selfconscious, and must have that magnetic "sex appeal" which is irresistible . . . It is a magnetic and peculiar force and you know it as soon as you come in contact.' Glyn herself even makes a cameo appearance in a restaurant scene in the film, again summarizing her views on sexual attraction: 'Self-confidence and indifference to whether you are pleasing or not – and something in you that gives the impression that you are not all cold. That's "It"!' She assures the hero that 'if you have "It" you will win the girl you love'.

But the film was to be a vehicle for Bow, not for Glyn, and the screenplay departs from the original story to that end. As adapted by two of Schulberg's staff writers, Hope Loring and Louis Lighton, the film version emphasizes the sex appeal of the young heroine over that of the manly lead. The film is also much lighter in tone than Glyn's rather ponderous romance, and aims for a more democratic touch. Where Glyn's story focuses on an aristocratic woman and a powerful self-made man, the film's heroine is the working-class Betty Lou Spence, and its department-store tycoon hero is in fact just the boss's son – far from being a Napoleon of business it is his first day running the family business.

In effect, the Loring–Lighton screenplay blends Glyn's *It* with a very familiar subgenre, the 'working girl'/Cinderella story. If the flapper had become a familiar Hollywood type by 1927, so had the feisty 'working girl' – the female factory-hand rarely appeared on screen in the 1920s, but shop-assistants, stenographers, typists, and personal secretaries appeared in droves, in part reflecting, in part mythologizing the changing nature of the work-place, as women increasingly entered the workforce as part of the expanding white collar service sector.[82] As Mary Ryan describes, 'by the late 1920s Hollywood seemed to take the work experience of young females for granted . . . and planted heroines firmly behind desks and counters.'[83] Planted firmly, but not permanently, of course: as Ryan points out, the usual trajectory of working-girl stories from *Ankles Preferred* (1926) to *Our Blushing Brides* (1930) was to chart the heroine's escape from behind the department-store counter (or out of the stockroom, as in another 1927 film, also part-scripted by Hope Loring, Mary Pickford's *My Best Girl*), usually into romance and marriage.[84]

Viewers of *It*, then, would have known what to expect, cued both by Bow's previous acting history and by generic markers. But tying Glyn's story to the department-store daydream in particular, also had the effect of tying sex appeal to consumer desire. As if to drive home the message that this is a film set in a consumer culture, the film opens with a shot of a huge sky-scraping rooftop sign for 'Waltham's – the World's Largest Store'. This opening shot tells us all that we need to know about the values of this film. Waltham's is America itself, the world's largest consumer society – here the business of America is literally business. In such a place we can expect romance to come under the sign of commerce, and for sexual allure and the spell of the commodity to mirror each other. The lofty sign confirms that the department store, like 'It', has its feet on the ground, but also its eyes on the firmament. Since we know that this is a romantic comedy, we might guess that some lucky girl will marry a Waltham, and that in doing so she will not simply marry merchandise – she will ascend into a veritable consumer heaven. This theme is reiterated later in the film when Betty Lou goes into a reverie at the sight of a newspaper advertisement for a dress sale at Waltham's – we are not quite sure if it is Waltham or the advertised couture that she is dreaming of. Our heroine's plebeian name, Betty Lou Spence (cf. Glyn's more patrician Ava Cleveland) even has a surname that augurs well for her future in this consumer world – Spence appears to be a portmanteau of 'spends' and 'expense'. Like another siren of the 1920s, Daisy Buchanan in *The Great Gatsby*, Betty Lou seems to link modern American womanhood to the sound of money.

After lingering on the Waltham's sign, the camera pans down many floors to show the street-level entrance, before a dissolve to the vast and bustling interior. A title tells us: 'Leaving his department store to his son, Cyrus T. Waltham has gone to Herrin, Illinois, for the shooting.' Thus when we see the man at the head of all this activity, Cyrus Junior, sitting at his imposing desk signing documents, we are not terribly impressed – where Glyn's John Gaunt is a self-made man of iron character, Cyrus represents second-generation wealth. Moreover, we learn that he has only recently shed his man-about-town persona when his best friend, the foppish Monty (a stereotyped chinless wonder played with comic gusto by William Austin) arrives with a huge bouquet that spells out 'Good Luck'. Work is clearly a novelty to both of them.

The 'It' theme is introduced when Monty picks up a copy of *Cosmopolitan*, and finds Glyn's story, *It*. The text, though, has been changed for comic effect. The camera zooms in on the following lines: 'Do you gather what I mean Grannie? [sc. No 'Grannie' features in Glyn's story, and if she did, it is unlikely that anyone would be telling her about 'It'.] "It" is that peculiar quality which some persons possess, which attracts others of the opposite sex. The possessor of "It" must be absolutely un-selfconscious, and must have that magnetic "sex appeal" which is irresistible . . . It is a magnetic and peculiar force and you know it as soon as you come in contact.' Further qualifications of 'It' are intercut with reaction shots from Monty: 'Mothers spoil boys with "It" . . . women never refuse them favors.' He admires himself in the mirror before exclaiming: 'Old fruit – you've got "It"!' He looks at Cyrus, and shakes his head dubiously: 'No, too bad, you haven't any "It".' The scene is played for laughs, and Glyn's theory is neatly undercut when Cyrus gives one probable popular reaction: 'Run away, Monty, the keepers are coming.'

We meet Bow's character for the first time when Cyrus and Monty go on an inspection tour of the store. She is visually coded as sexually appealing from the outset: Betty Lou stands behind the lingerie counter, demonstrating a nightdress by holding it against her own body. Besides making the link between women and merchandise, the scene makes clear the gender hierarchy: the many female employees are lined up behind their counters, while a handful of men stride around in control. Monty walks along the counters looking for a someone with 'It', but is disappointed until he sees Betty Lou. The film is mocking as much as exploiting a certain sort of voyeurism here, though. As Mary Ryan points out, lingerie scenes had become a cliché in 1920s film, and 'most every star who came to popularity in the 1920s played a lingerie scene'.[85] By literalizing this device, making Bow a lingerie sales-girl, *It* invites the audience to picture Bow in her underwear (as later they will see her), but it is also poking fun at the convention. Moreover, far from being simply part of the visual display, a commodity among commodities, Bow is represented as sexually aggressive from the outset, albeit in less dramatic ways than such smoldering sirens as Theda Bara. Before Monty sees her, we get her POV shot of Cyrus, with the delightful intertitle: 'Sweet Santa Claus, give me *him*!' She may be behind the counter, but the film empowers her to inspect and choose the goods *she* wants: the shop-girl has a shopping-list. The Cinderella theme is introduced when one of the other shop-girls suggests that she and Betty Lou could have a double wedding, with the Prince of Wales as the fourth party. But as a modern girl, it is a merchant prince that Betty Lou covets, not an aristocrat, and rather than waiting for her prince to come, she will go out and get him.

As the scene continues, the film picks up the thread of Glyn's *It* but develops a rather different version of the way in which sexuality works. When Monty spots Betty Lou and recognizes her as the personification of 'It' he exclaims to Cyrus: 'Look – if I ever saw "It", that's "It".' But Cyrus remains immune to Betty Lou's charms. He leans against her counter, but fails to notice her even when she disturbs him by tugging on an item of lingerie that is trapped between him and the counter. When she later tries to engineer a meeting at the close of business by strategically dropping her purse, he picks it up and hands it to her without a second glance. In the Loring–Lighton treatment of Glyn's story, then, the magical force of sex sometimes needs a little practical help, and Betty Lou has to rely on her native cunning as well as her personal allure. As the business world began to increasingly believe in the early twentieth century, it is not enough to have an attractive commodity: it must be placed before the consumer by advertising (between 1900 and 1925 spending on advertising went from $95.8 million to $923 million).[86] So when she overhears that Cyrus is dining that evening at the Ritz, Betty Lou gets Monty to invite her to dinner there too.

The democratic ethos of the film is consolidated in what follows, as the heroine allows Monty to take her home – on the bus. His car follows at a discreet distance, providing considerable fun for the children of Nolan Street, where Betty Lou lives. At home another aspect of the feisty shop-girl is introduced, as we see her playing with the baby of the young woman with whom she shares the small apartment: modern girl she may be, but she also has traditional motherly characteristics. Bow's playful screen presence is emphasized, her extraordinarily mobile features given full scope as she entertains the infant. Her room-mate spells out an alternative trajectory that Bow's character will not follow – Betty Lou wants love *and* marriage. The ensuing scenes contradictorily work to establish Betty Lou's can-do ethic, while also further establishing her as visual object: we see her improvise an evening dress out of the dress she is wearing, but we also see her shimmy into and out of clothes, and dance around as her friend literally dusts her with make-up. This sequence places Bow most firmly in the flapper mould, and is clearly designed solely to showcase Bow's erotic dynamism, which is given an extra peep-hole frisson by its appearing as a 'domestic' scene, rather than being motivated as, for example, a more typical flapper-movie dance-hall or party episode.

It is only when Cyrus sees Betty Lou at the Ritz in her eye-catching home-made dress, and surrounded by high society, that he finally notices her: Loring and Lighton's 'It', unlike Glyn's, is class-sensitive. As if to reassert her claims to her own concept, or to remind us of its place in this rags-to-riches fable, Glyn makes a cameo appearance as herself in this scene, and gives yet another gloss on 'It' to Cyrus. That Bow is the literal embodiment of the concept is confirmed when Cyrus's date, society blonde Adela Van Norman (Jacqueline Gadson), asks Cyrus if he believes in 'It'. He looks across at Betty Lou and says: 'I certainly do!' But a single sighting, even against the flattering backdrop of the Ritz, is still not enough – as with all advertising, including that for cinema stars, the message must be reinforced. When Cyrus is leaving with Adela and her mother (Julia Swayne Gordon) Betty Lou excuses herself by saying she has to make a telephone call from the lobby, and manages to be introduced to him. Despite his evident interest, the lingerie-selling Cinderella bets Cyrus that he won't recognize her the next time he sees her, and of course he does not the next day at the store (Figure 5). As a 'forfeit', he has to go out with her that evening – she wants them to 'go to the beach, and do it up right'.

The striking Coney Island amusement park sequence that follows continues the film's democratic motif, but it also seems to advance a meta-filmic argument about the nature of industrial entertainment. The rather stuffy Cyrus first has to relearn the pleasures of simple appetites – they eat hot dogs. But the mechanical attractions of the fairground also quite literally bring them closer together, in a sort of industrial mating: when they descend a giant slide, Betty Lou sits between Cyrus's legs; in the rolling barrel they are tumbled together. But the major attraction is the none-too-subtly titled 'Social Mixer' ride, where they and others sit in the middle of a spinning disc

5 Clara Bow and Antonio Moreno in a still from *It* (1927)

like a flat carousel or an over-sized centrifuge, until they are eventually flung
to the outside of the disc and more or less on top of each other. The scene
functions at a number of levels. Obviously in terms of the development of
the plot it is a highly sexually charged moment, and permits a degree of
on-screen physical intimacy between the characters that otherwise might
have attracted the wrath of the Hays office. Similarly, one needs no very
elaborate theory of the carnivalesque to see that the 'Social Mixer' dissolves
social hierarchies as well as gender barriers – millionaire and shop-girl
are quite literally thrown together. The carnivalesque, though, is a strictly
delimited zone. What makes the 'Social Mixer' sequence so interesting is
that the boundaries between it and what lies outside it are themselves weak.
On the one hand, the 'Social Mixer', like Waltham's, may be construed as
America itself, here in its putatively classless, 'Melting-Pot' aspect. More
significantly for our purposes, though, the 'Mixer' also functions as a mise-
en-abime of the cinema itself, another machine working to bring its users
together, regardless of class, specifically as consumers. The film's audience
are invited to recognize themselves as part of this imaginary community.
Moreover, while the Chicago Motion Picture Commission was worried

that the cinema was a threat to the national body, this sequence stresses that the machinic body can be a body for pleasure, and that industrial modernity can be, among other things, breathtaking fun. The machine, it seems to imply, whether that of the fairground or that of the cinema, can be thrilling, and can offer social and sexual liberation.[87]

But of course this is a romantic comedy, and trials must be endured before the lovers can be united. Carried away by the fun of the fair, Cyrus makes a grab for Betty Lou that she repulses irately. A further complication turns on Betty Lou's good-hearted efforts to help her friend, the young single mother with whom Betty Lou shares her apartment. To ward off two interfering do-gooders, Betty Lou pretends to be the baby's mother. A reporter (Gary Cooper, in an early uncredited appearance) and Monty also overhear her, though, and Cyrus comes to believe that his new love is an unmarried mother. Thinking that she can now never be his wife, he offers her a position as his mistress, but she recoils in horror: modern and earthy she may be, but like the heroines of many flapper films, Betty Lou turns out to be an old-fashioned girl at heart.

The two are reconciled again when Monty is bullied by Betty Lou into bringing her with him on a cruise on Cyrus's yacht, the *Itola*, in a location sequence filmed at Catalina Island. Cyrus is at first appalled to discover her aboard, since his other guests include Adela and Mrs Van Norman, but he melts when he looks at her, and proposes marriage. Betty Lou laughs off his proposal, seemingly determined to break his heart as he has broken hers. Resolution is provided when a small nautical disaster caused by Monty's erratic steering throws Betty Lou and Adela overboard. Again Betty Lou shows her resilience: she saves Adela before swimming off. Cyrus dives in too, and finds her hanging on to the ship's anchor in her now clingingly wet dress. The closing shot is of the two of them embracing, with part of the ship's name, the 'It' of *Itola* framed between them. Millionaire and lingerie sales-girl are reconciled by immersion in the sea, a liquid 'Social Mixer', or a cold version of the 'Melting Pot'. The millionaire gets a healthy shot of democratic vitality and Betty Lou gets the man she wanted from the start, as well as, one assumes, all the dresses in Waltham's. The bloodless socialites, on the other hand, Monty and the rescued Adela, are left to look on from the lifeboat, nothing but a pair of 'Itless Its', as he puts it.

READING *IT* THE FILM

The film was a huge success, grossing more than $1 million, and as B. P. Schulberg's son later recalled, Bow became 'not just a top box-office star but a national institution: The It Girl. Millions wore their hair like Clara's, pouted like Clara, and danced and smoked and laughed and necked like Clara.'[88] Her image saturated the country. Paramount founder Adolph Zukor claimed that, 'just as the land was overrun with "sheiks" in Valentino's heyday, there came into being a million or so "It" girls after [*It*]'.[89] A 'Clara Bow craze virtually swept the land (Figure 6). "It" Girl imitators were peeking from behind cash-registers and soda fountains and over store counters. The demand for henna hair dye soared as "The Bow Bob", a carrot-red short-cropped coiffure, became the rage in beauty shops throughout the nation.'[90] Fan mail poured in – Ripley's Believe It or Not reported that an entire car of the Los Angeles-bound mail-train was devoted to Bow's letters (Morella and Epstein, *The 'It' Girl*, 132). Publicists were not slow to take advantage of Bow's iconic status: in St Petersburg, Florida, one enterprising theatre manager advertised another Bow vehicle, *Hula* (1927), by creating life-sized cut-outs of Bow, mechanized to do the hula.[91]

Who was watching? To whom was Clara Bow, icon of 'It', offering a crash-course in How to be Modern and Sexy? It would be an error to assume that Bow was a commodified and sexualized image available only to the male gaze. Men were interested, certainly, but most contemporary accounts stress Bow's effect on *women*. It has become a commonplace of film history that the audience of the 1920s was mostly female, and while such claims have to be treated with some degree of caution, contemporary sources do identify women as the principal cinema audience. In a recent article on 1920s cinema fanzines, Gaylyn Studlar records that in 1924, *Photoplay* estimated that women comprised seventy-five per cent of the audience. In 1927, *Moving Picture World* gave the figure as eighty-three per cent, while the following year *The Exhibitors Herald/Moving Picture World* more circumspectly cited the 'established fact that women fans constitute the major percentage of patronage or at least cast the final vote in determining the majority patronage'.[92] But if these were the ones being 'trained' in modern American sexuality, they cannot simply be seen as the victims of the manipulations of the publicity departments, or indeed passive recipients of the images generated by the cinema apparatus. 'It' is not conferred unilaterally by the apparatus alone, but rather appears in the complex interaction of film, star, publicity, and audience. As Miriam Hansen has argued in the case of Valentino, high levels of audience investment suggest a form of bond between star and spectator that exceeds the control of the publicists. For these spectators the image of the star could offer utopian possibilities that were sometimes in conflict with the ideologies of the films themselves.[93]

6 A Clara Bow postcard from the 1920s

What possibilities did Bow suggest? Looking at the film with hindsight, Bow's most striking characteristic in this film, as elsewhere, is a vitality that goes beyond that of the dancing flapper. As in her other films, Bow is the most kinetic of actresses, even in otherwise quite static scenes. This quality appears to have been part of the off-screen as much as the on-screen Clara. Adolph Zukor recalls: 'it was an elemental magnetism – sometimes described as animal vitality – that made her the center of attention in any company'. As he accurately notes of the film, 'there is seldom, if ever, a moment . . . when she is in repose'.[94] It is that same dynamism that Gaylyn Studlar singles out as the subversive aspect of the film, arguing that Bow's dynamic eroticism remains 'uncurbed by [the film's] narrative closure' ('The Perils of Pleasure?', 282). Certainly Bow makes of the stock character of the 'working girl'-cum-flapper who marries up something altogether more interesting, a kinetic figure who emblematizes the syncopated rhythms of modernity itself, while also offering a thrilling image of the accelerated, nervous body. The modern body that cannot stay still, phobically evoked in the Chicago Motion Picture Commission reports of cinema-goers who suffer from St Vitus's Dance, is here celebrated. Sex appeal, 'It', becomes something very different to Glyn's powerful, unconsciously operative 'magnetism', which in the end still smacks of late Victorian earnestness. Through Bow, 'It' becomes *fun*.

Of course, in tune with the film's consumerist coding, this also means that sex could now take its place as another guiltless consumer pleasure, part of the shopper's paradise symbolized by Waltham's. In a period when the advertising industry was coming into its own, *It* was advertisement for fun, modern sexuality. From our own historical standpoint it is hard to see this as anything other than another part of the colonization of the unconscious and the commodification of the body. But this may be to shut down the significance of the film rather too quickly, and to bracket the fact that in the 1920s modernity did mean real historical change for some women. To Bow's countless fans and imitators, the women who were bobbing and dyeing their hair all over the United States to be just like Clara, perhaps she also offered a glimpse of a pleasurable sexuality, something earthy, but also something light, even euphoric.

AFTER *IT*

Glyn's career in Hollywood peaked with *It*, and the Bow vehicle that followed it, *Red Hair* (1928). A rather devil-may-care attitude to money reduced her Hollywood wealth considerably, and, after her return to England in 1929, a few disastrous investments in the precarious British film industry did further financial damage. Living in relatively modest circumstances – though still surrounded by tiger-skins – she continued to write until her death in 1943. The obituary in the *New York Times* quoted her own self-description as 'instinctively a high priestess of the God of love'.[95] While she kept up a few friendships, Hollywood for the most part forgot her. She does make a sort of reappearance, though, in the film that is perhaps the most poignant memorial to the silent cinema of the 1920s, Billy Wilder's *Sunset Boulevard* (Paramount, 1950). Gloria Swanson plays the part of former queen of the silent cinema, Norma Desmond, who lives in decaying splendour in a secluded mansion like a latter-day Miss Havisham, until a young screen-writer (William Holden) stumbles into her world. While researching this chapter at the Harry Ransom Center at the University of Texas, Austin, I happened upon a box in the Gloria Swanson Papers containing a leopard-print chiffon overskirt and matching leopard-skin sunglasses case. Watching the film again and looking through the publicity stills, I realized that this leopard-skin motif follows Norma Desmond throughout, from her head-scarves to the upholstery of her vintage Isotta Franchini limousine (in a nice touch her chauffeur, and former director and husband, is played by the director who almost bankrupted Swanson in the 1920s with *Queen Kelly*, Erich Von Stroheim). This is of course part of a more general attempt to capture the flavour of the 1920s, the past as another fabric, since animal skins were popular decorative items in an age of big-game hunting. But it is difficult not to conclude that this is also an oblique and bitter-sweet homage to another cat-lover, Madame Glyn (Figure 7), who made tiger-skin her personal signature, and that Swanson's acclaimed grande-dame manner in the film is modelled not on her own earlier self, but on her one-time colleague.

Bow went on to make many more films, among them her most successful (e.g. *Wings* (1927), *Red Hair* (1928), *Call Her Savage* (1932)). But Bow the actress found it hard to retain the invulnerable, spirited aura of Bow the icon (Figure 8). She suffered a nervous collapse during the making of *It*, and was dogged by poor mental health afterwards. She retired young: a series of scandals about her private life, her dissatisfaction with the limits the 'talkies' imposed on her dynamic acting (her Brooklyn accent was less of a problem), and the studio's cavalier treatment of her gave her little incentive to continue. In 1931 she married western actor Rex Bell (they visited Glyn in England on their belated honeymoon in 1933) and long outlived her fame, dying in 1965. To later commentators Bow would come to symbolize the tendencies of the whole decade, which was by then well and truly

7 Elinor Glyn, from the *Tatler*, 26 August 1931

mythologized as an era of madcap fun. Louise Brooks, an iconic figure of
the 1920s herself, writes of Bow, 'I thought she was the most marvelous
star of the 20s because she *was* the 20s . . . the real jazz baby.'[96] After Bow's
death in 1965, her front-page *New York Times* obituary struck a similar note,

8 Enlargement of a Clara Bow cigarette card for Army Club cigarettes, probably from the early 1930s

albeit with more gravitas: 'More than any other woman entertainer of her time, Clara Bow perhaps best personified the giddier aspects of an unreal era, the "Roaring Twenties".'[97]

Much of what Bow was for her era can never be recovered. Stardom is a two-way process, and if Bow was surrounded by a halo of earthy, modern sexuality, her fans helped to assign it to her. 'It', I have been arguing, took on its modern meaning when a late Victorian discourse of personality was combined in a heady cocktail (another 1920s invention) with diluted Freudianism, 1920s consumer culture, the iconogenic power of the last machine and of Hollywood publicity, and, not least, a young star of limitless dynamism. But 'It' may in the end be in the eye of the beholder as much as something there on the screen. As Simon Frith observes in a different context, 'stars, dull professionals, are made glamorous by the imagination and wit and excitement of their fans'.[98] Of course it is difficult to view *It* now without thinking that other '"It" Girls' have come and gone, and the phrase itself now circulates, shorn of historical context, as a convenient label for whichever minor celebrity holds the attention of the media for the moment. Whatever power was possessed by the original '"It" Girl', it is difficult to believe that it has been transferred whole to her many, many successors. And while Bow's performance is still luminous after some seventy odd years, one suspects that the real magic her fans saw in her has vanished along with those fans themselves.

CHAPTER 5

Crash: *flesh, steel, and celluloid*

For in love's field was never found
A nobler weapon than a wound
(Richard Crashaw, 'The Flaming
Heart' (1652))

For when I sleep or when I waken
A picture-film of me is taken.
And every time I sigh or laugh
It means another photograph
For, sad or merry, well or ill
The camera pursues me still,
Till ev'ry single thing I do
Is thus exposed to public view!
(*The Cinema Star* (1914), Act I)[1]

It would be possible to close this study by describing the ways in which an older machine world has been increasingly displaced by a new kind of technoculture. We could, for example, discuss here the social implications of the dimensionless environment of cyberspace; or the displacement of the cinema's indexical images by the more mediated simulacra of video and computer-generated images; or at another level the change from the bulky and *visible* industrial modernity of the nineteenth and early twentieth century to the invisible, silicon-based micro-technologies of the later twentieth century.

Others, though, have already done an excellent job of assessing the cultural impact of these shifts,[2] so I would prefer to turn in this final chapter to two closely related pieces of work that appear to ignore the new to meditate one more time, as it were, on the older machine culture that I have been exploring: J. G. Ballard's disturbing novel about a group of characters for whom sexuality comes to be complexly linked to car accidents, *Crash* (1973), and David Cronenberg's 1996 film version of that novel, also entitled *Crash*. If I began this study with a set of Victorian plays that celebrate narrow escapes from industrial collision, while also attesting to a fascination with such catastrophes, I am ending with a story that depends on the meeting of flesh and steel actually taking place – indeed being sought out.

Ballard is a writer who resists categorization, for some a science fiction writer, for others a figure from the late modernist avant garde. *Crash*, his best-known novel, is set in the present, though it seems to imagine future psychological dispositions. The central character/narrator, also called Ballard, and his wife, Catherine, are a couple before their time, 'early adopters'. Childless, seemingly without any significant family ties, they live in an apartment block outside London, an area dominated by the motorways and the background presence of Heathrow airport. They both pursue extra-marital sexual experiences, but far from being clandestine these are narrated to the other partner. Ballard and Catherine are, it might be surmised, representative of a set of newly affluent, post-war consumers, and devotees of the cult of experience – swingers, even. Catherine works in a wing of the commodity-experience economy – tourism. Ballard, though, represents one version of the intellectual elite of that society, a particular fraction of the professional managerial class: far from being a simple consumer, let alone a shop-worker like Betty Lou Spence in *It*, he works as a director of advertisements, shaping life-style fantasies that in an advanced consumer society come to fill the mental space once occupied by politics and class.

The events of the novel are quite literally set in motion when Ballard's car collides with that of Dr Helen Remington and her husband, killing the latter. An affair with his fellow crash victim leads to an encounter with the rogue scientist, Robert Vaughan, and gradually Ballard is drawn into a strange subculture of crash fetishism. Vaughan, the philosopher of this subculture, tells him that the automobile accident offers a 'benevolent psychopathology' that will free up human sexual energy. But this is not just a novel about people and cars: the auto-landscape of *Crash* is also a mediated landscape, one where the cinema's powerful magic is everywhere present. Dead celebrities are the gods of this world, and Vaughan's ultimate fantasy is to enter the dead star after-life by driving his Lincoln Continental into a car containing the actress Elizabeth Taylor, who is, as it happens, working on a film at Shepperton studios, where Ballard makes his advertisements.

Crash, then, revisits and puts in play a number of the themes that I have already touched on: the interplay of humans and technology imagined in terms of the collision; the emergence of a machine-mediated sexuality; the growth of a sexualized consumer culture; and the creation of a secular pantheon of screen gods and goddesses. The industrial accident, the parallel world of phantasmatic doubles, and the power of 'It' all intersect here. If we began with the way in which melodrama and sensation fiction come to terms with, while exploiting, the shocks of modernity, here we face an aesthetic that has incorporated shock as the dominant technique, though not quite in the way that Benjamin imagined film as doing. Both versions of *Crash* deal literally with the shocks and aftershocks of the collisions of bodies and machines, but they also set out metaphorically to shock the reader/viewer. The shocks of modernity are relayed not just by representing violent collisions but also by adapting the somatic aesthetic of melodrama's less innocent sibling, pornography. If melodrama was the appropriate visual style for mid-Victorian modernity, pornography seems the more appropriate form for a period when the public sphere is weak, and where the individualized, privatized consumer self is celebrated. What pornography and melodrama share, of course, is their appeal to the body, both seeking to excite the viewer, albeit in different ways. But they both also depend on explicitness. If melodrama aspired to render visible on stage social relationships, psychological and emotional states, and the very artifacts of modernity itself, the pornographic effect equally depends on showing/telling 'everything'. In the case of *Crash* this is a different kind of explicitness to that of mainstream pornography. The novel version in particular weds the permutations and combinations of the pornographic scenario to the explicit but affectless detail of the user's manual or the laboratory report: the net result chills, the sex scenes reading like so many autopsy transcripts.

Crash forsakes new machines for old, I have suggested, but it would be a mistake to see this contrast of new tech/old tech as absolute. The car is iconic of early twentieth-century modernity, so much so that the mass consumer economy takes its name from it – Fordism. But the car becomes more, not less, of an element of everyday life as the century progresses. Newer technologies also appear in the background of the text: television is an important context for the novel, and the airport is a significant presence. In any case, any hard-and-fast division between nineteenth- and twentieth-century technologies is a difficult one to sustain.[3] The telecommunications revolutions of the twentieth century were prepared for by such nineteenth-century technologies as the telegraph, which effected the epoch-making liberation of message from material object. Conversely, although the car conceived of as an individual machine harks back to older technologies, conceived of as part of a transport system, as traffic, it is very much a late twentieth-century concern. The idea of traffic and traffic systems leads us directly to information technology – in both the book and film versions

Vaughan is a former expert in computerized traffic systems. Moreover, as David Cronenberg has pointed out about his film version, the car contains *in parvo* a great deal more sophisticated technology than the combustion engine, from fibre-optic electronics to advanced metallurgy.[4] While it would be perverse, then, to read *Crash* as *primarily* about, say, late twentieth-century information technology, at some level, as in nineteenth-century melodrama, a more visible aspect of late modernity is being used to ponder the less visible.

ON THE ROAD

Before considering *Crash* in more detail, though, I want to outline some of the meanings that have accreted around the car in the twentieth century. Like the train, the car belongs to the nineteenth-century industrialization of transport. But from their nineteenth-century origins, railway and automobile transport have come to occupy quite different roles in our cultural imaginary. From its symbolic part in the 1860s as harbinger of modernity, the railway has come to connote organization, timetabling, state-controlled networks, and the submission of the individual's desires to the exigencies of public transport (though the train can also now be redolent of pastness, of a more leisurely, almost pastoral, transport era). But the car, through film and advertising in particular, has come to connote freedom, individualism, even anti-social rebellion, from the anarchic comedy of *How it Feels to be Run Over* (Hepworth, 1900) and Mack Sennett's 'Keystone Kops' in the 1910s, to the road-movie feminist revolt of *Thelma and Louise* (1991). (A similar mythology attaches to that other internal combustion-based transport, the motorbike, in such films as *The Wild One* (1954) and *Easy Rider* (1969).) This is in part understandable in light of the fact that the thrills of speed offered by the car can be placed in a broader historical series stretching back to the eighteenth century, as Jeffrey T. Schnapp has shown.[5] Schnapp sees a bifurcation between passenger-centred and driver-centred modes of transport at the beginning of the nineteenth century, which allows the latter to develop new modes of accelerated and intensified subjectivity, and the thrill of speed as a form of modern sublime. And yet, seen from a functionalist perspective, the two technologies do analogous work: both of them can be understood, in Peter Ling's words, as 'designed to expedite the flow of goods and services [and] thus to accelerate the circulation of capital and its eventual accumulation'.[6] They are both part of a more general dynamic of modernization and the concomitant transformation of the lived environment: together they have accomplished the incorporation of unique and remote regions into more homogeneous national systems; have reshaped the physical landscape; and, as we have already seen in the case of the railway, necessitated a retraining of the human sensorium to cope with a new experience of time and space, new levels of attentiveness, and new forms of distracted agency.

In the case of the car, though, there has been a greater degree of mystification of its systemic role in modernization. As Ling has argued, on the side of production the car stood with Fordism, the rationalized assembly line, de-skilling, and the installation of the individual worker as a cog in the productive mechanism; but on the side of consumption the car seemed to promise affordable individual mobility, new leisure potential, as well as the psychological compensations of speed (*America and the Automobile*, 4–8). In popular twentieth-century narrative, then, the car has been the vehicle of rebellion. Especially in the United States, it has been represented as offering access to the chronotope of the 'open road', and as promising the ascendancy of the individual (though also at times that of the family). For Ling, such technological fantasies are harder to sustain when the car is seen as part of the rationalization of transport imbricated in the logic of capitalism itself. Certainly when looked at in terms of the transport network – the provision of infrastructure, regulation of fuel prices, and the control of traffic – rather than in terms of the individual driver, the integrated economic role of automotive transport is more readily apparent.

In Britain, as in the United States, the post-war years saw increased government involvement in the provision of just such an integrated transport system. In the early 1950s in the United States, the Eisenhower administration advocated a new interstate highway network. Economic and safety reasons were cited, but civil defence was also an important concern – in the event of an atomic bomb attack by the Soviet Union, massive scale evacuation of cities was envisaged.[7] In Britain, work on the new motorway network started in 1956, and by 1972, the year before the publication of *Crash*, there were 1,000 miles of motorway. The Road Research Laboratory, which makes a cameo appearance in Ballard's novel, was initially concerned with road materials and engineering, but it expanded into the area of traffic and safety in the post-war years, and it continued to grow along with the new motorway system, from 1966 onwards using computer-based models in its work. Among its recommendations were safety barriers on central reserves (introduced in 1970) and a maximum speed limit of seventy miles per hour (introduced experimentally in 1965, adopted indefinitely in 1967): the mythology of the lone driver on the open road would have to accommodate itself to state regulation.

At the time that Ballard was writing the novel, then, the systemic, administered nature of car/road transport was more evident in the United States and Britain than it had ever been before, which to some extent may explain why he is not interested in exploring the open-road myth of speed and freedom. Even in the United States, while the car or motorcycle was a more fetishized commodity than ever, the fantasy of the open road was increasingly hard to sustain, as the downbeat ending of a film like *Easy Rider* (1969) suggests. (Indeed, the efforts of Ralph Nader, the consumer-rights advocate, to convince the American public that cars could be death-traps, might also be seen as part of this moment.) The roads in *Crash* are the roads of the edge-city commuter, roads to no-place, fibres knitting together an aura-less world of shopping centres, service stations, high-rise apartments, and huge carparks, all of which might be seen as the logical outcome of that draining of local aura instigated by the railway network in the Victorian period. While the iconic, frontier-pushing aspect of the space-age 1960s American car is evoked by Vaughan's 1963 Lincoln Continental, there is little sense here of the automobile as emblem of individual escape, as existential getaway car. Any such connotations are complicated by the fact that the 1963 Lincoln, a car named for an assassinated president, was also, of course, the car in which another American president, John F. Kennedy, was shot in Dallas – a special kind of car fatality, the novel notes, and one that closed down the New Frontier.

But if Ballard eschews the available popular cultural image of the car as vehicle of freedom, neither does he take the car/road system to be emblematic of some all-enveloping administered world, nor the car itself to be the metaphorical iron cage of modernity. Rather he seems to want to make the car/road system itself into a subject of fantasy investment. What attracts him is not the integrated system, but the strange fruit that grow in the cracks of the system, in the interstices of a gridded world (in this respect there are points of comparison with Thomas Pynchon's *The Crying of Lot 49* (1966), the WASTE network of that novel resembling the secret world of crash fetishists). The city of *Crash* might be the edge city of flyovers, and moulded concrete tower blocks for cars and people, but Ballard seems to be primarily interested in the ways in which these ostensibly sterile and rationalized spaces are re-mythologized, re-auraticized.

CRASH

In *Crash*, the industrial accident is finally allowed to happen. If the sensation drama of the 1860s inaugurated decades of fantasies of non-collision, fantasies of the machine avoided or defeated, *Crash* revisits that primal scene of people versus machines only to give up on its fantasy, to end the suspense. The dramatists of the mid-nineteenth century could still imagine men and women defeating the machine on its own terms, and imagine some postponement of the human/machine nexus, but by the second half of the twentieth century such a fantasy was a good deal less tenable, even if it continued to exert some appeal in popular culture. Giving up on the pastoral, Ballard's fiction assumes as one of its fundamental premises that our everyday experience, and indeed our imaginary, has been thoroughly mechanized. The lost children of Victorian melodrama offered a consolatory image of a vulnerable yet resilient humanity faced with a crushing modernity. Here they are pictured as the victims of a multi-car pile-up: '[Vaughan] dreamed of alienated brothers and sisters, by chance meeting each other on collision courses on the access roads of petrochemical plants, their unconscious incest made explicit in this colliding metal'.[8] Walter Benjamin theorized that the jostling of the street was part of the shock experience of modernity, a series of soft-machine collisions; for Ballard all encounters can be understood as crashes, all crashes can be interpreted as encounters. When people meet here it is quite literally 'by accident'.

According to Martin Bax, Ballard's friend and collaborator at the experimental magazine, *Ambit*, Ballard deals with a third phase of the industrial revolution – the phases of industrialization and consumerism being the first and second. For Bax, this third phase involves the full integration of technology and the human – 'we're no longer just biological organisms, we're bio-robotical organisms'.[9] In chapter 2 we encountered some early attempts to imagine the machinic body, including Miserrimus Dexter, Wilkie Collins's phobic vision of a man-machine in *The Law and the Lady*. At the centre of Ballard's novel is a different figure – not the nervous, galvanic body of the sensation novel, still less the euphoric body electric of the 1920s flapper, but the post-crash body, a body scarred but also strangely liberated and libidinized by the encounter with the machine. The alternative world for which Vaughan acts as gatekeeper, a world of scars and pain, scorched flesh and tortured metal, though also of Dionysian sexual release, opens to Ballard through his near-death experience. Indeed, the crash appears to act as a sort of baptism into the real: 'the crash was the only real experience I had been through for years. For the first time I was in physical confrontation with my own body, an inexhaustible encyclopedia of pains and discharges' (*Crash*, 39). But also, it appears, a catalogue of new pleasures.

The narrator, then, seems to suggest that the crash is a painful but necessary initiation into some more fundamental experiential realm. But whatever Ballard's crash opens up, it is not a world of unmediated corporeality. For one thing, the crash is the last step in a process rather than a radical departure – it transports Ballard to a new empire of the senses only because he has already been primed for it, has already been tutored by the mass-mediated society he inhabits. This is a society of the mechanical image: the nascent tendencies that Kipling saw at work in the 1900s, and which were already well established by the 1920s, are here taken for granted as part of the fabric of everyday life. For Ballard and his wife, Catherine, sex already recalls 'all those scenes of pain and violence that illuminated the margins of our lives – television newsreels of wars and student riots, natural disasters and police brutality which we vaguely watched on the colour TV set in our bedroom as we masturbated each other. This violence experienced at so many removes had become intimately associated with our sex lives' (37). Like one of Pavlov's unfortunate dogs, Ballard has already been conditioned to associate sex and violent death (cf. Pynchon again, specifically his interest in conditioned reflexes in *Gravity's Rainbow*, published in the same year as *Crash*).[10] Nor, indeed, is the link between transport technology and sex an entirely novel one for the Ballard character, since he tells us that two months before his accident he became sexually aroused at the airport 'by the conjunction of an air hostess's fawn gaberdine skirt on the escalator in front of [him] and the distant fuselages of the aircraft' (41). Before his fatal encounter with Helen Remington and her husband, he is already a conditioned machine fetishist: it is scarcely surprising that car crashes make his mouth water.

We begin to recognize that the 'real' of which Ballard gets a glimpse, and the alternative subculture to which he gains admittance, is just as mediated as the mainstream. His crash fetishism is continuous with his occupation as a director of advertisements – his current project in the novel being a high-budget advertisement for Ford's sports car range, in which he hopes to be able to use Elizabeth Taylor. Car advertisements in the 1970s (though not just then, obviously) worked very hard to make automobiles sexy, in the process having the presumed side effect of making sex automobilic. The cross-species intercourse between machines and people that Vaughan and Ballard imagine is at one level the logical outcome of advertising's efforts to anthropomorphize the object world. But the media have also helped to produce the novel's crash authority, Vaughan: the heavily scarred sexual pioneer was once a rising television personality. A minor media celebrity, he was 'one of the first of the new-style TV scientists' (63). Even Vaughan's sidekick and fellow crash fetishist, Seagrave, is himself a stunt driver, an expert in simulated crashes, photo-faking, as it might have been termed in the 1900s.

The clearest indicator that the crash does not represent some direct encounter with reality is that Vaughan's ultimate crash is to involve the death of Elizabeth Taylor, sometimes simply styled 'the film actress'. What Vaughan dreams of, in other words, is not a collision with a car containing an ordinary human body, but with the limousine containing the greatest film star of the time, and probably the world's most photographed woman in the 1970s, the '"It" Girl' of the moment. (Perhaps Vaughan is also inspired by the fact that she had already died as Gloria Wandrous in a car crash at the end of *Butterfield 8* (1960).) He imagines this fatal brief encounter as a ritual that will release the powerful sexual energy of the star, and immortalize her killer: 'With a little forethought she could die in a unique vehicle collision, one that would transform all our dreams and fantasies' (130). He tails off significantly: 'The man who dies in that crash with her . . .' (130). This ultimate crash never takes place successfully, though we get some idea of what is imagined when Seagrave pre-empts Vaughan's plan by dressing up as Taylor and crashing into the car of an unnamed minor celebrity. As described by the Ballard character, this is not just a deadly encounter of body and car, but of the technology-transformed star and her audience. The celebrity, or star, has already been transubstantiated by mechanical reproduction, her body morcellated by close-ups. What the crash means is a second transubstantiation, a more violent montage by glass and steel:

Her mutilation and death became a coronation of her image at the hands of a colliding technology, a celebration of her individual limbs and facial planes, gestures and skin tones. Each of the spectators at the accident site would carry away an image of the violent transformation of this woman, of the complex of wounds that fused together her own sexuality and the hard technology of the automobile . . . The automobile crash had made possible the final and longed-for union of the actress and the members of her audience. (189–90)

It is not clear whether the aura of the actress is being brought down to earth here, the Word, as it were, being made flesh, or whether it is the audience who are raised onto the magical dais of the celebrity. But either way, the crash is not represented as an encounter with some more concrete, or steely, reality, but with a higher level of the insubstantial – a cross between a night at the movies and the ritual of the mass.[11]

READING THE WRECKAGE

The most influential reading of *Crash* has been that of Jean Baudrillard, which situates Ballard's text as an exemplary postmodern artifact, one in which the novelistic problematics of surface/depth, illusion/reality, nature/artifice, and older characterological bases are forsaken for a world of pure simulacra, of circulating signs. Baudrillard welcomes *Crash* as 'the first great novel of the universe of simulation'. In Ballard's novel, he announces, 'no more fiction or reality, it is hyperreality that abolishes both'.[12] The novel represents a depthless, affectless world, beyond psychology, beyond the problematic of the alienated subject: 'No affect behind all that, no psychology, no flux or desire, no libido or death drive'.[13] And, one might add, no moral, no meaning beyond the endless circulation of cars, signs, and people who are not quite people. Yet there is evidence to suggest that Ballard's interpretation of mass-mediated society might be quite different to that of Baudrillard. In a July 1966 review essay, Ballard does refer to 'this moment, when the fictional elements in the world around us are multiplying to the point where it is almost impossible to distinguish between the "real" and the "false"'. But he assumes that the task of the arts is to 'isolat[e] the few elements of reality from this mélange of fictions'.[14] This is a position at some remove from Baudrillard's radical epistemological scepticism, which announces the impossibility of rescuing any such 'real' in a thoroughly mediated world in which simulation destabilizes the very opposition of real/false.

Rather than seeing Ballard as simply a post-structuralist *avant la lettre*, as it were, it is just as possible to locate what he describes as his 'overlit realm ruled by advertising and pseudo-events' within a more general drive in cultural theory and the arts to make sense of post-war consumer capitalism. The term 'pseudo-events', for example, seems to derive from Daniel J. Boorstin's 1962 study, *The Image, Or What Happened to the American Dream*, which offered a scathing critique of the consequences of the media's attempts to satisfy the public's increasing desire for novelty: heroes were being replaced by ephemeral celebrities; the media was generating news rather than reporting it; and reality itself was becoming a poor substitute for the 'Kodachrome original'.[15]

Roger Luckhurst has suggested another promising line of inquiry by arguing that we can also situate Ballard's work within the post-war avant garde.[16] This is particularly evident in Ballard's links to experimental post-war visual art, which seems to have impressed him far more than the psychological realism of contemporary British literature. Ballard has often noted how influential the Surrealists were for his early work, and he directly links what he sees as the appropriate territory for science fiction – mental or 'inner space', rather than 'outer space' – to the work of de Chirico, Dali, and others. His take on post-war British society was also informed by a native British visual arts source, the Independent Group, or IG, a group of young artists who met at the Institute of Contemporary Art (ICA) in the 1950s, and developed a British style of Pop art. Ballard became friendly with some of the members – Eduardo Paolozzi, Richard Hamilton, and Reyner Banham – who were reacting against what they perceived as the sterile formalism of the modernism promulgated by Herbert Read and the ICA.[17]

The IG drew on the ephemera of American-cum-international popular culture in an effort to escape the gravitational pull of contemporary British art. (As Ballard's own childhood was spent in the Americanized international quarter of pre-Second World War Shanghai, American popular culture must have seemed like a very natural source to him too.[18]) In 1956 Ballard attended the *This is Tomorrow* exhibition held by the IG at the Whitechapel Gallery, where pride of place was given to a 'pavilion' built by Richard Hamilton, John Voelcker, and John McHale. One wall of this confusing structure featured a fourteen-foot-high collage derived from a publicity poster for the film *Forbidden Planet*, in which a huge robot is seen carrying off the heroine; another wall displayed a large panoramic collage of Hollywood icons. Also on display was Richard Hamilton's 'famous little painting', as Ballard would later term it, a collage from 1956 entitled, *Just what is it that makes today's homes so different, so appealing?*[19] Hamilton appears to be a significant figure for *Crash* in a number of ways: in 1955 he put on an exhibition at the ICA entitled *Man, Machine and Motion*; in 1957 he produced a piece entitled *Homage à Chrysler Corp*; and in 1962 his wife, Terry O'Reilly, was killed in a car crash. *Just what is it* is not about cars, though, and yet it is a key artifact for Ballard's novel. It shows a modern household interior complete with modern couple. The male figure, apparently cut from a body-building magazine, holds an oversized lollipop, the female resembles a topless dancer, angled suggestively on a sofa, and fondling her left breast. The pair are surrounded by modern household appliances (a miniature female figure drags a vacuum cleaner), and icons of popular Americana – an American pulp magazine appears as a painting; a giant tin of ham rests on the coffee table; a Ford insignia decorates a lampshade; the television watches over it all from the background. This is not quite the 'overlit realm ruled by advertising and pseudo-events' that Ballard describes in his 1995 Preface to *Crash* (though this Preface substantially reproduces earlier comments, some of them ascribed to a fictional character in *The Atrocity Exhibition*). However, it is not hard to see how Hamilton's paper cut-out couple may have planted the germ for his own pair of jaded, childless, self-indulgent, and sexually obsessive super-consumers, Ballard and Catherine. In an essay from 1971 that seems to anticipate *Crash*, Ballard explicitly suggested that Pop art and (his kind of) science fiction shared the same subject matter, 'everyday life', which he glossed as 'the gleam on refrigerator cabinets, the contours of a wife's or husband's thighs passing the newsreel images on a colour TV set, the conjunction of musculature and chromium artifact within an automobile interior, the unique postures of passengers on an airport escalator'.[20] Every-day life, then, resembles Hamilton's collage in offering tableaux of bodies and machines within a shiny grotto of consumer goods and conveniences.

As Kristin Ross has illustrated in her study of modernization in post-war France, *Fast Cars, Clean Bodies* (1995), the cultural theorist, Henri Lefebvre, made *his* momentous 'discovery' of everyday life as an object of critical scrutiny in this same period, and Roland Barthes's *Mythologies* was not far behind. Ross highlights the extent to which French writers, like Ballard, began to register the presence of 'the newly vitalized unit of consumption energy . . . the couple, or jeune ménage'.[21] Midway between Lefebvre and Ballard, the Situationists were also investigating advertising and post-war consumer culture, the relationships between people and their built environments, and the cult of celebrity. Situationism is usually evoked now only with reference to Guy Debord's 1967 manifesto, *The Society of the Spectacle*, and the events of 1968 in France, but Situationism was a movement with a long genealogy of avant-garde practice as well as leftist critique, traceable back to Dada and Surrealism (already identified as a major influence for Ballard) as well as to Marx.[22] Debord's work closely resembles that of Baudrillard to the extent that it is concerned with the waning of reality under capitalism, but the politics of Debord's position are more legible, *The Society of the Spectacle* being essentially an attempt to bring Marx's account of the commodity (and Georg Lukács's *History and Class Consciousness*) to bear on post-war society. For Debord, capitalism, not the power of the media, has drained the world of its reality – the society of the spectacle is one where 'social life is completely taken over by the accumulated products of the economy'.[23] While mass media are a superficial example of the 'spectacle', the crucial fact is that 'the spectacle is capital accumulated to the point where it becomes image' (*The Society of the Spectacle*, 24). Marx was already in the nineteenth century arguing that under capitalist conditions of commodity exchange the fantastic had entered into the fabric of the real ('to find an analogy [to the commodity form] we must take flight into the misty realm of religion'),[24] but Debord extrapolates that analysis to late twentieth-century conditions, specifically to the Euro-American society of abundance. The society of the spectacle, then, is the society of the commodity fetish. As advertising, the commodity produces its own epic: 'of arms and the man the spectacle does not sing, but rather of passions and the commodity' (43). The car is a 'star commodity' (42), even if we might speculate that the car crash offers a more intense form of consumer experience than shopping.

As with Ballard, the cult of celebrity is central to Debord's fantastic world, the necessary concomitant of the replacement of citizens with privatized consumers, politics with lifestyles. The spectacle attenuates the public sphere, replacing human activity with passive contemplation: 'media stars are spectacular representations of living human beings, distilling the essence of the spectacle's banality into images of possible roles' (38). The celebrity becomes a sort of advertisement for the self. There are also, though, 'stars of decision' like J. F. Kennedy (also one of Ballard's key figures, especially in *The Atrocity Exhibition*) who offer fantastic and autonomous images of power divorced from the labour that makes power possible. But no matter how many star images or star commodities are consumed, the individual consumer 'can only get his hands on a succession of fragments of this commodity heaven' (43). The real and the false are practically indistinguishable, the world of politics and entertainment overlap, and people's primary passions are routed through commodities.[25] This is close to Baudrillard's vision, but in Debord it is always capital that is behind the wheel. There are also resemblances between Ballard's work and that of the other Situationists, in particular the Situationist use of 'psycho geography', which mimics scientific language for its own ends, an example of the pervasive Situationist technique of *détournment*, in which a text, or an image, could be 'borrowed' and redirected to other ends, a device that was itself borrowed by the Situationists from Surrealism. Its equivalent in Ballard's work is his use of scientific, medical, and other modes of writing – including pornography – for his own purposes. One of the direct sources for the vividly visceral descriptive prose of *Crash*, for example, is Jacob Kulowski's medical text-book, *Crash Injuries*, which, with the *Warren Commission Report* Ballard describes as one of his 'bibles'.[26]

While the tendency, then, has been to see *Crash* through a Baudrillardian lens as an exemplary postmodern text, the 'structure of feeling' within which it makes most sense may be that of the belated, post-war, modernist avant garde. The critique of post-war consumer culture developed by Boorstin, the Situationists, the IG, and others is very much there in Ballard, though in his work it becomes something rather different – he is, after all, writing a novel, not an essay. *Crash* enters fully into this enchanted world the better to understand it; it explores the ways in which people re-inject meaning into a commodified and thoroughly modernized world – it takes its mythology seriously. *Crash*, and the novels that follow it, *Concrete Island* and *High Rise*, all deal with situations in which individuals and groups re-mythologize what might at first appear to be completely administered environments. In *Concrete Island* a new Crusoe story unfolds in an artificial island created by the motorway system; in *High Rise* a new tribalism forms among the tenants of a state-of-the-art apartment building; and in *Crash* the protagonists cobble together a new religion-cum-sexuality out of the unlikely materials of the motorway system and Hollywood cinema.

MYTHOLOGIES

A new 'mythology' was exactly what Ballard saw himself as producing as early as 1966. In 'Notes from Nowhere: Comments on Work in Progress', an article he wrote for the science-fiction/avant-garde journal, *New Worlds*, he describes the 'manifest content' of his current work as 'the attempt to produce a new "mythology" out of the intersecting identities of J. F. K., Marilyn Monroe, smashed automobiles and dead apartments'.[27] The latent content, on the other hand, he explains, is his on-going concern for the geometric, for intersecting planes, indeed for the lived experience of space and time. This might seem like a description of *Crash*, but these concerns also run through Ballard's experimental novel of 1970, *The Atrocity Exhibition*, which at times reads like a set of notes for *Crash*. 'Novel' is scarcely the right term for *The Atrocity Exhibition*, which takes the form of a series of separate but linked narratives, most of which feature a disturbed central character who is obsessed with correspondences between the inner and outer worlds – more precisely, correspondences between mental and physical events, between parts of the body and the object world, and among different aspects of the object world. As Ballard described him in an interview, 'He has been shocked and numbed by the deaths of the Kennedys and Marilyn Monroe. To make sense of the modern world he wants to immerse himself in its most destructive elements.'[28] This character seems to reappear under different names in the separate chapters: Travis, Talbot, Traven, Tallis. He is surrounded by other semi-continuous characters, including his wife, his mistress, Catherine Austen (sometimes Austin, a nod to the capital of the state in which Kennedy's assassination took place, perhaps), Dr Nathan, his doctor (and/or colleague), and Karen Novotny.[29]

In a section entitled 'Planes Intersect', Dr Nathan offers some insight into the associative mental world of the Travis figure, though in fact he is also quoting Ballard's own essay, 'Notes from Nowhere':

Planes intersect: on one level, the tragedies of Cape Kennedy and Vietnam serialized on billboards, random deaths mimetized in the experimental auto-disasters of [sc. Ralph] Nader and his co-workers . . . On another level, the immediate personal environment, the volumes of space enclosed by your opposed hands, the geometry of your postures, the time-values contained in this office, the angles between these walls. On a third level, the inner world of the psyche. Where these planes intersect, images are born, some kind of valid reality begins to clarify itself. (*The Atrocity Exhibition*, 67)

It is this 'reality' that Travis seeks, but it is also Ballard's own mission as a novelist to save such fragments of reality from the media landscape, as the Surrealist painters had opened windows onto the real. Or, as he puts it in a different context, he wishes to capture moments when 'the conventional stage sets that are erected around us [and] from which we can never escape, are suddenly dismantled, and there's an element of magic involved'.[30]

Signalling the continuity between the two novels, the title *Crash* appears in *The Atrocity Exhibition* as an (undescribed) stage show and as a magazine. A character called Koester, a student in Travis's class, has produced *Crash!*, 'a magazine devoted solely to car accidents'. 'The dismembered bodies of Jayne Mansfield, Camus, and Dean presided over its pages, epiphanies of violence and desire' (31). Not only are some of the themes of *Crash* rehearsed in the earlier novel, but a number of the characters are introduced, including Vaughan, who first appears as a former day-patient at the clinic where Travis works/is treated. As in *Crash*, Vaughan is associated with cars and, more than in the later novel, with sexual violence. In *The Atrocity Exhibition*, though, it is the Travis character who desires some kind of sexual union with Elizabeth Taylor, though not 'in the literal sense', Dr Nathan assures Catherine Austin (77).

The car crash appears here in the terms that Vaughan will later use to describe it in *Crash*, though it is the Travis character who is credited with these ideas:

Talbot's belief . . . is that automobile crashes play very different roles from the ones we assign them. Apart from its ontological function, redefining the elements of space and time in terms of our most potent consumer durable, the car crash may be perceived unconsciously as a fertilizing rather than a destructive event – a liberation of sexual energy – mediating the sexuality of those who have died with an intensity impossible in any other form: James Dean and Miss Mansfield, Camus and the late President [sc. Kennedy]. (29)

The idea of the crash as something fertilizing directly anticipates the later novel, and here too it is linked to celebrity death. Kennedy's death becomes a special type of car crash, but so does the crucifixion: according to Dr Nathan, 'In 20th-century terms the crucifixion . . . would be re-enacted as a conceptual auto-disaster' (140). The outside world as much as the psyche is attributed manifest and latent content, and the special psychic role of the car is in part accounted for by the fact that much of twentieth-century technology – 'computers, pilotless planes, thermonuclear weapons' – refuse to reveal their 'latent identity', whereas the car makes itself available for psychodramas of aggression and desire (140). We begin to get a clearer sense why *Crash* downplays twentieth-century high tech to place the car centre stage.

FROM BLACK-AND-WHITE MAGIC TO COLOUR

The car and the media seem to offer access to a numinous realm inhabited by those film stars and celebrities who have died in traffic accidents (or in the case of Kennedy, less accidentally). In effect, then, Ballard returns us not only to the people versus machine scenarios of sensation drama, but also to the dimension of machine culture that we first encountered in chapter 3 – 'It', the personal magnetism magnified by the industrial magic of the cinema. While in the 1920s the concept (via Glyn) melded with notions of modern sexuality, consumerism, and the persona of Clara Bow to create the exhilarating '"It" Girl', here, as in Kipling's 'Mrs Bathurst', with its collation of film and death, it is the darker side of 'It' that is developed. In *The Atrocity Exhibition* and *Crash* Ballard dwells on what happens when the machine-transformed body of the star enters fully into our fantasy life. What happens when a screen goddess dies violently, as in the case of Marilyn Monroe or Jayne Mansfield? How does violent death overwrite existing sexual fantasy, and to what extent do cinema icons possess maleficent power? Ballard in effect addresses the black magic of celebrity culture. But where Kipling was speculating on the possible tendencies of the new medium in the light of its relation to the national trauma of the Boer War, Ballard is writing at a point when everyday life has been utterly saturated with the image, when the stars have quite literally become household names, and even household gods.

Whence Ballard's new mythology? One might speculate that here Ballard is drawing on the sinister anatomy of film given in one of the novels he acknowledges as among his favourites, Nathanael West's *Day of the Locust*, inspired in part by the hysteria surrounding the death of Valentino. (One can also point to the work of at least one of the science fiction writers that he grew up reading, Fritz Leiber, particularly the latter's 'The Girl with the Hungry Eyes'.) But *Crash* also explores modern celebrity culture by drawing fairly explicitly on some very venerable ideas. Rejecting the scientific ambitions of cultural theory, instead he takes flight into the misty realm of religion. To find the wounded body accorded the same iconic centrality, and to find similar fantasies of the collision of the human and the divine, we have to return to the theology of the late medieval period. Then, of course, the archetypal wounded body was that of Christ, represented in Books of Hours and in paintings as the Man of Sorrows, 'an image of Christ weary, bleeding, suffering, on whom are superimposed the crucifix and the wounds'.[31] His bleeding flesh testified to his human vulnerability but also symbolized his divine redemptive power. For more mystical writers, the wounds 'were literally an entry into Christ with whom they wished to be united in the spirit'.[32] The sacrifice of the mass, at which the body and blood of Christ were meant to be literally present, gave the participants access to Christ's redemptive body, though it also brought them together as a Christian community. In this sense the Eucharist was effectively the linchpin of the symbolic world of medieval Europe.

Ballard seems to suggest that the only way to understand the impact of violent celebrity death is in similar terms – the star crash is the closest thing we have to Calvary. As I noted earlier, one of the characters *in The Atrocity Exhibition* uses Alfred Jarry's painting, 'The Crucifixion Considered as an Uphill Bicycle Race' to speculate that if the crucifixion were to happen now it would be a car crash (140). But *Crash* seems to go further and suggest that this has already happened – violent celebrity deaths *are* modern myths of resurrection, of the union of church and godhead, audience and star. Ballard imagines just such a world of bloody communion: 'I visualized the injuries of film actresses and television personalities, whose bodies would flower into dozens of auxiliary orifices, points of sexual conjunction with their audiences formed by the swerving technology of the automobile' (180). The language recalls not so much pornography as the devotional baroque poetry of the seventeenth century, the mystical work of Richard Crashaw, for example (in this light Vaughan's name is perhaps meant to remind us of the mysticism of Thomas Vaughan).

The followers of the latter-day Vaughan, then, are creating their own ritual, their own auto-mass, by staging car accidents. This mass/crash connection is made more explicit in one of the novel's unstaged crashes: 'The last of the ambulances drove away . . . pervasive sexuality filled the air, as if we were members of a congregation leaving after a sermon urging us to celebrate our sexualities with friends and strangers, and were driving into the night to imitate the bloody Eucharist we had observed with the most unlikely partners' (157). Vaughan even collects relics, taking a piece of blood-stained seat-leather from the later crash involving a television actress: 'It lay between us like a saintly relic, the fragment of a hand or shinbone. For Vaughan this piece of leather . . . contained all the special magic and healing powers of a modern martyr of the super-highways . . . stained with the blood that had flowed from her wounded genital orifice' (188). When he himself is 'martyred', his car will take on a similarly numinous aspect for his followers.

Crash dusts off some of the paradoxes of late medieval theology and politics for a celebrity age: on the one hand the star is seen as meta-physical, immortal; on the other he or she is all too real, all too much exposed to the frailty of the flesh. Christ's corporeal aspect created a significant problem for the medieval church. How could Christ be at once immortal and mortal? The difficult question of Christ's 'two natures' became a fertile source of theological debate, and indeed of heresy (specifically the Arian heresy). Later this Christological problem was bequeathed to late medieval political theory, where it became the concept of 'the king's two bodies'.[33] The king was a 'Corporation Sole', partaking of both body 'natural and corruptible' and a 'body politic', which was in theory immortal. This also meant that the king, through his 'superbody' could be present in his courts, for example, even though he was not physically present. In effect, this theory offered a way of harmonizing ancient practices of personal kingship and aspects of the modern disembodied state. Thus the king could die, but his body politic would be transferred to another body natural, and kingship itself would be intact (the king resembles an actor in a role that is always filled, an idea with which Shakespearean drama sometimes flirts). But as in the case of the Eucharist and the mass, this theory also meant that the people were intimately bound to him: people and king formed one body – they were the 'mystic members' of which he was the head (Kantorowicz, *The King's Two Bodies*, 15), just as Christ was the head of the body of the church.

Stars have their own 'two natures'. That is to say, the 'parallel world of phantasmatic doubles' we met in chapter 3 takes on a somewhat different aspect in a celebrity culture, where it is joined with the star's 'It'. Just as there is a body natural and a body politic, so there is an actual Elizabeth Taylor with a 'body natural', and her cinematically and publicity-transformed 'superbody', which enjoys immortality, omnipresence, and a sort of hyper-sexuality. Vaughan's fantasy is to somehow access the immortal status of the superbody by dying in a collision with the body natural. He imagines this moment as also being a fateful collision of bodies and machine, a grotesque threesome involving himself, his car, and Taylor, 'her uterus pierced by the heraldic beak of the manufacturer's medallion, his semen emptying across the luminescent dials that registered for ever the last temperature and fuel levels of the engine' (8). (The most immediate reference here appears to be to the myth of Leda and the swan, and W. B. Yeats's version of it as the origin of the Trojan war, 'A shudder in the loins engenders there / The broken wall, the burning roof and tower / And Agamemnon dead'.[34]) Of course Vaughan fails: instead of dying in a mythopoeic collision with Elizabeth Taylor, he dies when his car collides with a busload of tourists from the airport:

Driven on a collision course towards the limousine of the film actress, his car jumped the rails of the London Airport flyover and plunged through the roof of a bus filled with airline passengers. The crushed bodies of package tourists, like a haemorrhage of the sun, still lay across the vinyl seats when I pushed my way through the police engineers an hour later. Holding the arm of her chauffeur, the film actress Elizabeth Taylor, with whom Vaughan had dreamed of dying for so many months, stood alone under the revolving ambulance lights. As I knelt over Vaughan's body she placed a gloved hand to her throat. (7)

In a sort of reversal of roles, the actress for a brief moment becomes a spectator at a 'real-life drama', but the impossibility of any union with Elizabeth Taylor the icon is underlined by Vaughan's ignominious end. Hoping to cross the line between spectators and spectacle, and to take his place in the modern, media-inflected pantheon, he dies instead amidst the most scorned of all consumers, the package tourists. While the narrator sees Vaughan's death as itself a fertilizing event, it is scarcely a very auspicious end for the protomartyr of a new religion.

CRONENBERG/BALLARD/*CRASH*

I want to finish by moving from a shocking novel to a medium that, as montage, incorporates shock as its principle – film – and to a film director who more than most has worked with shock as content: David Cronenberg. According to Ballard himself, the first screenplay for *Crash* was written by Heathcoate Williams, and it relocated the action of the novel to that quintessential city of the car, Los Angeles. The film company that took an interest in it wanted Jack Nicholson to star. Ballard, for one, didn't like the treatment, and thought that it 'Disney-fied' his novel – not easy to imagine. Happily, when a film version of the novel was finally made it was by the uncompromising Canadian director, David Cronenberg, rather than someone more attuned to mainstream Hollywood.[35]

Cronenberg's avowed early ambition was 'to show the unshowable... speak the unspeakable'.[36] His brand of horror has not been the suspense horror of the unseen, but of the *seen*, a particularly visceral style that he has consistently employed, exploiting, like Ballard, the horror potential of bio-science and medicine. His career and that of Ballard have displayed a curious synchronicity, his work from the 1970s echoing the themes of Ballard's 1970s technology 'trilogy', *Crash, Concrete Island*, and *High Rise*. The science fiction/horror feature, *Shivers* (1975), for example, is set in the Starliner Towers apartments, a luxurious, self-contained complex for those weary of the dangers and personal confrontations of urban living, almost a mirror image of the apartment complex in Ballard's *High Rise* (also 1975). In Ballard's novel, the highly sophisticated apartment dwellers become increasingly tribalized, and open warfare breaks out among floors. In *Shivers*, mutant parasites infect the cocooned and isolated residents, turning them into a frenzied, blood-thirsty mob, and producing a spree of sex and violence. In the film's final sequence the residents drive off in a convoy to pass on the parasite, just as *High Rise* envisages the chaos spreading to other buildings. In another curious convergence, Ballard and Cronenberg both use crashes in their work to signal some transformation in their characters. Where the Ballard character experiences an awakening after his crash (and Vaughan's career as a television pundit is ended by a motorbike crash), Johnny Smith, the protagonist of *The Dead Zone* (1983), begins to see visions of the future after a car crash. In Cronenberg's earlier *Rabid* (1976), the crash victim becomes a vampire after a tissue transplant goes wrong. Cronenberg himself has remarked upon the curious links between their quite different bodies of work, comparing *Crash*'s Vaughan to Darryl Revok, the rogue scientist of his own 1981 film, *Scanners*: 'my own creatures... were emerging at the same time Ballard was writing his creatures'.[37] While Ballard initially used the generic licence of science fiction, Cronenberg moved into the relative mainstream from another disreputable genre, horror (indeed for a brief period, through his involvement with the production and distribution company, Cinepix, he was on the edge of the porn industry). Significantly, while they are thus both associated with 'marginal' genres, both have used the freedom this has given them to pursue avantgarde ends. (Interestingly, both are also drawn to the formally radical work of William Burroughs: Ballard lists him as one of the few contemporary authors writing in English who interests him, while in 1991 Cronenberg made a film version of Burroughs's cult novel, *The Naked Lunch*, based on his own screenplay.[38])

Like Ballard's novel, the film *Crash* is both unrelenting in its intention to show us things, and yet extremely stylized. The distanced tone of the original is kept; Ballard's detailed and clinical descriptions of crash injuries and sex-acts have their visual equivalent in the slow pace of the editing and the cool lighting – much of the action takes place at night, and blue, metallic grey, and the dull orange of brake-lights predominate. Thanks to the virtuoso cinematography of Peter Suschitzky, one could say of the visual composition what Ballard says elsewhere about Surrealist painting, that it has 'a glassy isolation, as if all the objects in its landscapes had been drained of their emotional associations, the accretions of sentiment and common usage'.[39] The exterior shots of the edge city and the interiors alike appear drained of history. In this respect the use of Cronenberg's home town, Toronto, rather than London as a setting works well, the former city's reputation for sanitized affluence offering a perfect backdrop. Even more than in Ballard's novel the characters occupy a completely built environment: they are almost invariably either indoors or in their cars – the only 'nature' that is to be seen is the grass that occupies the space between highways. Cronenberg even alters the original story to situate Ballard and Helen Remington's first car-bound sexual encounter in a multi-storey carpark (in the novel it is on a service road), a nod, perhaps, to the thousands of film and television drama scenes that depend on that most anonymous and rationalized of non-places.

The performances, especially those of James Spader and Deborah Kara Unger as Ballard and Catherine, are in keeping with the other aspects of the mise en scène, subdued and unhurried almost to the point of parody. The impersonal quality of their conversations is mirrored in their sex-ual encounters, which are just as central here as in the novel. Indeed, as Cronenberg points out, the sex scenes *are* the film. Whereas in mainstream Hollywood films such scenes provide 'lyrical little interludes', here they 'are absolutely the plot and the character development'.[40] This most obvi-ously describes Ballard and Catherine's relationship. The film opens with Catherine having sex with a stranger (we assume) in an airplane hangar; in the next sequence Ballard has sex with a co-worker in the studio camera room. Later we see them discussing and partially re-enacting these sex acts at home, evidently a key aspect of their relationship. These collisions with strangers appear to be part of a search for some piece of fresh experience: when Ballard asks Catherine if she reached orgasm with the stranger, she wistfully says, 'maybe the next one'.

But there are a whole set of other couplings through which at one level *Crash* rehearses the permutational and combinational logic of pornography: Ballard has sex with Helen; Vaughan fondles Helen while Ballard watches; Vaughan has sex with Catherine in the backseat of a car while Ballard watches; Ballard has sex with Gabrielle, Vaughan's partner; Ballard has sex with Vaughan; Gabrielle and Helen have sex. The final scene returns us to Ballard and Catherine embracing next to her wrecked car. And yet the film's peculiarly passionless atmosphere is preserved. This is, of course, a deliberate effect rather than some kind of failure – Cronenberg even cut footage of Ballard having sex with his secretary because they appeared to have too much 'chemistry'. For the same reason sex in the film is rarely face to face. Cronenberg notes that this helped 'that sort of "disconnected" thing . . . It's more "how do you have sex when you're not quite having sex with each other?"'[41]

HOLLYWOOD LEGENDS

There are a number of other significant respects in which the film departs from the novel. For practical reasons, one assumes, Cronenberg drops the Elizabeth Taylor references from his treatment. Rather than dying in an attempt to fuse himself with Elizabeth Taylor, Vaughan is killed when he loses control of his Lincoln while trying to drive Catherine off the road. Nonetheless Cronenberg makes Hollywood celebrity death a central part of his film – if anything it is an even more important part of the film than it is of the book, adding a layer of self-reflexivity to its treatment of Ballard's themes.

In the novel, Helen and Ballard go to see a re-enacted car crash, supervised and in part performed by Vaughan, high-priest at this auto-mass. But whereas in the novel the simulated crash is a recent one from the newspapers, 'a multiple pile up in which seven people had died on the North Circular Road during the previous summer' (85), in the film Vaughan stages the legendary auto-death of James Dean, making it into an elaborate set-piece, a drama within the drama. (The choice of Dean is presumably over-determined: besides his cult status, he was Taylor's co-star in *Giant* (1956), and she was reportedly grief-stricken by his death.) In this memorable sequence Ballard and Helen are part of a small crowd that has gathered by night at what appears to be a race-track to watch Vaughan's car-theatre. Vaughan, dressed in overalls, is all showman. He strides around menacingly with the microphone, intoning Dean's last words, 'That guy's got to see us', before explaining the crash scenario to the captivated audience. It is a piece for three players: Vaughan and two stuntmen, Colin Seagrave and Brett Trask. Vaughan introduces the cast of characters: Hans Vudrich, the German mechanic, sent over by the Porsche factory with the 550 Spyder that Dean raced in; James Dean himself, played by Vaughan's friend Seagrave, and, in the other car, Trask playing the college student Donald Turnipseed, driving home to Fresno for the weekend. Dean and the mechanic are heading for the race-track at Salinas. Dean and Turnipseed 'would meet for one moment, but it was a moment that would create a Hollywood legend', Vaughan states solemnly, before the cars back up and hurtle at each other. As with all the crashes in the film (except those the characters watch on video) there is no slow-motion, and the collision is over in a second, making the aftermath all the more unnerving. While Trask staggers from his car, Vaughan and Seagrave lie still, as if dead or seriously hurt. The camera lingers on the vapour rising from the crushed grille of Turnipseed's car before we see Vaughan come slowly to life and again address the crowd in hushed tones. Vudrich would spend the year in hospital, he tells us, and Turnipseed was dazed, but essentially unhurt, but 'James Dean died of a broken neck and became immortal'.

Dean is thus the film's exemplary instance of celebrity death, though others are mooted, notably Jayne Mansfield. Whereas in the novel Seagrave kills himself dressed as Elizabeth Taylor, in the film he is re-enacting the death of Mansfield, complete with wig and artificial breasts. These changes do mark a shift of emphasis from novel to film. In a later scene in which he lists other celebrity auto-deaths – those of Albert Camus, Nathanael West, Grace Kelly – Vaughan stresses that it is the nexus of celebrity and violent auto-death that is his real 'project'. When Ballard reminds him that he had earlier announced that his project was the reshaping of the human body by technology (which certainly *is* one of J. G. Ballard's themes), Vaughan dismisses this as 'a crude sci-fi concept'. What is important about technology is that it allows 'a liberation of sexual energy that mediates the sexuality of those who have died with an intensity impossible in any other form'. This is very close to Ballard's vision towards the end of *Crash*, which I quoted earlier (it does not reappear in the film): 'I visualized the injuries of film actresses and television personalities, whose bodies would flower into dozens of auxiliary orifices, points of sexual conjunction with their audiences formed by the swerving technology of the automobile' (180).

In fact, the film, like the novel, ends by partly undercutting this idea, though in a different way. Vaughan's death-by-bus is replicated, but this time he has been attempting to crash into Catherine, not Elizabeth Taylor. As in the novel, his sexuality is indeed 'mediated' for those left behind. Gabrielle and Helen have sex in the back of his crashed car at the pound, drawn by its vestigial sexual aura. More significantly, though, Ballard becomes himself a Vaughan figure. He and Catherine rescue Vaughan's Lincoln from the pound, and in the film's final sequence we see Ballard recklessly driving the battered but roadworthy Lincoln. After a moment we realize that he is in fact playing out Vaughan's last car scene – he pursues Catherine's silver sports car, and, unlike Vaughan, succeeds in pushing it off the road (though it is evident that she is also playing a part in this auto-drama). We see Catherine's body prone next to the overturned car, and, as with Vaughan and Seagrave in the earlier staging of James Dean's death, we are unsure for a moment whether she is alive or not. Echoing their conversation about sexual adventures with other people at the start of the film, Ballard whispers to her 'maybe the next one'. It may at first appear that they are acting out Vaughan's life, as if he really has become a dead celebrity like Dean. But in fact it is Vaughan who has been incorporated into *their* sexual routine, like, we presume, many others before him – they are vampires of experience. As coolly as ever they are looking for a fresh piece of consumer experience in an eternal present. While the novel ends on a messianic note, with Ballard carrying on Vaughan's project, Cronenberg ends by showing us how the guru-like Vaughan is swallowed up by the super-consumer couple. I have argued that Baudrillard's postmodern lens is the wrong one to apply to *Crash* the novel, and to an extent this is also true of *Crash* the film, which still works within an older avant-garde problematic. But the film's protagonists do lend themselves to analysis in Baudrillard's terms – they represent not only the death of affect, but indeed of narrative progress itself.

While the film, like the book, seems to take it as axiomatic that there is no longer an outside to machine culture, and that the pastoral impulse of the railway rescue is no longer possible, the critical response suggests that the pastoral survives in some unlikely places. Although the film won a Special Jury Prize at Cannes (some jury members publicly declaring their abstention), the result left many critics as cold as the film itself. According to Kenneth Turan writing in the *Los Angeles Times*, *Crash* was 'so far from being involving or compelling, so intentionally disconnected from any kind of recognizable emotion, that by comparison David Lynch's removed *Lost Highway* plays like *Lassie Come Home*'.[42] Roger Ebert recognized the same distancing effect at work in the film, but described it in more approving terms, arguing that 'Cronenberg [had] brought a kind of icy, abstract purity to his subject'.[43] The most revealing comment, though, came from Desson Howe in the *Washington Post*, who complained that Cronenberg's work 'exud[ed] a replicant-like coolness'.[44] 'Replicants', of course, are the bio-robotic organisms, almost indistinguishable from humans, who appear in Phillip K. Dick's classic science fiction novel, *Do Androids Dream of Electric Sheep?*, and Ridley Scott's 1982 film version, *Blade Runner*. One way of telling the replicants from humans is an 'empathy test' – humans are supposed to be more empathetic than machines. What Howe and other mainstream critics appear to have objected to, then, is that the film refuses our emotional investment – the characters are unsympathetic, more like machines than humans. In a neat paradox, a film that is very much about the way in which audiences identify with, worship, and fall in love with projected screen images itself makes it difficult to behave like a 'fan'. In effect what Cronenberg attempts is a piece of modernist defamiliarization, refusing us any comfortable point of identification, including that of formalist delight in the film's cool tones. To the extent that we are frustrated spectators, the film forces us to acknowledge our own desires, our own learned investment in the superbodies on the screen. We are reminded not only of how the cinema machine normally works, but also of the fact that it cannot work without us as part of the mechanism.

If the characters embrace the crash, the collision with technology, it is because that nineteenth-century fantasy of escape from the locomotive, from machine culture, or modernity tout court is no longer viable. Insofar as they seem to welcome the meeting of flesh and steel, Ballard, Vaughan, and the others might indeed be seen as 'replicants'. It seems odd, then, to accuse the film of registering this as effectively as possible through its chilliness. What is striking about Howe's criticism (and similar critiques of the film) is that this point either escapes him, or is seen to be irrelevant. I would suggest that this is principally because he is working with a particular theory of what cinema is, or does: cinema is meant to be affective, and we are meant to be affected. In chapter 4 I suggested that *It* identifies the cinema with the 'Social Mixer', acknowledging its own ideological role in the United States of the 1920s in creating a national imagined community around sexualized consumerism. In the 1990s the assumption would appear to be that cinema is not so much a 'Mixer' as an empathy test. But this is also to deliberately forget that the cinema experience is also an industrial one, and that no less than the collisions of *Crash*, it depends on the body transformed by the machine – not just that of the attentive spectator, but also that of the star as mechanical superbody. We may go to the cinema to feel more alive, or more human, but that only works to the extent that we are engaged by the cinema machine, and because the cinema produces icons of identification and desire that are, quite literally, more than human.

For all that recent popular and intellectual culture appears to be fascinated by the cyborg, or the android, or the replicant (for example, in such films as *Terminator* (1984), and *Artificial Intelligence: A.I.* (2001), such novels as William Gibson's influential *Neuromancer* (1984), and such critical works as Donna Haraway's *Simians, Cyborgs, and Women* (1990)), at some level we still like to define our humanity against machines. What shocked critics the most about *Crash* was not the sex or the crashes per se, but that it denied us our moment of non-mechanical empathy, our espresso shot of affect. If the intellectual separation of humans and machines represented a basic tenet of industrial modernity, we may not have left that moment behind just yet. Melodrama offered thrills and tears that reassured the audiences of a mechanical age that they themselves were flesh and blood. The Victorian theatre-goer dreamt of beating the train, of saving that body, which was also his or her own, from the path of whatever it was that hurtled towards it along the tracks. Locomotives may no longer steam their way through our dreams, and melodrama has acquired a pejorative sense outside of critical discourse, but we appear to retain our own pastoral fantasies of modernity thwarted.

Notes

INTRODUCTION

1. See, for example, Igor Kopytoff, 'The Cultural Biography of Things: Commoditization as Process', in Arjun Appadurai, ed., *The Social Life of Things: Commodities in Cultural Perspective* (Cambridge: Cambridge University Press, 1986), 64–91, and Bruno Latour, *We Have Never Been Modern*, trans. Catherine Porter (Hemel Hempstead: Harvester Wheatsheaf, 1993). See also Bill Brown, 'Thing Theory', *Critical Inquiry*, 28.1 (Autumn 2001), 1–21.
2. Fredric Jameson, *The Political Unconscious: Narrative as a Socially Symbolic Act* (Ithaca: Cornell University Press, 1981), 236.
3. On Britain's eccentric relation to modernism see, for example, Perry Anderson, 'Modernity and Revolution', in Cary Nelson and Lawrence Grossberg, eds., *Marxism and the Interpretation of Culture* (Urbana and Chicago: University of Illinois Press, 1988), 317–33 (323).
4. Mark Seltzer, *Bodies and Machines* (New York and London: Routledge, 1992), 21.
5. Seltzer, *Bodies and Machines*, 135–45, and *passim*. Seltzer notes that the term 'machine culture' was used by Thorstein Veblen, among others, at the end of the nineteenth century.
6. Tim Armstrong, *Modernism, Technology and the Body: A Cultural Study* (Cambridge: Cambridge University Press, 1998); Christoph Asendorf, *Batteries of Life: On the History of Things and Their Perception in Modernity* (Berkeley and Los Angeles: University of California Press, 1993); Lynne Kirby, *Parallel Tracks: The Railroad and Silent Cinema* (Exeter: University of Exeter Press, 1997); Tom Gunning, 'From the Kaleidoscope to the X-Ray: Urban Spectatorship, Poe, Benjamin, and *Traffic in Souls* (1913)', *Wide Angle*, 19.4 (October 1997), 25–61, and many other articles; Seltzer, *Bodies and Machines*.
7. Alain Corbin, *Time, Desire and Horror: Towards a History of the Senses*, trans. Jean Birrell (Cambridge: Polity Press, 1995), ix.
8. Jonathan Crary, *Suspensions of Perception: Attention, Spectacle, and Modern Culture* (Cambridge, MA: MIT Press, 1999), 2.
9. Ben Singer gives an excellent account of the range of meanings of the term modernity in his recent *Melodrama and Modernity: Early Sensational Cinema and Its Contexts* (New York: Columbia University Press, 2001), chapter 1.

10. On this continuity see Anne Friedberg, *Window Shopping: Cinema and the Postmodern* (Berkeley: University of California Press, 1993).
11. Crary, *Suspensions of Perception*, 21–3.
12. Kirby, *Parallel Tracks*, 2–3, and *passim*.
13. See, for example, Charles Musser, *The Emergence of Cinema: The American Screen to 1907*, vol. 1 of Charles Harpole, ed., *History of the American Cinema* (Berkeley: University of California Press, 1994), 429–31, and Kirby, *Parallel Tracks* 45–6. Cf. Friedberg, *Window Shopping*, 20–9 on such earlier forms of machine-assisted virtual mobility as the diorama.

1 SENSATION DRAMA, THE RAILWAY, AND MODERNITY

1. H. G. Wells, *Anticipations of the Reaction of Mechanical and Scientific Progress Upon Human Life and Thought* (1901; Mineota, New York: Dover, 1999), 3.
2. *The Era*, 3 October 1868, 330.
3. James L. Smith notes that versions of Moncrieff's *The Scamps of London* also opened at Sadler's Wells (10 September 1868), the Whitechapel Pavilion (17 October) and the Grecian Saloon in Hoxton (26 October), and that by the end of the year there were productions at Highbury, Greenock, Brighton, Dublin, Hull, and Leeds. See his *Victorian Melodramas: Seven English, French and American Melodramas* (London: Dent, 1976), 222.
4. *The Era*, 6 September 1868, 15.
5. See A. Nicholas Vardac, *Stage to Screen: Theatrical Method from Garrick to Griffith* (Cambridge, MA: Harvard University Press, 1949), 48–9 for a description of the special effects of a United States production of *After Dark*. A critic of the English production refers to a 'velocipede locomotive'. See 'A Little Light Upon "After Dark"', *The Mask* (September 1868), 237–43 (243).
6. *The Times*, 17 August 1868, 4.
7. *The Era*, 13 September 1868, 11. See George C. D. Odell, *Annals of the New York Stage*. 15 vols. (New York: Columbia University Press, 1927–49), IX, 302–4 on Daly's production.
8. Smith, *Victorian Melodramas*, 220–1.
9. *The Era*, 29 March 1863, 11.
10. *The Era*, 8 April 1866, 11.
11. Daly v. Palmer et al. Case No. 3552, Circuit Court, S.D., New York. See also Richard Fawkes, *Dion Boucicault: A Biography* (London: Quartet Books, 1979), 173, and Selden Faulkner, 'The Great Train Scene Robbery', *The Quarterly Journal of Speech*, 39.1 (February 1964), 24–8. In 'Captain Tom's Fright' the hero, a railway engineer, is tied to the main railway line by his mutinous crew, but disaster is averted because the train goes by him on a temporary side track.
12. See 'A Little Light Upon "After Dark"', 240.
13. 'A Little Light Upon "After Dark"', and see Smith, *Victorian Melodramas*, 222.

14. Walter Benjamin, 'On some Motifs in Baudelaire', in Hannah Arendt, ed., Harry Zohn, trans., *Illuminations* (New York: Schocken Books, 1985), 155–200 (165).
15. See 'A Little Light Upon "After Dark"', 243, and Jean Louis Comolli, 'Machines of the Visible', in Teresa de Lauretis and Stephen Heath, eds., *The Cinematic Apparatus* (London and Basingstoke: Macmillan, 1980), 121–42 (122). On Victorian visual culture see also Anne Friedberg, *Window Shopping: Cinema and the Postmodern* (Berkeley: University of California Press, 1993).
16. On the Victorian urban imaginary see, for example, Peter Stallybrass and Allon White, *The Politics and Poetics of Transgression* (Ithaca: Cornell University Press, 1986), 125–48.
17. Ben Singer, *Melodrama and Modernity: Early Sensational Cinema and its Contexts* (New York: Columbia University Press, 2001), 133.
18. Frank Rahill, *The World of Melodrama* (University Park and London: Pennsylvania State Press, 1967), 15. Cf. Daniel Gerould, 'Melodrama and Revolution,' in Jacky Bratton, Jim Cook, and Christine Gledhill, eds., *Melodrama: Stage, Picture, Screen* (London: British Film Institute, 1994), 185–98 (185), and Peter Brooks's 'Melodrama, Body, Revolution' in the same volume, 11–24.
19. See Brooks, 'Melodrama, Body, Revolution', in Bratton et al., *Melodrama*, 11–24, and his earlier *The Melodramatic Imagination: Balzac, Henry James, Melodrama, and the Mode of Excess* (New Haven and London: Yale University Press, 1976), 14–20.
20. Singer, *Melodrama and Modernity*, 137.
21. Martha Vicinus, '"Helpless and Unfriended": Nineteenth-Century Domestic Melodrama', *New Literary History*, 13.1 (Fall 1981), 127–43 (128).
22. Elaine Hadley, *Melodramatic Tactics: Theatricalized Dissent in the English Marketplace, 1800–1885* (Stanford: Stanford University Press, 1995), 3. On the public sphere in relation to melodrama see, for example, Lynn M. Voskuil, 'Feeling Public: Sensation Theater, Commodity Culture, and the Victorian Public Sphere', *Victorian Studies*, 44.2 (Winter 2002), 245–74, and Matthew Buckley, 'Sensations of Celebrity: Jack Sheppard and the Mass Audience', *Victorian Studies*, 44.3 (Spring 2002), 423–63. The most impressive of the recent accounts, though it is more focused on American material, is Singer's *Melodrama and Modernity.*
23. See Rahill, *The World of Melodrama*, 85. On 'social energy' see Stephen Greenblatt, 'The Circulation of Social Energy', in Nicholas B. Dirks, Geolt Eley, and Sherry B. Ortner, eds., *Culture/Power/History: A Reader in Contemporary Social Theory* (Princeton: Princeton University Press, 1994), 504–19. For contemporary accounts of the kaleidoscope aspect of urban life see Tom Gunning, 'From the Kaleidoscope to the X-Ray: Urban Spectatorship, Poe, Benjamin, and *Traffic in Souls* (1913)', *Wide Angle*, 19.4 (October 1997), 25–61 (32–3).
24. On melodrama's relation to detective narratives see Martin Meisel, 'Scattered Chiaroscuro: Melodrama as a Matter of Seeing', in Bratton et al., *Melodrama*, 65–81.

25. See Vicinus, '"Helpless and Unfriended"', 130.

26. Dion Boucicault et al., *The Poor of New York* (1857), Dicks Standard Plays, no. 381 (London: John Dicks, 1883).

27. Singer argues that melodrama is essentially a working-class form, but his account is principally concerned with American 10–20–30 drama from the 1880s on. The Victorian melodrama of the 1860s seems often to be aimed squarely at the middle class.

28. Rahill, *The World of Melodrama*, 86–7. On the influence of *Les Bohémiens de Paris* see Katherine Newey, 'Attic Windows and Street Scenes: Victorian Images of the City on the Stage', *Victorian Literature and Culture*, 25.2 (1997), 253–62.

29. On stage versions of Egan's novel, see Maurice Willson Disher, *Blood and Thunder: Mid-Victorian Melodrama and its Origins* (London: Frederick Muller, 1949), 120, and Rahill, *The World of Melodrama*, 214–15.

30. Jerrold Seigel, *Bohemian Paris: Culture, Politics, and the Boundaries of Bourgeois Life, 1830–1950* (New York: Penguin, 1987), 6. Seigel is describing French attitudes to Bohemia, but the same would appear to be true of British culture.

31. Dion Boucicault, 'Leaves from a Dramatist's Diary', *North American Review*, 148 (1889), 228–36 (230), and see Allardyce Nicoll, *A History of Late Nineteenth-Century Drama, 1850–1900*, 2 vols. (Cambridge: Cambridge University Press, 1949), I, 85.

32. Boucicault was the principal writer of *The Poor of New York*, but he was assisted by three American journalists. See Fawkes, *Dion Boucicault*, 94. In the edition of the play published in *French's Standard Drama* the play is described as 'By the **** Club'.

33. *The Era*, 16 August 1868, 11. Cf. the less enthusiastic review in the *Illustrated London News* (15 August 1868, 151).

34. Fawkes, *Dion Boucicault*, Rahill, *The World of Melodrama* and Michael Booth in *Hiss the Villain: Six English and American Melodramas* (London: Eyre and Spottiswoode, 1964) credit Boucicault with introducing the term. The OED's first citation is from the journal of Mrs Sam Cowell, describing a tour of America with her husband, the comic singer: (13 March 1860) 'After tea we went to "The National Theatre" [sc. Cincinnati] and saw Matilda Heron, in a "new sensation Drama" called "Mathilde" . . . full of strong and immoral situations.' According to Henry Morley, writing in the mid-1860s, '"sensation play" was a popular Americanism introduced by Mr Boucicault'. See his *Journal of a London Playgoer from 1851 to 1866* (London, 1866), 366–7. See also Vardac, *Stage to Screen*, 41–2.

35. 'On 2 Roundabout Papers which I Intended to Write', in *The Oxford Thackeray*, 20 vols. (London: Oxford University Press, 1908), XVII, 526–36 (529).

36. Richard Altick, *Deadly Encounters: Two Victorian Sensations* (Philadelphia: University of Pennsylvania Press, 1986), 139.

37. See Tom Gunning, 'The Horror of Opacity: The Melodrama of Sensation in the Plays of André de Lorde', in Bratton et al., *Melodrama*, 50–61 (52).

38. See Vardac, *Stage to Screen* for an argument for Boucicault's influence on early cinema. Singer's *Melodrama and Modernity* provides a detailed argument for the melodrama-film nexus.

39. See Michael Booth, *Victorian Spectacular Theatre, 1850–1910* (Boston, London, and Henley: Routledge, 1981), 63. A recent publication from the Society for Theatre Research, *British Theatrical Patents, 1801–1900* (London: Society for Theatre Research, 1996), gives some idea of the level of technological innovation in this period.

40. Michael Booth, *English Melodrama* (London: Herbert Jenkins, 1965), 169, and *Victorian Spectacular Theatre*, 68.

41. See Schivelbusch, *The Railway Journey: The Industrialization of Time and Space in the Nineteenth Century* (1977; Berkeley: University of California Press, 1986), 33–44.

42. See Schivelbusch, *The Railway Journey*, 119–23.

43. See Nicoll, *A History of Late 19th-Century Drama* 1, 8, 27, and Michael R. Booth, *Theatre in the Victorian Age* (Cambridge: Cambridge University Press, 1991), 14.

44. For Dionysius Lardner's advice to travellers, see *Railway Economy: A Treatise on the New Art of Transport* (1850; Newton Abbot: David and Charles, 1968), 284–96.

45. L. T. C. Rolt, *Red for Danger: A History of Railway Accidents and Railway Safety*, revised with additional material by Geoffrey Kitchenside (London and Sydney: Pan, 1978), 23.

46. Rolt, *Red for Danger*, 24.

47. Fawkes, *Dion Boucicault*, 16. On 2 April 1838 Boucicault gave up the railway and took to the boards of the Theatre Royal, Cheltenham, under the name Lee Moreton.

48. See Fawkes, *Dion Boucicault*, 197–202. For an account of the collision, see Rolt, *Red for Danger*, 114–19.

49. Schivelbusch, *The Railway Journey*, 130.

50. Schivelbusch, *The Railway Journey*, 83. See H. B. Irving's 'The First Railway Murder', in Jonathan Goodman, ed., *The Railway Murders* (Bath: Chivers Press, 1992), 9–44 for an account of the Briggs murder.

51. *Illustrated London News*, 29 August 1868, 206.

52. *Illustrated London News*, 29 August 1868, 204.

53. This is the version of the scene quoted in Daly v. Palmer rather than that in the privately printed version of the play contained in the collection of the University of Kent at Canterbury (the National Library of Ireland possesses a microfilm version of these plays, which I have relied on for the purposes of this chapter). The Daly v. Palmer version contains some changes in dialogue and gives more extensive stage directions.

54. Cf. Daly's *Under the Gaslight*, where the modernity of the train is matched by the modernity of the heroine.

55. Jonathan Crary, *Suspensions of Perception: Attention, Spectacle, and Modern Culture* (Cambridge, MA: MIT Press, 1999), 21–3, and *passim*.

56. For an account of modernization that stresses its thrills rather than its traumas, see Jeffrey T. Schnapp, 'Crash (Speed as Engine of Individuation', *Modernism/Modernity*, 6.1 (1999), 1–49.

57. A contemporary reviewer describes him as a 'fashionable scamp'. See *The Era*, 16 August 1868, 11.

58. 'Silver Hell' appears to have been a generic name for gaming houses. In W. T. Moncrieff's *The Scamps of London* (1843), Morris's equivalent, Mr Hawksworth Shabner, is 'principal proprietor of a Silver Hell in the West End, director of a company, capital 1 million, bill discounter, and Anythingarian when there's anything to be got'.

59. See Bryan Cheyette, *Constructions of 'the Jew' in English Literature and Society: Racial Representations, 1875–1945* (Cambridge: Cambridge University Press, 1993), xi, 1–54, and *passim*, and Michael Ragussis, *Figures of Conversion: 'The Jewish Question' and English National Identity* (Durham, NC and London: Duke University Press, 1995), 211–33.

60. Cited in Colin Holmes, *Anti-Semitism in British Society, 1876–1939* (London: Edward Arnold, 1979), 64.

61. Colin Holmes, *John Bull's Island: Immigration and British Society, 1871–1971* (London: Macmillan, 1988), 66.

62. *The Times*, 29 May 1863, 5.

63. The use of 'sh' for 's' and other consonants is a part of the British stereotype of 'the Jew' in the nineteenth century. See, for example, the excerpts from *Punch* reproduced in Anne and Roger Cowen, *Victorian Jews through British Eyes* (Oxford: Oxford University Press, 1986).

64. Henry Llewellyn Williams's *After Dark* (London, 1880 (?)), 2, 'Founded on the Popular Drama by Dion Boucicault.'

65. *Daily Telegraph*, 15 August 1868, 3. *The Times* also objected that Murray gave a 'Milesian accentuation to a Hebrew dialect' (17 August 1868, 4).

66. On the perception that British Jews had a special affinity for prostitution, see Holmes, *Anti-Semitism in British Society*, 44–6.

67. On hostility to commerce and (especially) industry within English culture, see Martin J. Wiener's *English Culture and the Decline of the Industrial Spirit, 1850–1980* (Harmondsworth: Penguin, 1985).

68. On the transformation of London transport in the 1860s, see Theo Barker, *Moving Millions: A Pictorial History of London Transport* (London: London Transport Museum, 1990), 39.

69. Sander Gilman, *The Jew's Body* (New York and London: Routledge, 1991), 169–93, esp. 173–4. On Jews as 'the people of the night', see Léon Poliakov, *The History of Anti-Semitism*, 4 vols. (Oxford: Littman Library/Oxford University Press, 1974–85), IV. 34. On the racial indeterminacy of Jewish characters in later British literature see Bryan Cheyette, 'Neither Black nor White: The Figure of 'the Jew' in Imperial British Literature', in Linda Nochlin and Tamar Garb, eds., *The Jew in the Text: Modernity and the Construction of Identity* (London: Thames and Hudson, 1995), 3–41, and his *Constructions of 'the Jew' in English literature, and Society*. For a short survey of the figure of 'the Jew' in English

literature, see Harold Fisch, *The Dual Image: A Study of the Jew in English Literature* (London: World Jewish Library, 1971).

70. See, for example, the cartoon of Disraeli as Fagin in *Punch*, 9 November 1867, reproduced in Anne and Roger Cowen, *Victorian Jews through British Eyes*, 30.

71. Gilman notes that blacks and Jews are paired in this way at least as early as William Hogarth's *A Harlot's Progress* (1731) (*The Jew's Body*, 121).

72. Michael Ragussis, 'The "secret" of English Anti-Semitism: Anglo-Jewish Studies and Victorian Studies', *Victorian Studies*, 40.2 (Winter 1997), 295–307 (298).

73. Gilman, *The Jew's Body*, 99–101.

74. See Gilman, *The Jew's Body*, 31, 96–7.

75. On the underground, the sewer, and the nineteenth-century city as a networked, integrated system, see Rosalind Williams, *Notes on the Underground: An Essay on Technology, Society, and the Imagination* (Cambridge, MA and London: MIT Press, 1990), 70–3. See also Stallybrass and White, *The Politics and Poetics of Transgression*, 125–48.

76. See T. C. Barker and Michael Robbins, *A History of London Transport: Passenger Travel and the Development of the Metropolis*, 2 vols. (London: Allen and Unwin, 1963–74), I, 117.

77. See Barker and Robbins, *A History of London Transport*, I, 118. But having summarized popular anxieties, the article goes on to suggest that the public will be 'agreeably surprised' at how dry, bright and odourless the new system will be. In a humorous sketch of modern life from 1904, 'In the Tube', one character, a 'Typical Briton' rhetorically asks: 'Is this the good old Anglo-Saxon? Are they to burrow like sewer-criminals?' See *The Windsor Magazine*, 20 (June–November 1904), 238.

78. On the currency of the image of the 'dirty' Jew in nineteenth-century Britain, see Frank Felsenstein, *Anti-Semitic Stereotypes: A Paradigm of Otherness in English Popular Culture, 1660–1830* (Baltimore and London: Johns Hopkins University Press, 1995), 257–9.

79. T. S. Eliot, 'Burbank with a Baedeker: Bleistein with a Cigar', in *T. S. Elliot: Collected Poems, 1909–1962* (London and Boston: Faber and Faber, 1974), 42–3.

80. Cf. Alan Trachtenberg, *The Incorporation of America: Culture and Society in the Gilded Age* (New York: Hill and Wang, 1992), 133, on the 'backstage' of modernity. See also Gunning, 'From the Kaleidoscope to the X-Ray', 39.

81. Cited in Vardac, *Stage to Screen*, 49.

82. See Ben Singer, 'Female Power in the Serial-Queen Melodrama: The Etiology of an Anomaly', *Camera Obscura*, 22 (1990), 90–129, and Lynne Kirby, *Parallel Tracks: The Railroad and Silent Cinema* (Exeter: University of Exeter Press, 1997).

2 SENSATION FICTION AND THE MODERNIZATION OF THE SENSES

1. Oscar Wilde, *The Importance of Being Earnest* (1895), in *The Importance of Being Earnest: A Reconstructive Critical Edition*, ed. Joseph Donohue and Ruth

Berggren (Gerrards Cross, Bucks: Colin Smythe, 1995). Hereafter cited paren-thetically in the text by page number.

2. *The Times* (London), Saturday 10 June 1865, 9.

3. Quoted in Peter Ackroyd, *Dickens* (New York: HarperCollins, 1990), 961. I have drawn substantially on Ackroyd's description of the accident and its aftermath, 951–64.

4. *The Letters of Charles Dickens*, ed. Walter Dexter, 3 vols, 1858–70 (London: The Nonesuch Press, 1938), III, 424.

5. In a letter to Arthur Ryland, *Letters*, III, 428.

6. Wolfgang Schivelbusch, *The Railway Journey: The Industrialization of Time and Space in the Nineteenth Century* (1977; Berkeley: University of California Press, 1986), 137–8.

7. Wilkie Collins, *The Woman in White*, ed. Harvey Peter Sucksmith (1859–60; Oxford: Oxford University Press, 1991), 15. Hereafter abbreviated *W* and cited parenthetically in the text by page number.

8. Mrs Oliphant, 'Sensation Novels', *Blackwood's*, 91 (1862), 564–84 (572). Cf. Rae Beth Gordon, 'From Charcot to Charlot: Unconscious Imitation and Spectatorship in French Cabaret and Early Cinema', *Critical Inquiry*, 27.3 (2001), 515–49.

9. For a summary of the arguments over the retraining required by modernity, see Ben Singer, *Melodrama and Modernity: Early Sensational Cinema and its Contexts* (New York: Columbia University Press, 2001), chapter 4.

10. See Herbert Sussman, 'Cyberpunk Meets Charles Babbage; The Difference Engine as Alternative Victorian History', *Victorian Studies*, 38.1 (1994), 1–23 on the devaluation of technology within Victorian literary culture. See also Sussman's earlier work on Victorian attitudes to machine culture, *Victorians and the Machine: The Literary Response to Technology* (Cambridge, MA: Harvard University Press, 1968). On the ambivalence of British attitudes to economic and technological modernization, see Martin J. Wiener, *English Culture and the Decline of the Industrial Spirit, 1850–1980* (Cambridge: Cambridge University Press, 1981).

11. On earlier discourses of nervousness, see Peter Melville Logan, 'Narrating Hysteria: *Caleb Williams* and the Cultural History of Nerves', *Novel*, 29.2 (1996), 206–22 (206).

12. See Fredric Jameson's *Postmodernism, or, The Cultural Logic of Late Capitalism* (Durham, NC: Duke University Press, 1991), 14, and 11–16.

13. On the break with older modes of experiencing art, see Gianni Vattimo, *The Transparent Society* (Baltimore: Johns Hopkins University Press, 1992), 45–61.

14. Walter Benjamin, *Illuminations*, ed. Hannah Arendt, trans. Harry Zohn (New York: Schocken Books, 1985), 155–200.

15. Simmel's essay is reprinted in *On Individuality and Social Forms: Selected Writings* edited and introduced by Donald N. Levine (Chicago and London: University of Chicago Press, 1971), 324–39.

16. The locus classicus is Wordsworth's 1800 Preface to the *Lyrical Ballads*.

17. See Winifred Hughes, *The Maniac in the Cellar* (Princeton: Princeton University Press, 1980), 5; Mrs Oliphant, 'Novels', *Blackwood's*, 102 (1867), 257–81 (258).
18. See Hughes, *The Maniac in the Cellar*, 19, and see Catherine Peters, *The King of Inventors: A Life of Wilkie Collins* (Princeton: Princeton University Press, 1991), 227, and 227–45.
19. D. A. Miller, *The Novel and the Police* (Berkeley and Los Angeles: University of California Press, 1988), 146.
20. Oliphant, 'Sensation Novels', 572.
21. H. L. Mansel, 'Sensation Novels', *Quarterly Review*, 113 (1863), 481–514 (482).
22. Cf. Ann Cvetkovich, *Mixed Feelings: Feminism, Mass Culture, and Victorian Sensationalism* (New Brunswick: Rutgers University Press, 1992), 212 n.4.
23. Wilkie Collins, *Armadale* (Oxford and New York: Oxford University Press, 1989), 576.
24. Cf. Mark Seltzer, *Bodies and Machines* (New York and London: Routledge, 1992), 17, and Lynne Kirby, *Parallel Tracks: The Railroad and Silent Cinema* (Exeter: University of Exeter Press, 1997), 66–73.
25. See Dolf Sternberger, *Panorama of the Nineteenth Century*, trans. Joachim Neugroschel (Oxford: Blackwell, 1977), 17–38. See also Seltzer, *Bodies and Machines*, Anson Rabinach, *The Human Motor: Energy, Fatigue, and the Origins of Modernity* (New York: Basic Books, 1990), and Paul Virilio's *Speed and Politics: An Essay on Dromology* (New York: Semiotext(e), 1986).
26. Schivelbusch, *The Railway Journey*, 139. See also Armand Mattelart, *Mapping World Communication: War, Progress, Culture* (Minneapolis and London: University of Minnesota Press, 1994), chapter 1.
27. *The Lancet*, 4 January 1862, 15. See Schivelbusch, *The Railway Journey*, chapter 7, for a detailed account of the medical response to railway travellers.
28. Wilkie Collins, *The Moonstone* (London and Melbourne: Dent, 1984), 380.
29. *The Lancet*, 11 January 1862, 51.
30. 'Walter', *My Secret Life*, 11 vols. (Privately printed, 1882–92); reprinted 3 vols. (London: Arrow, 1994).
31. On the erotics of machines see Seltzer, *Bodies and Machines*, 17–21 and 25–44; Christoph Asendorf, *Batteries of Life: On the History of Things and their Perception in Modernity* (Berkeley and Los Angeles: University of California Press, 1993), 105–8; and on the train and sexuality in early cinema, see Kirby, *Parallel Tracks*, 75–131. Cf. Dickens's Mrs Gamp in *Martin Chuzzlewit* (1843–4; Oxford: Clarendon Press, 1982), who comments on the effects of railway travel on the other side of the reproductive process (626).
32. See *Punch*, 51 (1866), 70.
33. Quoted in Jack Simmons, *The Railway in England and Wales 1830–1914*, vol. 1, *The System and its Working* (Leicester: Leicester University Press, 1978), 230. See also Schivelbusch, *The Railway Journey*, 82.
34. Peters, *The King of Inventors*, 231.
35. Jenny Bourne Taylor, *In the Secret Theatre of Home: Wilkie Collins, Sensation Narrative and Nineteenth-Century Psychology* (London and New York: Routledge, 1988), 3.

36. Taylor, *In the Secret Theatre of Home*, 4.
37. See George Miller Beard, *American Nervousness: its Causes and Consequences* (New York, 1881), vi.
38. See Schivelbusch, *The Railway Journey*, 122. Cf. Benjamin on the shock-experience of the crowd, *Illuminations*, 176.
39. Schivelbusch, *The Railway Journey*, 43. On world time, see Stephen Kern, *The Culture of Time and Space 1880–1918* (Cambridge, MA: Harvard University Press, 1983), 11–15.
40. Alfred Haviland, *Hurried to Death: Especially Addressed to Railway Travellers* (London, 1868), 22.
41. For a survey of the appearance of railways and railway accidents in Victorian fiction, see Myron F. Brightfield, *Victorian England in its Novels (1840–1870)*, 4 vols. (Los Angeles: University of California Library, 1968), III, 189–212, and Richard D. Altick, *The Presence of the Present: Topics of the Day in the Victorian Novel* (Columbus: Ohio State University Press, 1991).
42. See Bret Harte, *Condensed Novels, and Other Papers*, with comic illustrations by Frank Bellew (New York: G. W. Carleton, 1867), 51–90.
43. Cited in Taylor, *In the Secret Theatre of Home*, 1.
44. Stephen Knight, 'Regional Crime Squads: Location and Dislocation in the British Mystery', in Ian A. Bell, ed., *Peripheral Visions: Images of Nationhood in Contemporary British Fiction* (Cardiff: University of Wales Press, 1995), 27–43.
45. M. E. Braddon, *Lady Audley's Secret* (1862; Oxford: Oxford University Press, 1998), 251.
46. See Peters, *The King of Inventors*, 260–1, 267, 291, though see above on the dangers of travel with female passengers.
47. Wilkie Collins, *The Law and the Lady* (1874–5), ed. Jenny Bourne Taylor (Oxford: Oxford University Press, 1992), 206.
48. On the ways in which Darwinism altered the terms of the body/machine problematic, see Sussman, *Victorians and the Machine*, 135–61.
49. Walter Pater, *The Renaissance: Studies in Art and Poetry* (1873; London: Macmillan, 1910), 234.
50. See Christopher Craft, 'Alias Bunbury: Desire and Termination in *The Importance of Being Earnest*', *Representations*, 31 (Summer 1990), 19–46.
51. Wilde, *The Importance of Being Earnest*, 316.
52. Cited in Schivelbusch, *The Railway Journey*, 54 n.8.

3 THE BOEROGRAPH

1. Rudyard Kipling, *Something of Myself and other Autobiographical Writings*, ed. Thomas Pinney (Cambridge: Cambridge University Press, 1991), 124–5.
2. Anne Friedberg, *Window Shopping: Cinema and the Postmodern* (Berkeley: University of California Press, 1993). Lynne Kirby, *Parallel Tracks: The Railroad and Silent Cinema* (Exeter: University of Exeter Press, 1997), 2–3, and *passim*.
3. See, for example, Charles Musser, *The Emergence of Cinema: The American Screen to 1907*, vol. 1 of Charles Harpole, ed., *History of the American Cinema* (Berkeley: University of California Press, 1994), 429–31, and Kirby, *Parallel*

Tracks, 45–6. Cf. Friedberg, *Window Shopping*, 20–9, on such earlier forms of machine-assisted virtual mobility as the diorama.

4. Roland Barthes, *Camera Lucida: Reflections on Photography*, trans. Richard Howard (London: Jonathan Cape, 1982).

5. See Bill Brown, 'How to do Things with Things (A Toy Story)', *Critical Inquiry*, 24.4 (Summer 1998): 935–64 (941 n.10).

6. Musser, *The Emergence of Cinema*, 24–5.

7. Tom Gunning, 'Phantom Images and Modern Manifestations: Spirit Photography, Magic Theater, Trick Films, and Photography's Uncanny', in Patrice Petro, ed., *Fugitive Images: From Photography to Video* (Bloomington and Indianapolis: Indiana University Press, 1995), 42–71.

8. Barthes, *Camera Lucida*, 88.

9. I am grateful to Keith Williams for highlighting the specificity of Wells's theory of the cinematic future, in 'Seeing the Future: Visual Technology and Dystopia in the Early Writing of H. G. Wells', a paper delivered at the Technotopias conference at the University of Strathclyde in July 2002.

10. John Barnes, *The Beginnings of the Cinema in England 1894–1901*, 5 vols. (Exeter: University of Exeter Press, 1988), III, 16.

11. Thomas Pakenham, *The Boer War* (London: Weidenfeld and Nicolson, 1997), 572. I am indebted to Pakenham's lucid and comprehensive account. Further references in parentheses in the text.

12. Tabitha Jackson, *The Boer War* (London: Channel 4 Books, 2001), 184.

13. For a contemporary British reaction to the continental reports, see Arthur Conan Doyle, *The War in South Africa: Its Cause and Conduct* (London: Smith, Elder, 1902), 116. On continental hostility see, for example, J. B. Priestley, *The Edwardians* (Harmondsworth: Penguin, 2000), 36–45.

14. See (Lord) Robert Blake's Preface to Emanoel Lee, *To the Bitter End: A Photographic History of the Boer War 1899–1902* (Harmondsworth: Penguin, 1986), ix.

15. See Raymond Sibbald, *The Boer War: The War Correspondents* (Stroud: Alan Sutton, 1993), 47–82.

16. On the political sympathies of the audiences for early cinema, see Richard Maltby, Introduction to Barnes, *The Beginnings of the Cinema*, v, xviii–ix.

17. Barnes, *The Beginnings of the Cinema*, v, 122.

18. See Barnes, *The Beginnings of the Cinema*, IV, 7, and *passim*; Maltby, Introduction to Barnes, *The Beginnings of the Cinema*, v, xxix; and Musser, *The Emergence of Cinema*, 225–6, 261. But cf. Luke McKernan, 'Sport and the First Films', in Christopher Williams, ed., *Cinema: The Beginnings and the Future. Essays Marking the Centenary of the First Film Show Projected to a Paying Audience in Britain* (London: University of Westminster Press, 1996), 107–16.

19. Lee, *To the Bitter End*, 4–10.

20. Sibbald, *The Boer War*, 70.

21. Sibbald, *The Boer War*, 52.

22. See, for example, the *Times* description of the enemy position at Colenso, in Sibbald, *The Boer War*, 78.

23. See Paul Virilio, *War and Cinema: The Logistics of Perception* (London and New York: Verso, 1989), 59.
24. Kipling, *Something of Myself*, 93.
25. Letter to Mr Brooks, dated 21 March 1901, in Thomas Pinney, ed., *The Letters of Rudyard Kipling*, 4 vols. (Basingstoke: Macmillan, 1990–99), III, 46–7.
26. See Tom Gunning, 'From the Kaleidoscope to the X-Ray', 33.
27. Barnes, *The Beginnings of the Cinema*, III, 60.
28. William Kennedy-Laurie Dickson, *The Biograph in Battle: Its Story in the South African War Related with Personal Experiences* (London: Fisher Unwin, 1901), and Barnes, *The Beginnings of the Cinema*, v, 61–77.
29. Barnes, *The Beginnings of the Cinema*, IV, 218.
30. Barnes, *The Beginnings of the Cinema*, IV, 76. See Maltby, Introduction to Barnes, *The Beginnings of the Cinema*, v, xxiii. Cf. Robert Sklar, *Movie-Made America: A Cultural History of American Movies* (London: Chapell, 1978), 21.
31. Barnes, *The Beginnings of the Cinema*, IV, 72–6.
32. Barnes, *The Beginnings of the Cinema*, IV, 73 and Maltby, Introduction, v, xxx.
33. See Kevin Brownlow and John Kobal, *Hollywood: The Pioneers* (London: Collins, 1979), 81, and Virilio, *War and Cinema*, 14–15.
34. Barnes, *The Beginnings of the Cinema*, IV, 68.
35. See, for example, the Thomas-Edison advertisement in the *Manchester City News* for Saturday 8 June 1901, 1.
36. *Daily Dispatch*, Tuesday 18 June 1901, 8.
37. *The Photographic Chronicle*, 1 August 1901, cited by Simon Popple in 'The Diffuse Beam: Cinema and Change', in Williams, ed., *Cinema: the Beginnings and the Future*, 97–106 (100–1). I am indebted to Popple's article for first bringing this episode to my attention.
38. Popple, 'The Diffuse Beam', 100.
39. See Kirby, *Parallel Tracks*, 64–5, and Ian Christie, *The Last Machine: Early Cinema and the Birth of the Modern World* (London: BBC Educational Developments, 1994), 15.
40. Rudyard Kipling, *Traffics and Discoveries* (1904; Harmondsworth: Penguin, 1992), 279. Subsequent references are given in parentheses in the text.
41. Barthes, *Camera Lucida*, 14, 96; André Bazin, 'The Ontology of the Photographic Image', in Bazin, trans. Hugh Gray, *What is Cinema?*, 2 vols. (Berkeley, University of California Press, 1967), 1, 9–16.
42. Angus Wilson, *The Strange Ride of Rudyard Kipling: His Life and Works* (London: Secker and Warburg, 1977), 221.
43. Lord Birkenhead, *Rudyard Kipling* (London: Weidenfeld and Nicolson, 1978), 331.
44. J. M. S. Tompkins, *The Art of Rudyard Kipling* (London: Methuen, 1959), 90n.
45. On this dimension of the collection, see Hermione Lee's Introduction to the Penguin *Traffics and Discoveries*, 7–29.
46. Pinney, ed., *Letters*, III, 146–7.
47. Kipling, *Something of Myself*, 101.

48. Martha Banta, *Imaging American Women: Idea and Ideals in Cultural History* (New York: Columbia University Press, 1987), 208.
49. See also Banta, *Imaging American Women*, 723 n.51.
50. See Kenneth S. Lynn, *Charlie Chaplin and His Times* (London: Aurum, 1998), 41.
51. Barnes, *The Beginnings of the Cinema*, v, 8–10.
52. Published in the 'Song' series of postcards by Bamforth (author's own collection).
53. On the technological context of *Heart of Darkness*, see Ivan Kreilkamp, 'A Voice Without a Body: The Phonographic Logic of *Heart of Darkness*', *Victorian Studies*, 40.2 (Winter 1997), 211–44.
54. Cf. André Bazin's comments in his essay 'What is Cinema?'

4 'IT': THE LAST MACHINE AND THE INVENTION OF SEX APPEAL

1. Quoted in Booton Herndon, *Mary Pickford and Douglas Fairbanks* (London: W. H. Allen, 1978), 6.
2. *Traffics and Discoveries* (1904; Harmondsworth: Penguin, 1992), 185.
3. On the paradoxical phenomenon of modern primitivism, see Marianne Torgovnick, *Gone Primitive: Savage Intellects, Modern Lives* (Chicago: Chicago University Press, 1990).
4. Cf. contemporary references in the *Little Review* to Chaplin as a 'mob god'. Cited in Kenneth S. Lynn, *Charlie Chaplin and His Times* (London: Aurum, 1998), 162.
5. Chris Marker, *Immemory* (Interactive CD-ROM, Centre Pompidou/Les films de l'Astrophore, 1999). One of the first films he saw was *Wings* (1927), with Clara Bow.
6. Alexander Walker, *Stardom: The Hollywood Phenomenon* (Harmondsworth: Penguin, 1974), 5.
7. See Ian Christie, *The Last Machine: Early Cinema and the Birth of the Modern World* (London: BBC Educational Developments, 1994), 71–6 on 'the extraordinary sexual power of the new medium' (74).
8. Two classic accounts are Jean-Louis Baudry's 1975 essay, 'The Apparatus: Metapsychological Approaches to the Impression of Reality in Cinema', reprinted in Philip Rosen, ed., *Narrative, Apparatus, Ideology* (New York: Columbia University Press, 1986), 299–318, and Laura Mulvey's 'Visual Pleasure and Narrative Cinema', *Screen*, 16.3 (Autumn 1975), 6–18. For a survey of apparatus and post-apparatus theories, see Judith Mayne, *Cinema and Spectatorship* (London: Routledge, 1993).
9. Contrast the Benjamin of 'The Work of Art in the Age of Mechanical Reproduction' with that of 'On Some Motifs in Baudelaire', both in Hannah Arendt, ed., Harry Zohn, trans., *Illuminations* (New York: Schocken Books, 1985), 217–51, and 155–200. See also Miriam Bratu Hansen, 'Benjamin and Cinema: Not a One-Way-Street', *Critical Inquiry*, 25.2 (Winter 1999), 306–43.

For a summary of the influence of the 'modernity thesis' in film studies, see Ben Singer, *Melodrama and Modernity* (New York: Columbia University Press, 2001).

10. Miriam Hansen, 'Early Cinema: Whose Public Sphere?', in Thomas Elsaesser and Adam Barker, eds., *Early Cinema: Space, Frame, Narrative* (London: BFI, 1997), 228–46.

11. Billie Melman, *Women and the Popular Imagination in the Twenties: Flappers and Nymphs* (New York: St Martin's Press, 1988). In Britain the invidious attention attracted by the flapper seems to have been focused by resistance to the proposed enfranchisement of women under thirty, eventually secured in 1928.

12. For accounts of Glyn's chequered life, see Anthony Glyn, *Elinor Glyn* (London: Hutchinson, 1955); Meredith Etherington-Smith and Jeremy Pilcher, *The 'It' Girls: Lucy, Lady Duff Gordon, the Couturière 'Lucile,' and Elinor Glyn, Romantic Novelist* (London: Hamish Hamilton, 1988); Joan Hardwick, *Addicted to Romance: the Life and Adventures of Elinor Glyn* (London: André Deutsch, 1994); and Glyn's own *Romantic Adventure: Being the Autobiography of Elinor Glyn* (New York: E. P. Dutton, 1937). I am indebted to all of these for the synopsis of Glyn's career that follows.

13. Cited in Etherington-Smith and Pilcher, *The 'It' Girls*, 107.

14. On Famous Players-Lasky's in the 1920s, see Richard Koszarski, *An Evening's Entertainment: The Age of the Silent Feature Picture 1915–28*, vol. III of Charles Harpole, ed., *History of the American Cinema* (Berkeley, University of California Press, 1994), 69–74, 228. On Hollywood and European passion, see Robert Sklar, *Movie-Made America: A Cultural History of American Movies* (London: Chapell, 1978), 100.

15. *Shadowland*, May 1921, Box 580, clipping folder 66 of the Gloria Swanson Papers at the Harry Ransom Center for the Humanities, University of Texas, Austin.

16. 'Mirrors of Screenland', May 1922, source unidentified, Gloria Swanson Papers, Scrapbook 16, Box 573.

17. On the evolution of the star system in the cinema, see Walker, *Stardom*, 15–20 and 359–65; and Richard Dyer, *Stars* (London: BFI, 1998), 9–10. Cf. Eileen Bowser, *The Transformation of Cinema, 1907–1915*, vol. II of Charles Harpole, ed., *History of the American Cinema* (Berkeley: University of California Press, 1994), 112.

18. Jesse L. Lasky (with Don Weldon), *I Blow My Own Horn* (London: Victor Gollancz, 1957), 141.

19. See the many advertisement and promotional articles in the Paramount publicity folder for the film, Gloria Swanson Papers, Scrapbook 70, Box 581.

20. See, for example, the article 'My Glorious Career' from *Movie Weekly*, 1921, Gloria Swanson Papers, Scrapbook 72, Box 581.

21. Source? (Georgia), 22 May 1921, 'Gloria Gives an Estimate of Herself', Gloria Swanson Papers, Box 580.66.

22. Glyn, *Romantic Adventure*, 294.

23. The Taylorology website http://www.silent-movies.com/Taylorology/ reproduces descriptions of the Hollywood social events of 1921. The articles cited are
from the *Los Angeles Examiner*, 16 March 1921 (Taylorology 20); the *New York
Telegraph*, 10 April 1921 (Taylorology 20); *Photoplay*, 21 June 1921 (Taylorology
44); and the *Los Angeles Express*, 1 September 1921 (Taylorology 20).

24. Etherington-Smith and Pilcher, *The 'It' Girls*, 20; Anita Loos, *A Girl Like I*
(London: Hamish Hamilton, 1967), 119.

25. Budd Schulberg, *Moving Pictures: Memoirs of a Hollywood Prince* (London:
Allison and Busby, 1993), 169.

26. For a more complimentary description, see the interview with Mary Miles
Minter reproduced from the *Honolulu Advertiser* of 26 March 1922 in
Taylorology 37.

27. Gloria Swanson, *Swanson on Swanson* (London: Michael Joseph, 1981), 159.

28. Sklar notes that Los Angeles was known as the nation's 'leading open-shop,
non-union city', *Movie-Made America*, 67–8.

29. Loos, *A Girl Like I*, 119.

30. Lasky, *I Blow My Own Horn*, 141.

31. Swanson, *Swanson on Swanson*, 163.

32. Leatrice Gilbert Fountain, with John R. Maxim, *Dark Star* (London: Sidgwick
and Jackson, 1985), 93.

33. Proud of her move to the other side of the cameras, she framed the $7.50
cheque she received from DeMille for her efforts in *The Affairs of Anatol*, or so
she reported to the readers of 'In Filmdom with Elinor Glyn', Gloria Swanson
Papers, Scrapbook 35, Box 553.

34. Fountain and Maxim, *Dark Star*, 92. Fountain claims that Glyn was hired by
a number of studios to give deportment classes to executives and stars (92).

35. On 'cultural capital', see Pierre Bourdieu, trans. Richard Nice *Distinction: A
Social Critique of the Judgment of Taste* (Cambridge, MA: Harvard University
Press, 1984).

36. Glyn, *Romantic Adventure*, 300.

37. For some support for her boast that she discovered Gilbert, see Harry Carr's
Untold Tales of Hollywood, serialized in *Smart Set* magazine from December
1929 to February 1930, reproduced in Taylorology 43.

38. Swanson, *Swanson on Swanson*, 160.

39. Glyn, *Romantic Adventure*, 299–300.

40. Full-page advertisement for *Beyond the Rocks*, *Seattle Times*, 12 May 1922, Gloria
Swanson Papers, Scrapbook 16, Box 573A.

41. *Washington Press* (Spokane), 22 March 1921, Gloria Swanson Papers, Scrapbook 35, Box 553.

42. See Sumiko Higashi, *Cecil B. DeMille and American Culture: The Silent Era*
(Berkeley: University of California Press, 1994).

43. Etherington-Smith and Pilcher, *The 'It' Girls*, 233–4.

44. David Stenn, *Clara Bow: Runnin' Wild* (New York: Cooper Square, 2000), 76.

45. Elinor Glyn, *'It' and Other Stories* (London: Duckworth, 1927), 10. Subsequent
references in the text.

46. Cited in Etherington-Smith and Pilcher, *The 'It' Girls*, 241. On 'sex appeal', see Robert Graves and Alan Hodge, *The Long Week-End: A Social History of Great Britain, 1918–1939* (1940; New York and London: W. W. Norton, 1994), 129.

47. Grace Wilcox, 'Fashions of the Screen', unknown magazine, 12 March 1921, 13, Gloria Swanson Papers, Scrapbook 73, Box 582.

48. Daniel Pick, *Svengali's Web: The Alien Enchanter in Modern Culture* (New Haven and London: Yale University Press, 2000), 169. Cf. Christoph Asendorf, *Batteries of Life: On the History of Things and Their Perception in Modernity* (Berkeley and Los Angeles: University of California Press, 1993), 153–6.

49. Cited in Valerie Steele, *Fashion and Eroticism: Ideals of Feminine Beauty from the Victorian Age to the Jazz Age* (New York and Oxford: Oxford University Press, 1985), 213–14.

50. See George Robb, 'Race Motherhood: Moral Eugenics vs Progressive Eugenics, 1889–1929', in Claudia Nelson and Ann Sumner Holmes, eds., *Maternal Instincts: Visions of Motherhood and Sexuality in Britain, 1875–1925* (Basingstoke: Macmillan, 1997), 58–74.

51. Cited in Angelique Richardson, 'The Eugenization of Love: Sarah Grand and the Morality of Genealogy', *Victorian Studies*, 42.2 (Winter 1999/2000), 227–55 (240).

52. On the relations between psychoanalysis and some of its less successful competitors, see Pamela Thurschwell, *Literature, Technology, and Magical Thinking* (Cambridge: Cambridge University Press, 2001).

53. On Freud's American visit, see, for example, Ellen K. Rothman, *Hands and Hearts: A History of Courtship in America* (Cambridge, MA and London: Harvard University Press, 1987), 260.

54. Interview with Glyn in the *Chicago Record-Herald*, 27 April 1908, in the Robinson Locke Scrapbook in the collection of the New York Public Library Center for the Performing Arts.

55. Frederick Lewis Allen, *Only Yesterday: An Informal History of the 1920s* (1931; New York: John Wiley and Sons, 1997), 75.

56. Allen, *Only Yesterday*, 160.

57. A. Glyn, *Elinor Glyn*, 293.

58. Marjorie Rosen, *Popcorn Venus: Women, Movies, and the American Dream* (London: Peter Owen, 1975), 118.

59. Proofs of 'In Filmdom with Elinor Glyn', Gloria Swanson Papers, Scrapbook 35, Box 553.

60. I have drawn heavily on Paula S. Fass's excellent account, *The Damned and the Beautiful: American Youth in the 1920s* (Oxford: Oxford University Press, 1979), chapter 2, for this thumbnail sketch of historical transition.

61. Rothman, *Hands and Hearts*, 242. See also, for example, Milton Rugoff, *Prudery and Passion* (London: Granada, 1972), 354, 356, 365.

62. See Pamela S. Haag, 'In Search of "The Real Thing": Ideologies of Love, Modern Romance, and Women's Sexual Subjectivity in the United States, 1920–40',

in John C. Fout and Maura Shaw Tantillo, eds., *American Sexual Politics: Sex, Gender, and Race since the Civil War* (Chicago and London: University of Chicago Press, 1993), 161–92 (167).

63. Fass, *The Damned and the Beautiful*, 7, 13.
64. Ben B. Lindsey and Wainwright Evans, *The Companionate Marriage* (London: Brentano's, 1928), 66–7.
65. On the pre-war origins of many of these fashions, see Steele, *Fashion and Eroticism*, 223–6. While the war did not produce these changes, Steele argues, it probably hastened them.
66. Rothman, *Hands and Hearts*, 292–3. One of the best sources on such changes is still Robert S. Lynd and Helen Merrell Lynd, *Middletown: A Study in Contemporary American Culture* (London: Constable, 1929). See especially 137–40.
67. On women's clothes in the 1920s, see Steele, *Fashion and Eroticism*, 236–42; on petting, see Fass, *The Damned and the Beautiful*, 264, 450 n.7. On Glyn's hostility to petting, see A. Glyn, *Elinor Glyn*, 292.
68. Lynd and Merrell Lynd, *Middletown*, 138–9.
69. Percy Marks, *The Plastic Age* (London: Selwyn and Blount, 1924), 53.
70. Lynd and Merrell Lynd, *Middletown*, 266.
71. 'Pictures Changing American Faces, Says Henry Clive', *Tacoma Washington Ledger*, 19 June 1921. Gloria Swanson Papers, Scrapbook 64, Box 580. On earlier French theories of nervous audiences and unconscious imitation, see Rae Beth Gordon, 'From Charcot to Charlot: Unconscious Imitation and Spectatorship in French Cabaret and Early Cinema', *Critical Inquiry*, 27.3 (Spring 2001), 515–49.
72. See Sklar, *Movie-Made America*, 124, 135–7. See also Gaylyn Studlar, 'The Perils of Pleasure? Fan Magazine Discourse as Women's Commodified Culture in the 1920s', in Richard Abel, ed., *Silent Film* (London: Athlone Press, 1996), 263–97 (276–7).
73. On Glyn's own response to the attacks on Hollywood, see her 'Justice and Fair Play for Film Folk', in the *Los Angeles Examiner*, 20 February 1922, reproduced in Taylorology 49. On Hays and censorship, see Richard Maltby, *Harmless Entertainment: Hollywood and the Ideology of Consensus* (Metuchen, NJ: Scarecrow, 1983), 94–117.
74. See Lynn, *Charlie Chaplin and his Times*, 271.
75. Swanson, *Swanson on Swanson*, 173.
76. See Stenn, *Clara Bow*, 107. For a vivid contemporary portrait of Bow, see Harry T. Brundidge's *Twinkle, Twinkle, Movie Star!* (1930; New York and London: Garland, 1977), 1–13.
77. Joe Morella and Edward Z. Epstein, *The 'It' Girl: The Incredible Story of Clara Bow* (New York: Delacorte Press, 1976), 84.
78. See Schulberg, *Moving Pictures*, 170; and Stenn, *Clara Bow*, 81–2.
79. Etherington-Smith and Pilcher, *The 'It' Girls*, 242.
80. Cited in Koszarski, *An Evening's Entertainment*, 89. Cf. A. Glyn, *Elinor Glyn*, 306.

81. Glyn performed similar promotional work with John Gilbert. See Fountain, *Dark Star*, 94.

82. See, for example, Julie A. Matthaei, *An Economic History of America: Women's Work, the Sexual Division of Labor, and the Development of Capitalism* (New York: Schocken Books, 1982), 282.

83. Mary P. Ryan, 'The Projection of a New Womanhood: The Movie Moderns of the 1920s', in Jean E. Friedman and William G. Shade, eds., *Our American Sisters: Women in American Life and Thought* (Boston: Allyn and Bacon, 1976), 366–84 (375).

84. On the social mobility of 'working girls' in Hollywood cinema of the 1920s, see also M. Rosen, *Popcorn Venus*, 78–85.

85. Ryan, 'The Projection of a New Womanhood', 369.

86. Matthaei, *An Economic History of America*, 236.

87. On the history of the thrill in modernity see Jeffrey T. Schnapp, 'Crash (Speed as Engine of Individuation)', *Modernism/Modernity*, 6.1 (1999), 1–49.

88. Schulberg, *Moving Pictures*, 170.

89. Adolph Zukor, *The Public is Never Wrong. The Autobiography of Adolph Zukor, with Dale Kramer* (London: Cassell & Co., 1954), 176.

90. Morella and Epstein, *The 'It' Girl*, 117.

91. Koszarski, *An Evening's Entertainment*, 39–40.

92. Studlar, 'The Perils of Pleasure?', 263.

93. Miriam Hansen, *Babel and Babylon: Spectatorship in American Silent Film* (Cambridge, MA: Harvard University Press, 1991), 18, 245–68 *passim*.

94. Zukor, *The Public is Never Wrong*, 176, 179.

95. *New York Times*, 22 September 1943, Gloria Swanson Papers, Scrapbook 35, Box 553.

96. Quoted in Kevin Brownlow and John Kobal, *Hollywood: The Pioneers* (London: Collins, 1979), 179.

97. Quoted in Koszarski, *An Evening's Entertainment*, 307.

98. Simon Frith, *Sound Effects: Youth, Leisure, and the Politics of Rock 'n' Roll* (New York: Pantheon, 1982), 265.

5 *CRASH*: FLESH, STEEL, AND CELLULOID

1. *The Cinema Star: A New Musical Farcical Comedy in Three Acts* from the German Operette, *Kino Königin* by Georg Okonkowski and Julius Freund, English version by Jack Hulbert. Lyrics, Henry Graham. Music, Jack Gilbert (London: Chapell, 1914).

2. See, for example, Donna Haraway, *Simians, Cyborgs, and Women: The Re-Invention of Nature* (London: Free Association, 1990); David Harvey, *The Condition of Postmodernity: An Enquiry into the Origins of Cultural Change* (Oxford and Cambridge, MA: Blackwell, 1990); Fredric Jameson, *Signatures of the Visible* (New York and London: Routledge, 1990), Perry Anderson, *The Origins of Postmodernity* (London: Verso, 1998), chapter 4.

3. Cf. Anne Friedberg's argument that there is no abrupt rupture between the modern and the postmodern in *Window Shopping: Cinema and the Postmodern* (Berkeley: University of California Press, 1993).

4. Chris Rodley, ed., *Cronenberg on Cronenberg*, revised edition (London and Boston: Faber and Faber, 1997), 203.

5. Jeffrey T. Schnapp, 'Crash (Speed as Engine of Individuation)', *Modernism/Modernity*, 6.1 (1999), 1–49.

6. Peter J. Ling, *America and the Automobile: Technology, Reform and Social Change* (Manchester: Manchester University Press, 1990), 1. On the impact of the car on all aspects of American life, see David L. Lewis and Laurence Goldstein, eds., *The Automobile and American Culture* (Ann Arbor: University of Michigan Press, 1983). On specifically British cultural accretions to the car, see Sean O'Connell, *The Car in British Society: Class, Gender and Motoring* (Manchester and New York: Manchester University Press, 1998), 185–217 and *passim*.

7. George Charlesworth, *A History of British Motorways* (London: Thomas Telford, 1984), 34–5.

8. J. G. Ballard, *Crash* (1973; London: Vintage, 1995), 13. Subsequent references are given in parentheses in the text.

9. 'Interview with Martin Bax', in *Re/Search*, 8/9, special issue on Ballard, ed. V. Vale and Andrea Juno (1984), 36–41 (36).

10. The science-fiction/avant-garde journal, *New Worlds*, with which Ballard was associated in the 1960s and 1970s, published Pynchon's 'Entropy'. Another interesting coeval text is Michel Foucault's *History of Sexuality* (1976), which, as the title suggests, also presents sexuality as anything but 'natural'.

11. Cf. David Lodge's *The Picturegoers* (London: MacGibbon & Kee, 1960), which also explores the mass/movies connection.

12. Jean Baudrillard, *Simulacra and Simulation* (1981; Ann Arbor: University of Michigan Press, 1994), 118–19.

13. Baudrillard, *Simulacra and Simulation*, 112.

14. Ballard, 'Review of Patrick Waldberg's *Surrealism* and Marcel Jean's *History of Surrealist Painting*', *New Worlds*, 50, 164 (July 1966), 141–6 (145–6).

15. Daniel J. Boorstin, *The Image, Or What Happened to the American Dream* (London: Weidenfeld and Nicolson, 1962), 14.

16. Roger Luckhurst, *'The Angle Between Two Walls': The Fiction of J. G. Ballard* (Liverpool: Liverpool University Press, 1997), 73–117.

17. See Juno and Vale, eds., *Re/Search*, 8/9 (1984), especially the biographical section, 'From Shanghai to Shepperton', 112–24; and Eugenie Tsai, 'The Sci-Fi Connection: the IG, J. G. Ballard, and Robert Smithson', in Lawrence Alloway et al., *Modern Dreams: The Rise and Fall of Pop* (New York: ICA, 1988), 70–6.

18. 'They had American-style houses, air-conditioning and refrigerators, and American cars. I never saw an English car until I came to Britain in 1946. We had Coca-Cola – and American-style radio stations.' 'From Shanghai to Shepperton', *Re/Search*, 112.

19. Cited in Tsai, 'The Sci-Fi Connection', 72.

20. 'Fictions of Every Kind', in Juno and Vale, eds., *Re/Search*, 8/9 (1984), 98–100, originally published in *Books and Bookmen*, February 1971.

21. Kristin Ross, *Fast Cars, Clean Bodies: Decolonization and the Reordering of French Culture* (Cambridge, MA: MIT Press, 1995), 59.

22. See Sadie Plant, *The Most Radical Gesture: The Situationist International in a Postmodern Age* (London and New York: Routledge, 1992), and Peter Wollen, 'The Situationist International', *New Left Review*, 174 (March/April 1989), 67–96.

23. Guy Debord, trans. Donald Nicholson-Smith, *The Society of the Spectacle* (1967; New York: Zone, 1994), 16.

24. Karl Marx, trans. Ben Fowkes, *Capital: A Critique of Political Economy*, 3 vols. (London: Penguin, 1990–3), I, 165.

25. Indeed, Ballard at one point had plans for a more direct use of Situationist-type techniques – he planned to use Arts Council funding to display a sort of collage-novel on advertising billboards, and in 1970 he mounted an exhibition of crashed cars at the New Arts Lab in London. Ballard describes it as 'a speculative illustration of a scene in *The Atrocity Exhibition*'. It ran from 4 to 28 April 1970. See Vale and Juno, eds., *Re/Search*, 8/9 (1984), 154. On the car 'happenings' staged by Jim Dine and Claes Oldenburg in the 1960s, see Schnapp, 'Crash', 49 n.100.

26. See Juno and Vale, eds., 'Interview', in *Re/Search*, 8/9 (1984), 9, 10. Ballard's associate at *Ambit*, Martin Bax, on the other hand, traces Ballard's use of found materials to Eduardo Paolozzi. See Vale's 'Interview with Martin Bax' in the same issue of *Re/Search*, 39.

27. J. G. Ballard, 'Notes from Nowhere: Comments on Work in Progress by J. G. Ballard', *New Worlds*, 50, 164 (July 1966), 147–51 (150).

28. 'Interview with Douglas Reed' in *Books and Bookmen*, April 1970, Vale and Juno, eds., quoted in *Re/Search*, 8/9 (1984), 154.

29. On the significance of Novotny's name, see Luckhurst, '*The Angle Between Two Walls*', 106.

30. 'Interview by Graeme Revell', in Vale and Juno, eds., *Re/Search*, 8/9 (1984), 42–52 (47).

31. Miri Rubin, *Corpus Christi: The Eucharist in Late Medieval Culture* (Cambridge: Cambridge University Press, 1991), 308.

32. Rubin, *Corpus Christi*, 303.

33. The classic discussion of this idea is Ernst H. Kantorowicz, *The King's Two Bodies: A Study in Medieval Political Theory* (1957; Princeton: Princeton University Press, 1997), with a new preface by William Chester Jordan. I am grateful to Jennifer Wicke for highlighting Kantorowicz's relevance to contemporary media culture in a talk given at the Projecting the Nation conference at the Irish Film Centre, Dublin, in November 1996, '"Birth of an Otion": Why there are no Women in National Cinema'.

34. W. B. Yeats, 'Leda and the Swan', in A. Norman Jeffares, ed., *Yeats' Poems* (Dublin: Gill and Macmillan, 1989), 322.

35. Juno and Vale, eds., 'Interview', in *Re/Search*, 8/9 (1984), 12.

36. Rodley, *Cronenberg on Cronenberg*, 189–90.

37. Rodley, *Cronenberg on Cronenberg*, 192.

38. Ballard lists *The Naked Lunch* as one of his top-ten books (cited in *A User's Guide to the Millennium: Essays and Reviews* (New York: St Martin's Press, 1997), 182, from Antonia Fraser, ed., *The Pleasure of Reading*. Other books in the list include Nathanael West's *The Day of the Locust* and Baudrillard's *America*. In one respect Cronenberg also resembles the novel's Ballard character – he has worked as a director of commercials, including advertisements for Nike and Caramilk.

39. 'The Coming of the Unconscious', a review essay first published in *New Worlds*, 50, 164 (July 1966), reprinted in Vale and Juno, eds., *Re/Search*, 8/9 (1984), 102–4.

40. Rodley, *Cronenberg on Cronenberg*, 199.

41. Rodley, *Cronenberg on Cronenberg*, 198.

42. Kenneth Turan, 'Cronenberg on a "Crash" Course with Eroticism', *Los Angeles Times*, Friday 21 March 1997, reprinted in the CalendarLive film review database http://www.calendarlive.com.

43. Roger Ebert, Review of *Crash*, *Chicago Sun-Times*, 3 March 1997, reprinted at http://www.suntimes.com/ebert/ebert_reviews/1997/03/032101.html.

44. Desson Howe, 'Crash: Wham, Bam, No Thank You, Ma'am', *Washington Post*, 21 March 1997, 8.

Index